Praise for *Shadows of Glory*

"The World Series has been baseball's greatest event for more than 100 years. I was fortunate enough to play for three straight World Series winners with the Swingin' Oakland A's. This entertaining book recounts some fascinating but lesser-known World Series stories, which baseball fans of all ages should find enjoyable."

—**Sal Bando,** third baseman and captain for the 1972, 1973, and 1974 world-champion Oakland A's; member of Athletics Hall of Fame

"Beating the Houston Astros in the National League playoffs and the Kansas City Royals in the World Series in 1980 was the high point of my major-league career. If you're an avid baseball fan, this is a must-read book—you will like reading this collection of interesting and unusual World Series stories."

—**Larry Bowa,** shortstop for the 1980 world champion Philadelphia Phillies; member of the Phillies Wall of Fame

"Playing in three World Series in the 1980s was a great honor. *Shadows of Glory* captures the excitement and intensity of what the Fall Classic is all about in a behind-the-scenes look at the games. A great read for any baseball fan!"

—**Tom Herr,** second baseman for the 1982 world-champion St. Louis Cardinals and 1985 and 1987 Cardinals World Series teams; member of Cardinals Hall of Fame

"There are a million ways to consume baseball these days, from your phone or your watch or your high-def TV. You might even enjoy a throwback day at the ballpark. And there's always advanced analytics if none of the above lights your fuse. The real baseball fan, however, knows the medium is subordinate to the story—the human interaction that makes the sport so rich. That's where *Shadows of Glory* excels. It delves deeper than the pixels and numbers to explore baseball's World Series history as never told before. Thanks to their old-school reporting and research, Dave Brown and Jeff Rodimer have written a must-read account of what really happened on and off the field, weaving through generations of anecdotes. It's a celebration of baseball but, most importantly, an education. You'll have trouble putting this book down."

—**Bob Klapisch,** baseball columnist, *Newark Star-Ledger*; co-author, *New York Times* best-seller, *Inside the Empire: The True Power Behind the New York Yankees*

"The best baseball stories are tales that draw back the curtain of history and take you places you never expected to go. That's the inspiration behind this fun, creative book by Dave Brown and Jeff Rodimer, and I'm all in on this project. From Cliff Lee's emergency subway ride to a Game 1 World Series start to a pitcher who got arrested hours before he took the mound in a World Series, these are amazing stories that need to be told. I'm so glad that Dave and Jeff agree!"

—**Jayson Stark**, senior baseball writer, the *Athletic*; honored in Cooperstown by the MLB Hall of Fame as the winner of the 2019 BBWAA Career Excellence Award

"One of the amazing things about broadcasting Major League Baseball games is the chance you will see something for the first time. Dave Brown and Jeff Rodimer have written a fun book containing facts and anecdotes about some classic World Series memories. And for this lifelong baseball fan, they have managed to bring to light many new and less well-known stories of the Fall Classic. This is a must-read for all baseball fans, but especially for those who savor new information."

—**Chris Wheeler**, broadcaster for the Philadelphia Phillies (1977–2013); author, *View from the Booth: Four Decades with the Phillies*

"Dave Brown and Jeff Rodimer tell the stories of some of the most fascinating and previously unexplored moments in World Series history. *Shadows of Glory* is a book for *every* baseball fan, hard-core and casual alike. A wonderful read!

—**Greg Brown**, broadcaster for the Pittsburgh Pirates (1994–present)

"No event in sports provides more great stories than baseball's World Series. Going back to the first Series in 1903, an endless number of very special events and accomplishments have occurred. *Shadows of Glory* provides some wonderful accounts of the history and excitement produced by our national pastime. Having attended eight different World Series, I can truly say that this book adds to the great memories that I've acquired."

—**Rich Westcott**, baseball writer and historian; author of twenty-seven sports books

Shadows of Glory

SHADOWS OF GLORY

Memorable and Offbeat World Series Stories

DAVE BROWN AND JEFF RODIMER

Foreword by Mark Teixeira, 2009 World Series champion

LYONS
PRESS

Essex, Connecticut

An imprint of Globe Pequot, the trade division of
The Rowman & Littlefield Publishing Group, Inc.
4501 Forbes Blvd., Ste. 200
Lanham, MD 20706
www.rowman.com

Distributed by NATIONAL BOOK NETWORK

British Library Cataloguing in Publication Information available

Library of Congress Cataloging-in-Publication Data
Names: Brown, David W. (David Wesley), 1960- author. | Rodimer, Jeff, author.
Title: Shadows of glory: memorable and offbeat World Series stories / Dave Brown and Jeff
   Rodimer; foreword by Mark Teixeira.
Description: Essex, Connecticut: Lyons Press, 2024. | Includes index.
Identifiers: LCCN 2023043728 (print) | LCCN 2023043729 (ebook) | ISBN 9781493081295
   (trade paperback) | ISBN 9781493079698 (epub)
Subjects: LCSH: World Series (Baseball)—History.
Classification: LCC GV878.4 .B76 2024 (print) | LCC GV878.4 (ebook) | DDC
796.357/646—dc23/eng/20231025
LC record available at https://lccn.loc.gov/2023043728
LC ebook record available at https://lccn.loc.gov/2023043729

CONTENTS

FOREWORD

If you play baseball long enough, you're bound to find yourself in some interesting situations. If you're a fan of the game, you've most likely seen things that you couldn't believe. These are some of the reasons we love the sport; it's an imperfect game played by imperfect men. Sometimes those men have stories that need to be shared with the world, because it wouldn't be fair to the rest of us to keep them a secret.

I've played baseball from the time I could walk and, after playing for fourteen years in the major leagues, I have my fair share of great stories to tell. Some I'm proud of and want to tell the whole world; others are probably better left to die, never to be told again. Like the time I was traded from the Texas Rangers to the Atlanta Braves but didn't know for twelve hours because my phone got waterlogged and stopped working while I was fishing on an off day. (No, that story is not in this book.)

When Jeff Rodimer and Dave Brown reached out to talk about the 2009 World Series, I thought it was to get content for a book about the Yankees or that Series versus the Philadelphia Phillies. I'm always excited to talk about that season, and, as the first baseman of that team, I had plenty of interesting information to share about the new Yankee Stadium, our rabid fan base, and my uber-talented teammates who carried us to a world championship. While Jeff and Dave were happy to hear about my home run off Hall of Famer Pedro Martinez in Game 2 of that Series, they really wanted to talk to me about—wait for it—Phillies starting pitcher Cliff Lee's pregame commute from Manhattan to the Bronx. Huh?

Lee's performance in Game 1 of that Series at Yankee Stadium was one of the best pitched games I've ever been a part of. Unfortunately, I was on the wrong end of that stick. After my first at-bat that game (a strikeout in the first inning), I knew it was going to be a long night for my Yankees teammates at the plate. Lee pitched a complete game, allowing six hits and striking out 10. Knowing now the behind-the-scenes account of Lee's crazy day makes his outing even more incredible.

And that's what makes *Shadows of Glory* such a special book. There is plenty written about the greatest players and the greatest teams in baseball history. I know all about the Roger Maris–Mickey Mantle home run chase of 1961, and I was a kid growing up in Baltimore when Cal Ripken played in 2,632 consecutive games. But what a lifelong baseball fan like me really enjoys is reading about the greatest STORIES in baseball history: some funny, some sad, some crazy enough that they have to be true because you couldn't make them up. Who knew that shoe polish would have a major impact in not one but TWO different World Series games?

Shadows of Glory brings these stories to life, to be treasured by baseball fans of all generations. Even when the authors are retelling events from over one hundred years ago, I feel a part of the moment and can imagine myself being in the stands, on the field, or in the locker room. It's these stories that make baseball America's favorite game and why fans of all ages will enjoy turning these pages. This book is not just for hard-core fans who follow the stats of their favorite players; casual fans will treasure these stories just the same.

I am honored to be a small part of this piece of baseball history and hope that the stories told in the pages to follow will help you remember why you love baseball.

Mark Teixeira, 2009 World Series champion

INTRODUCTION

Jeff and I met in 1979 when I joined his fraternity at Gettysburg College in Central Pennsylvania. We connected quickly, in part because both of us had been hard-core baseball fans since we were young boys. I came from outside of Philadelphia, so I was naturally a Phillies fan; Jeff grew up in North-Central New Jersey and chose the Yankees over the Mets as his team. In college, Jeff and I became best friends, which we have remained for more than forty years. Our mutual passion for baseball is a big reason for our long-lasting friendship.

But Jeff and I haven't just cheered on our teams over the years—our love of baseball has run deeper than that. We have always relished the minutiae of the sport: the stats, the trivia, and the stories, especially the behind-the-scenes stories about the players, managers, teams, and games.

Of course, watching the World Series each October has been a highlight for us. In 1973, several years before Jeff and I met, while we were slogging our way through adolescence, we watched drama unfold in the World Series between the Mets and the Oakland A's. Charlie Finley, the despotic owner of the A's, impulsively tried to kick second baseman Mike Andrews off the team for committing two errors in the 12th inning of the second game. The methods that Finley used to replace Andrews on the roster, and the aftermath of this escapade, were remarkable.

When we were in college, Jeff's Yankees squared off against the LA Dodgers in the 1978 Fall Classic. It was amazing to watch Brian Doyle, who was filling in for the injured Willie Randolph and who collected just 32 hits in his major-league career, accomplish a hitting feat for the Yankees in the Series, a feat that several all-time Yankees greats never did.

We also read about some unbelievable World Series happenings from the early part of the twentieth century, such as when Connie Mack, manager of the Philadelphia Athletics, picked a bottom-of-the-rotation pitcher to start the opener of the 1929 Series—and the outcome was incredible. We were floored to learn that during the rain-filled Game 7 of the 1925 World Series, the commissioner of baseball declared to Clark Griffith, owner of the Washington Senators, that his team was the world champion—but Griffith did not confirm this declaration.

Fellow baseball junkies would share with us stories that they had heard, such as the tale of the pitcher Rube Marquard, who was arrested for scalping tickets on the morning of a World Series game in 1920 and released in time to pitch in the game that afternoon.

Jeff and I got to talking one day and asked ourselves: Wouldn't stories like these, about lesser-known, offbeat World Series moments, make for an interesting book? We noted that there are many famous World Series stories, including Don Larsen's perfect game in '56, Bill Buckner's blunder to end Game 6 in '86, and Kirk Gibson's walk-off home run to end Game 1 in '88. These are iconic moments for sure, but we decided that plenty has been written about them already. We wanted to take a different tack and focus on the stories that many baseball fans may *not* have heard about. If a story left us wondering, "Could that really have happened during baseball's premier event?" then we wanted to look into it.

So, we had Finley's shenanigans, Marquard's scalping adventure, and those few other stories for starters. We needed to do more research to "know what we didn't know." We rolled up our sleeves and scoured books as well as articles in newspapers and magazines and on websites. We interviewed players who participated in World Series. We watched YouTube videos of World Series action. After writing about fourteen stories, we hit a wall but kept going. Finally, we came up with a total of eighteen World Series stories, ranging in era from 1918, when World War I, the Spanish flu, and Babe Ruth collided, to 2016, when the Cubs broke a drought that lasted more than a century by bringing a world championship to Chicago.

A conversation with Bob Cvornyek, a professor at Florida State, inspired us to look at the Negro World Series. This great event, played for four years in the 1920s before taking a hiatus and resuming for seven more years in the 1940s, put on display some of the best players ever to put on a baseball uniform. Sure enough, stories from the 1942 Negro World Series fit so perfectly with the theme of the book that we never really debated whether to include it!

That's our story behind *Shadows of Glory*. Hope you enjoy reading the stories.

Dave Brown and Jeff Rodimer

PART I

OWNERS, UMPIRES, AND COMMISSIONERS—OH MY!

The Andrews Affair

IT IS NOT OFTEN THAT THE HOME CROWD—LET ALONE A NEW YORK crowd—gives a standing ovation to a visiting player, but it happened in Game 4 of the 1973 World Series. The chain of events that precipitated the standing O remains one of the biggest controversies in World Series history.

The Fall Classic that year pitted the New York Mets against the defending champion Oakland Athletics. The '73 Mets still had a core of players from the 1969 Miracle Mets, including Tug McGraw, Ed Kranepool, Cleon Jones, and Bud Harrelson (all of whom once played for Casey Stengel), along with Tom Seaver, Jerry Grote, and Jerry Koosman. Joining them were the new additions John Milner, Rusty Staub, Jon Matlack, George Stone, Felix Millan, and the forty-two-year-old Willie Mays, who was acquired early in the 1972 season from the San Francisco Giants.

Sadly, Gil Hodges was no longer at the helm, having died suddenly of a heart attack before the beginning of the 1972 season. Another Casey Stengel favorite and former Yankees manager, Yogi Berra, had replaced Hodges and was in his second year as manager.

After a strong start to the season, the injury bug hit the Mets hard, and by the end of June they were in last place. Pitcher Matlack was sidelined in May after taking a line drive to the head in a game played against Atlanta, and serious injuries to Grote, Harrelson, and Jones later in the season left the team at the bottom of the division through the end of August.

In September, however, fortunes shifted for the Metropolitans. Though they were nine games under .500 at the beginning of the month, no other team had taken control of the pennant race, so the Mets found themselves only 5½ games out of first place, trailing the Montreal Expos, the Chicago Cubs, the Pittsburgh Pirates, and the first-place St. Louis Cardinals. With injured players healing and a dominant pitching staff, the Mets edged into first place on September 21 after a three-game series sweep of the Pirates at Shea Stadium. Their record stood at a pedestrian 77–77, but they went on to win five of their last seven games to finish with 82 wins during the year, good enough to win the division by a game and a half over the Cardinals. They had passed five teams during the month and closed out the season on a 20–8 run.

Tom Seaver anchored a strong pitching staff, and flaky southpaw Tug McGraw, who coined the team's catchphrase, "Ya gotta believe," was a dominant closer for the Mets down the stretch with a 0.88 ERA in September. In typical Tug fashion, McGraw bought himself a bunch of National League Championship Series tickets in anticipation of a post-season run and then left them in a briefcase on the roof of his car while searching for his keys. He drove away, leaving the tickets to fly off his car onto the side of the road.

Conversely, Oakland had little difficulty in winning the American League's Western Division. Led by manager Dick Williams, the team had won the World Series the year before, defeating the Cincinnati Reds whose roster then featured Pete Rose and Johnny Bench. The team hovered around the .500 mark for two months in 1973 but then got hot. They took over first place for good in mid-August, never relinquishing their division lead during the rest of the season. Superstar Reggie Jackson was the American League's MVP, and Oakland boasted three 20-game winners: Catfish Hunter, Vida Blue, and Ken Holtzman.

Bombastic, controlling, and contentious Charlie Finley owned the Oakland team. He bought the team in December 1960, when it was still in Kansas City. Forty-two years old at the time, Finley had made millions as the owner of an insurance company in Chicago. Unlike many other baseball owners, who defer to their general managers for person-nel decisions, Finley was heavily involved in deciding what players his team drafted and traded. For the first seven years that Finley owned the Athletics, they were dreadful; they never finished higher than eighth place in the American League's ten-team league; nor did they end the season within 20 games of first place. But then Finley moved his club to Oakland in time for the 1968 season, and they started to turn the corner, recording a winning record during their first year on the West Coast.

In 1970, Finley began phasing out the Athletics team name in favor of the "A's." In 1971, the A's made the playoffs, the first time the franchise had earned a postseason berth since 1931, when the club was in Philadelphia. In 1972, Finley, always trying out gimmicks to promote the team, offered to pay a bonus to any player who grew a mustache by Father's Day. Every player took him up on his offer. So did Williams. The A's became known as the "Mustache Gang" and won the World Series in 1972. But, despite the team's success, the players and Williams clashed with the overbearing Finley.

In the early summer of 1973, the twenty-two-year-old second baseman Manny Trillo was called up to the A's from the team's Triple-A affiliate in Tucson, Arizona. Finley had selected Trillo from the Philadelphia Phillies in the 1969 Rule 5 draft and watched him progress steadily through the A's minor league system. Trillo played briefly for the A's as a backup to the veteran Dick Green following his June call-up but was returned to the minors before rejoining the big club in September. His first year in the big leagues would be a memorable one.

In July 1973, the A's signed second baseman Mike Andrews, who had been released by the Chicago White Sox two weeks earlier. Williams, who had managed Andrews on the Boston Red Sox years earlier, favored the move. In 1967, when Williams took over the manager's job for Boston, Red Sox fans were not optimistic about the season. The team was coming off eight consecutive losing years. But, that year, under Williams's strong leadership, the Red Sox caught fire and edged out three teams to win the American League pennant. According to the Society for American Baseball Research, when the Red Sox reached first place and seemed to have a chance to win the pennant, "[i]t became the summer of the 'Impossible Dream.'" Rookie second baseman Andrews was a key part of the team's success. He hit .263, including .342 in September, as the Red

Sox fought off the White Sox, the Detroit Tigers, and the Minnesota Twins to emerge as American League champions. And, though the Red Sox lost to the Cardinals in seven games in the World Series that year, Andrews played well, hitting .308.

Despite Andrews's leading American League second basemen in errors in 1970, 1971, and 1972, Williams thought that, with his scrappy play and valuable postseason experience, Andrews would be a good mid-season acquisition for the A's and a better alternative as a backup to Dick Green than the light-hitting Ted Kubiak.

It quickly became apparent to the A's that Andrews was not what they had bargained for. He was having difficulty making routine throws from second, though he claimed his arm was fine. Williams finally announced that he would be limiting Mike to pinch-hitting duties along with occasional appearances in the newly created position of designated hitter.

Heading into the postseason, Finley wanted Trillo, whom he coveted, on the A's twenty-five-man roster. But, because he was not on the team on September 1, the A's had to obtain approval from the Baltimore Orioles, their opponent in the American League Championship Series to add him to the roster. The Orioles did not object to the addition of Trillo, so he was added to the roster, though he did not play in the five-game series in which the A's knocked off the Orioles.

The A's headed back to the World Series to face the winner of the National League Championship Series between the Mets and the heavily favored Cincinnati Reds. The series would come down to whether the Mets' pitching could keep the Big Red Machine in check long enough to give their meager offense a chance to score a few runs. Aside from John Milner's 23 homers and Rusty Staub's 76 RBIs (to go along with a .279 batting average), the Mets lineup had failed to provide much pop during the regular season.

The Mets starting pitching prevailed, holding the powerful Reds to just seven earned runs in a wild and brawl-filled five-game National League Championship Series. Game 3 at Shea, most memorably, featured fisticuffs between Pete Rose and Bud Harrelson in a bench-clearing melee that ended with Reds pitcher Pedro Borbon furiously chewing on a Mets cap he had mistakenly donned at the end of the fight—to the delight of the Mets faithful. The Mets outscored the Reds 23–8, despite hitting a mere .220 as a team. Seaver and company held the Reds to a team batting average of .186, and, while their .509 regular-season winning percentage is still the lowest ever for a pennant winner, the Mets were now on a roll.

Finley, who was still recovering from a heart attack suffered on August 7, insisted that Trillo be included on the team's roster for the World Series. It was odd that Finley had such strong feelings about the subject, because, while Trillo went on to have a stellar seventeen-year major-league career, which included starting at second base for the 1980 world champion Phillies, at that point in his career he had just 12 major league at-bats. But Finley was a control freak, and he wanted his guy on the roster.

Unlike the Orioles, the Mets denied the A's request to add Trillo to the roster. This move so incensed Finley that, before Game 1 of the World Series at Oakland-Alameda County Coliseum, he ordered the public-address announcer to tell fans to scratch Trillo from their programs because the Mets had not allowed the move. Baseball commissioner Bowie Kuhn later fined Finley for his irreverence.

The opener was played in Oakland before a less-than-capacity crowd and would be a matchup between two lefties, the A's veteran Ken Holtzman and the Mets' twenty-three-year-old Jon Matlack. The A's won the game 2–1, pushing across two unearned runs in the bottom of the third after Mets second baseman Felix Millan let a grounder by Bert Campaneris go between his legs, allowing Holtzman to score from second.

Campy then stole second and came home on a single to right by Joe Rudi. Third baseman and team captain Sal Bando sent Rudi to third with a single to center that Mays misplayed for an error. But Matlack stopped the bleeding, getting Jackson to foul out to short for the third out. Holtzman and the A's bullpen, with four innings of shutout ball, made the two runs stand up for the victory. It would be a bad series for second basemen and for Willie Mays—a story line that would play out in full during Game 2.

Game 2 may not have been the pivotal game of the Series but it would be a critical one for the Mets. It would also indisputably be the wildest and most memorable game of the Series.

On paper it looked like another pitching duel between two great lefties—Vida Blue for the A's and Jerry Koosman for the Mets. The A's jumped on Koosman in the first when Cleon Jones lost a routine fly off the bat of Rudi in the sun, which fell for a double. Bando drove him home, and Jesus Alou plated Bando with a two-out double to left.

After putting up runs in the second and third innings on homers by Jones and Wayne Garrett, the Mets scored four runs in the sixth inning to take a 6–3 lead. The onset of the A's Game 2 fielding woes contributed mightily as reliever Darold Knowles, with the bases loaded, induced a one-out comebacker from pinch-hitter Jim Beauchamp. Knowles lost his balance and, stumbling toward first, threw the ball to the backstop, allowing the Mets to score their fifth and sixth runs. It was the A's second of five errors that day. But it would get lost in the shuffle of what was to come.

The A's got one back in the seventh when Jackson doubled to right, scoring Campaneris. In the top of the ninth, Yogi Berra was faced with a dilemma. Mays had been benched after Game 1 in favor of Staub, who was still hurting with a separated throwing shoulder. The Mets needed offense, though, so the starting lineup included Staub in right field with Don Hahn returning to center. After Staub led off the ninth with a single, Berra sent Mays in to pinch-run for him. Staub simply couldn't throw, and, though Mays had shoulder issues of his own by then, he must have seemed the better defensive option to Yogi, who was otherwise out of outfielders. When Milner followed with a single, Mays stumbled and almost fell over the second-base bag, which couldn't have heartened Berra. Blue Moon Odom, now in his second inning of relief, retired the next two Mets and kept the A's deficit at two runs.

In the bottom of the ninth, Mays trotted out to right field and began to warm up. But, at the last second, he jogged over to center field, and Don Hahn switched over to right. Pinch-hitter Deron Johnson immediately made the Mets pay for this decision when he lined a ball to center. Mays appeared to lose the ball in the sun and, at the last second, tried to come in to make the catch, falling to the ground as his right leg slipped out from underneath him. Johnson ended up on second with a double. Tug McGraw, who had come in at the beginning of the sixth inning, recovered to retire the next two A's. But, after a walk to Bando, Jackson and Gene Tenace came up with dramatic back-to-back two-out hits to tie the game 6–6 and send it into extra innings.

After the game, the Say Hey Kid was quoted as saying "The sun hit me right in the face" and "I couldn't see the balls at all." Reggie Jackson also struggled with the sun, and Cleon Jones called the Coliseum "the worst sun field I've ever seen." He added, "An outfielder has no chance. You gotta know it's bad because if anybody can handle it, you know Willie can."

The game might have ended in the 10th inning had it not been for a blown call by the home-plate umpire Augie Donatelli. Bud Harrelson led off with a single, and McGraw sacrificed him to second. Wayne Garrett then smacked a hard grounder off the first-base bag. Tenace made a great play to corral it, but his throw to Rollie Fingers, who was covering first, took the pitcher's foot off the base, putting Mets runners on first and third with one out. With the infield in, Felix Millan lofted a fly to short left. Harrelson had made up his mind to tag up and go for the lead run. Joe Rudi circled the ball, getting into prime throwing position. His throw home was off line and Harrelson never slid, running past catcher Ray Fosse as he gamely tried to swipe tag Harrelson before he got to the plate. Harrelson scored standing up, but Donatelli called him out, causing a near riot at the plate. The image of Mays, who was on deck, on his knees at the plate, pleading with Donatelli to change the call, is iconic. Berra came out of the dugout and flew at Donatelli, demanding to know just where Fosse had touched Harrelson. Slow-motion replays showed that his tag had missed Bud completely. But Augie had the final say, and the double play ended the inning.

Soon the fireworks would really start as Mike Andrews took center stage. He had grounded out as a pinch-hitter in the bottom of the eighth inning and stayed in the game to play second base. With the score still knotted at 6–6 in the top of the 12th, the Mets put runners on first and third against Fingers, now pitching in his third inning. After a strikeout and a pop out, Mays atoned for his earlier misplays by singling in the go-ahead run. It would be the last hit of his illustrious career. Cleon Jones kept the rally going by hitting a single to load the bases.

Williams replaced Fingers with southpaw Paul Lindblad, who induced left-handed batter John Milner to hit a ground ball to second base. But Andrews let the ball go through his legs, and two more runs scored. The next batter, Jerry Grote, hit a grounder to second, but Andrews's throw appeared to pull first baseman Tenace's foot off the bag for his second consecutive error, and the Mets scored their fourth run of the inning. And, though slow-motion replay showed that the throw beat the runner and that Tenace had managed to keep his foot on the bag, Grote was ruled safe by umpire Jerry Neudecker—the second big blown call by the umpiring crew that day. Perhaps a more experienced first baseman would have made the play more elegantly, but Tenace was in the first year of his full-time transition from catcher to first baseman, and his awkward footwork may have influenced the umpire's call. The A's scored a run in the bottom of the 12th, aided by another fielding miscue by Mays on a fairly routine ball off the bat of Jackson that went for a triple, but it was too little, too late. The Mets won the game 10–7 and evened the Series.

After the game, in the Mets clubhouse, Mays reiterated to reporters what he had announced in September: he was retiring after the World Series. With the exception of an at-bat as a pinch-hitter, he would not appear in the Series again. He was rightfully proud of his remarkable career and, during the season, had let teammates know that he was struggling to play up to his own standards. A total pro, he didn't want to cause Yogi Berra more headaches by forcing him to make any special accommodations for him, given the thrashing Yogi was taking in the papers during the team's spell in last place. (A running joke in the press was whether Berra or embattled president Richard Nixon would be fired first.)

"It's a helluva way to go out," Mays said. "I was very excited. I guess I'm just an emotional guy, but I try not to show it on the field. A week ago, I didn't think I'd be in a World Series. Now this." Tug McGraw fondly remembered how well Mays blended into the Mets clubhouse, saying that it felt like he had been a Met for twenty years.

Meanwhile, a drama was unfolding in the A's clubhouse. When Finley saw Andrews make errors on consecutive plays in the 12th inning, he was furious: If Trillo were playing second, he would have fielded Milner's ground ball cleanly and thrown him out. The Mets would have been held to one run, and the A's might have won the game.

Hastily, Finley cooked up a scheme to force Andrews off the team and replace him with Trillo. Before the game was over, from his box along the third-base line, Finley called the A's team physician, Dr. Charles Hudson. Dr. Hudson then contacted the team orthopedist, Dr. Harry Walker, and directed him to evaluate Andrews when the game was over.

After the game, Andrews accepted accountability for the loss. In describing his first error to the *New York Times* reporter Leonard Koppett, Andrews said, "I have no excuses. I put my glove down for the ball and thought I had it." When asked about the absence of Trillo from the World Series roster as a reason for the loss, Williams refused to take the bait and tersely said, "Let's face it, when you get down to the 25th man, you're in trouble."

When Andrews left the dugout after the game, he was told to report to the trainer's room to see Dr. Walker for an examination of his right shoulder and arm. He was then sent to the manager's office, where Finley presented him with a paper that contained the following statement, signed by Dr. Walker:

> Mike Andrews has a history of chronic shoulder disability. He is unable to play his position because of a bicep tenosynovitis of the right shoulder. It is my opinion he is disabled for the rest of the year.

Finley insisted that Andrews express his concurrence with Dr. Walker's statement by signing under the words "I agree to the above."

"Finley told me, 'If you want to help this team, the best thing you can do is step aside and let us put Manny [Trillo] in there,'" Andrews later recalled. "He kept beating me down, and finally I just signed it." Andrews caught the next flight home to Massachusetts.

The next day, as they were boarding the flight to New York for Game 3, the A's players noticed that Andrews was not there. When they learned about Finley's shenanigans, they were furious. Sal Bando, in a conversation shortly before he passed away in January 2023, confirmed that the players knew that Andrews had arm issues when he came to Oakland, but outfielder Joe Rudi echoed the sentiments of his teammates when he said, "We weren't going to let Finley get away with making Andrews the scapegoat."

The players voted to boycott the rest of the Series if Andrews was not reinstated. Later they decided against a boycott because they didn't want to disappoint the A's fans. In those days the players' union was nowhere near as strong as it is today, and many players didn't have agents to look after them. Some players feared speaking out "because we might be here next year" and they didn't want to be on Finley's bad side. Help would have to come from somewhere else. In the meantime, as an act of solidarity, at the suggestion of their captain, Sal Bando, they wore black patches with Andrews's number 17 taped on their uniforms during their workout at Shea Stadium the day before Game 3. Williams was so fed up with Finley that he told his players he intended to resign at the conclusion of the World Series.

While the players and manager were seething, Finley held a press conference to announce "the injury" and his hope to activate Trillo in place of Andrews, whose play he was dissatisfied with. Help arrived when Kuhn intervened and blocked Finley's attempt to replace Andrews with Trillo, stating that Major League Baseball's rules provide for a substitution of a player in a postseason series only if he is injured during the series.

Kuhn didn't dispute that Andrews had health issues, only that the doctor's letter contained "no suggestion that this condition has changed or worsened since the Series began or that he has been injured in the Series." He added, "The fact that he was used in game No. 2 by the Oakland club would appear to indicate the contrary." Furthermore, "the handling of the matter by the Oakland club has had the unfortunate effect of unfairly embarrassing a player who has given many years of able service to professional baseball."

Finley was livid. "It is my ball club, my money and I don't appreciate anyone telling me how to spend my money to run my business," he barked. Of Kuhn, whom Finley once called "the village idiot," he said, "I don't think the commissioner treated us fairly." Dismissing the idea that his actions embarrassed Andrews, Finley retorted, "I sure as hell was embarrassed by what the commissioner did."

With this controversy swirling around the World Series, the A's beat the Mets 3–2 in Game 3 at Shea Stadium. It was another extra-inning game—this time the A's came out on top by scoring a run in the top of the 11th inning.

Following Kuhn's ruling, Williams and the A's players welcomed Andrews back to the team for Game 4. It was all Mets from the start as they knocked out Holtzman in the first inning with three runs. Then, after the A's scored one in the top of the fourth, the Mets added three more in the bottom of the inning to give starter Jon Matlack a 6–1 lead.

Matlack cruised along through seven innings with the same 6–1 lead when Williams called on Andrews to pinch-hit for relief pitcher Horacio Pina to lead off the top of the eighth. When number 17 walked to the plate, the sold-out Shea Stadium crowd of more than fifty-four thousand rose to give Andrews a standing ovation. Andrews grounded out to third base, and while he was trotting back to the A's dugout, the Mets fans gave him another ovation. It would be the last at-bat in Andrews's major league career. Finley did not stand—he remained in his seat, defiantly waving an A's pennant.

Moved by the gesture from the New York fans, not always known for their sympathetic ways, Andrews told a *New York Daily News* reporter, "The ovation gave me chills, it surprised me. I don't think I've ever had a standing ovation in my life. To me that meant everything." The Mets closed out the game, winning 6–1, to even the Series. Andrews did not appear during the rest of the Series. The Mets came within a game of capturing the World Series, as Jerry Koosman and McGraw combined on a three-hit shutout in Game 5, beating the A's, 2–0. When asked years later if the A's were concerned about being down three games to two, Bando replied, "No. We were the defending champs and we knew we had a really good team."

The resilient A's bounced back and won the final two games back in Oakland, 3–1 and 5–2, for their second straight world championship. Reggie Jackson delivered big hits in both games and was named MVP of the World Series.

The A's won the Series, but the Mets won the battle of the statistics, outhitting and outpitching the A's by most statistical measures. Staub, despite the separated shoulder and missing Game 1, led all hitters with a .423 average and 11 hits, while MVP Jackson and Rudi led the A's, both hitting over .300 and supplying most of the power for Oakland. Darold Knowles set a record by appearing in all seven games for the A's as a relief pitcher.

Soon after the Series ended, Williams made good on his promise to resign as A's manager. In announcing his decision, he told the media, "All the recent fuss had nothing to do with it. I'm leaving with the most cordial relations with Mr. Finley and the whole club." In reality, Williams could not stand Finley, and his handling of the Andrews matter was the final affront.

Williams was offered the job as the New York Yankees manager, but he had one year left on his contract with the A's, and Finley would not let him out of the contract without compensation from the Yankees. Bill Virdon was hired instead as the Yankees manager. When Williams was offered the job as manager of the last-place California Angels in the middle of the 1974 season, Finley did not object. After the Angels, Williams managed the Montreal Expos (taking them to their first division title in 1981), the San Diego Padres (leading them to their first World Series in 1984), and the Seattle Mariners.

Yogi Berra, however, managed to outlast Richard Nixon by a year before being fired in August 1975, as the Mets struggled to compete for the division title. Finally, in 1977, Mets chairman Donald Grant (with an assist from some of the New York press) delivered a knife to the hearts of Mets fans when he traded Tom "the Franchise" Seaver to the Reds. The Mets then went into an ugly tailspin that lasted through the 1983 season, while, over the years, their fans were treated to watching Seaver throw his only no-hitter in a Reds uniform and win his 300th game at Yankee Stadium as a member of the Chicago White Sox.

Even without Williams at the helm, the A's did not miss a beat. Finley rehired Alvin Dark, who had managed the club when it was still in Kansas City in 1966 and part of 1967 before he was fired. Dark had managed the San Francisco Giants to the National League pennant in 1962, losing to the Yankees in the World Series. In 1974, Dark led the A's to their third consecutive world championship, beating the Los Angeles Dodgers in the World Series in five games.

The A's won another division title in 1975. But, despite the team's exceptional run, many of the players wanted out. They had had enough of Finley. As Bando noted, "Most players—prior to the 1973 season anyhow—would consider Mr. Finley a father figure. [But] with his heart attack, things started to change; he became more vindictive."

In 1976, with unrestricted free agency looming, Finley sold Vida Blue to the Yankees for $1.5 million and sent stars Joe Rudi and Rollie Fingers to the Red Sox for $1 million each. He didn't want to pay them the salaries they would surely earn as free agents, and he didn't want to be left empty-handed when their contracts expired and they could simply walk away. Within days, commissioner Kuhn, invoking his ability to make decisions in "the best interests of baseball," voided the transactions.

The stubborn Finley was furious and told manager Chuck Tanner (the replacement for Alvin Dark, whom Finley fired for failing to make it to the World Series in 1975) not to play his three stars as he furiously tried to mount a $10-million lawsuit against Kuhn and Major League Baseball. A threatened strike by the A's players on June 27 caused Finley finally to relent, but his actions put a major dent in any chance that the A's had of catching the Kansas City Royals, and they finished the season 2½ games behind Kansas City. Bando also remembered that two-week period as the straw that broke the A's back that season.

Free agency was in full swing and, by 1977, several key players had been traded or signed as free agents with another team: Catfish Hunter, Reggie Jackson, Vida Blue, Rollie Fingers, Sal Bando, Joe Rudi, and Bert Campaneris. The team was so decimated that they finished in last place, behind the Seattle Mariners, a first-year expansion team. In 1979, the team finished with an anemic 54–108 record. Fan interest in Oakland had dwindled so much that the team averaged fewer than four thousand fans per game that season. In 1980, Finley bailed out and sold the A's. He returned to Chicago to run his insurance company.

After the '73 World Series, Finley, predictably, began the process of releasing Andrews. Even though the A's had won the Series, he couldn't resist taking one last personal swipe at Andrews in an interview with *The Sporting News*. Citing a clause from baseball's waiver rules, he said, "Any team that wants him can have him for $1."

Andrews was only thirty years old, but he was finished as a major league player. He sued Finley for $2.5 million for trying to humiliate him during the Series and settled out of court for an undisclosed sum. He made efforts to contact almost every major league team in the off season but could generate no interest in his services, despite his claims that his arm was fine (though he did admit to having developed a mental block in his first season with the White Sox that affected his throwing). He sat out the 1974 season, played a season in Japan in 1975, and then called it quits. After retiring from baseball, Andrews spent twenty-five years as chairman of the Jimmy Fund of the Dana-Farber Institute in Boston, an organization that raises money for cancer research.

Many players have committed errors in the World Series, some of which were costly. But no player's error set off the firestorm that Andrews's pair of miscues did in the 1973 World Series.

Dick Williams (left) with Mike Andrews. Williams lobbied the A's to acquire Andrews in 1973, but in Game 2 of the 1973 World Series, Andrews committed two late-inning errors, triggering a chain of events with owner Charlie Finley attempting to kick him off the roster only to be overruled by Commissioner Bowie Kuhn. *New York Daily News Archive/New York Daily News via Getty Images*

2

Time-Out to a Title

AN EARTHQUAKE DELAYED GAME 3 OF THE 1989 WORLD SERIES
between the Oakland A's and the San Francisco Giants by ten days. A
confluence of unusual events caused an even longer hiatus between games
in the 1942 Negro World Series between the Kansas City Monarchs and
the Homestead Grays.

The Monarchs had played in the first Negro World Series in 1924,
squaring off against the Hilldale Daisies. The Monarchs played in the
Negro National League (NNL), which was founded in 1920 and made
up primarily of midwestern teams. Hilldale, located in the Philadelphia
suburb of Darby, was part of the upstart Eastern Colored League (ECL),
which debuted in 1923. The ECL consisted of teams from the East
Coast as well as a squad from Cuba and other Latin American countries
that played only road games. When Ed Bolden, head of the ECL and
also owner of the Hilldale club, approached Rube Foster, founder of the
NNL, about a World Series between the two leagues that fall, Foster
would not agree to it because he was angry that the ECL had raided
players from his league's teams.

In 1924, Foster relented and agreed that the NNL would participate
in a World Series. He and Bolden decided to use a best-of-nine format,
which Major League Baseball had followed in its first World Series in
1903 and again from 1919 to 1921. The two men decided that not all of
the games would be played in the participants' cities—the games would
be divided among Philadelphia, Baltimore, Kansas City, and Chicago.

That 1924 Negro World Series (also called the Colored World Series) was a classic, nip-and-tuck duel between the Monarchs and the Daisies, and it went to the hilt. In each of the last seven games, the victor scored the winning run in the team's last at-bat. Hilldale took a 3–1 lead in the Series (with one tie), but Kansas City stormed back to win four of the last five games. Black fans, proud of the high caliber of baseball displayed in the two leagues, hoped the winner of the Negro World Series would face the winner of the MLB World Series, but it did not happen.

The Negro World Series continued for the next three years, with the leagues sticking to the best-of-nine format. When the ECL dissolved midway through the 1928 season, the Negro World Series went by the wayside as well. There would not be another Negro World Series for fifteen years. The American Negro League was created in 1929, as the Great Depression started to cripple the country's economy, but lasted just one season. The NNL folded in 1931 after a twelve-year run. The East-West League kicked off in 1932, but, like the American Negro League, it failed to survive more than one year.

A second incarnation of the NNL began play in 1933. The new NNL initially featured teams in Baltimore, Chicago, Pittsburgh, Indianapolis, Nashville, Homestead (a steel town outside of Pittsburgh), and Columbus, Ohio. Teams came and went during the season. The Indianapolis team moved to Detroit within the first month, and, not long after, Homestead was expelled for stealing players from Detroit. The Columbus team moved around Ohio during the season, first to Akron and then to Cleveland. Baltimore bailed out before the season's end.

What would become a signature event in Negro League baseball started on September 10, 1933, at Chicago's Comiskey Park, home of the major league White Sox: the East-West All-Star Game. The first MLB All-Star Game was also played in 1933. The majority of the contestants in the East-West Game played for the Pittsburgh Crawfords and the Chicago American Giants.

The new NNL struggled but survived for the next three years. Seasons were split into halves; the first-half winner faced the second-half winner in a series to determine the league champion. Negro League seasons were much shorter than major league seasons. While MLB played a 154-game season, Negro League teams usually played between fifty and eighty official league games per season. And though all MLB teams would play the same number of games per season—154, give or take a game or two—teams in the Negro Leagues sometimes played hugely disparate numbers of games in a season. Furthermore, teams also played nonleague exhibition games against teams outside of the Negro Leagues and, at times when there were two leagues, games against teams in the other league. The exhibition games did not count in the standings or toward the players' statistics.

In 1937, for the first time in five years, a second league was formed, the Negro American League, and this one was not short-lived. Primarily Midwestern teams played in the new league, while Eastern teams competed in the NNL. Because of the frosty relationship between owners in the two leagues, the World Series was not reinstituted. The Kansas City Monarchs and the Homestead Grays won their respective league titles in '37.

Over the next four years, league officials periodically discussed a merger of the two leagues and a revival of the Negro World Series, but neither materialized, for the most part because of the ongoing bickering between team owners, who accused each other of violating contracts and stealing players. The East-West All-Star Game continued to be a hit—the biggest event in the Negro baseball world. The game was so popular that it outdrew the MLB All-Star Game twice in the 1930s and would do so six more times in the 1940s. Sportswriters chose the players for the MLB All-Star Game, but fans voted for the players who made the East-West Game. Black fans relished the opportunity to participate in the process of picking the players and year after year sent in hundreds of thousands of ballots. In addition to instilling a feeling of racial pride, the East-West Game was profitable for the Negro Leagues because all the teams shared part of the gate receipts.

In February 1942, the owners held a meeting at which an agreement was formalized to play a World Series, the first in the Negro Leagues since 1927. The 1920s Negro World Series were played in October, coinciding with the MLB World Series. The '42 Negro Series and subsequent Negro Series started in September and usually concluded that month; two of the Series went into the first week of October. The owners switched to a best-of-seven format. The Series pitted the traditional Negro League powerhouses, the Grays and the Monarchs, against each other; each team had won its league pennant in five of the previous six years. From 1940 to 1942, the Grays played half of their home games in Pittsburgh and half in Washington, DC; the team was sometimes referred to as the Washington-Homestead Grays.

The Monarchs and the Grays each featured a legendary Negro League player, an all-time great, a future member of the Baseball Hall of Fame: pitcher Leroy "Satchel" Paige of the Monarchs and catcher Josh Gibson of the Grays.

Paige was the undisputed face of the Negro Leagues. He was a racial pioneer who displayed showmanship and swagger. By 1942, Paige had been toiling in the Negro Leagues for fifteen years, with stops in Birmingham, Cleveland, New York, and Pittsburgh before Kansas City. He also pitched outside the United States, including in the Dominican Republic and Mexico, and led a group of Negro League players in barnstorming tours that included games against teams consisting of major league players headed up by star pitchers Dizzy Dean of the St. Louis Cardinals and Bob Feller of the Cleveland Indians.

Paige was a dominant pitcher who relied on an arsenal of pitches that included a fastball, a forkball, a screwball, and a hesitation pitch, all of which he threw with impeccable accuracy. Satchel's pitching philosophy was simple: "Just take the ball and throw it where you want to. Throw strikes. Home plate don't move." Paige made a great impression on Dizzy Dean when they barnstormed together. "If Satch and I were pitchers on the same team," Dean, the National League's last 30-game winner, said, "we would clinch the pennant by July 4 and go fishing until World Series time."

Gibson and Paige were teammates and batterymates with the Pittsburgh Crawfords for three years in the early 1930s. In 1930, when he was eighteen, Gibson broke into the Negro Leagues. Over the next ten years, he played primarily for Pittsburgh and Homestead but spent most of 1940 and 1941 playing in Cuba, Mexico, and Puerto Rico. He was mainly a catcher, but he played some first base, third base, and outfield as well.

He was an exemplary batter—he regularly hit for a high average with tremendous power. He was known for his prodigious home runs—some of his bombs reportedly traveled more than five hundred feet. Monte Irvin, who played for a decade for the Newark Eagles, followed by eight years in the majors, mostly with the New York Giants, said, "I played with Willie Mays and against Hank Aaron, and they were tremendous players, but they were no Josh Gibson."

It is difficult to compare the statistics that Paige, Gibson, and their fellow players compiled in the Negro Leagues to the stats of major league players of the time because of the shorter seasons in the Negro Leagues. According to Paige's Negro League stats, he never won more than 13 games in a season, and his season high in innings pitched was 185. But he won about two games for every game he lost and struck out more than four batters for every walk he issued in his Negro League career. In two seasons before 1942 and two after, his ERA was less than 2.00.

Gibson's log of his time in the Negro Leagues reveals that he topped out at 20 home runs in a season. But he is credited with leading his league in home runs nine times and in RBIs seven times, and he won three batting titles.

The Grays and the Monarchs played two exhibition games against each other during the '42 season, and both times the Grays won in extra innings and Paige was the losing pitcher. Some of the pre–World Series hype concerned Paige's determination to atone for those two losses.

A unique feature of Negro League baseball was that some players became umpires when they retired, and this World Series included three men who had played in the inaugural Negro World Series in 1924. Phil Cockrell was a longtime pitcher for the Hilldale Daisies, who lost the opening game of the Series. Hosley "Scrip" Lee was a teammate of Cockrell on the '24 Daisies. Bullet Rogan, a fine pitcher for the Monarchs throughout the 1920s, won two games in the '24 Series. The Negro Leagues used three umpires for a game, and the crews were shuffled from game to game. Lee, Cockrell, and Rogan each served as an umpire in one of the '42 Series games.

Game 1 was played at Griffith Stadium in Washington. The Senators and the Boston Red Sox played an American League regular-season game that afternoon. Afterward, the stadium was vacated and cleaned, and the Grays and the Monarchs took the field to play the opener of the Negro World Series under the lights. MLB did not incorporate night games into the World Series until twenty-nine years later, in 1971, when the Pittsburgh Pirates faced the Baltimore Orioles. Night baseball during the regular season also began in the Negro Leagues before it did in MLB. In 1929, J. L. Wilkinson, co-owner of the Monarchs, bought a set of fifty-foot portable generator light towers that were used for the first time in a game in 1930. These towers allowed the Monarchs to play day-night doubleheaders. The Monarchs also rented out the lighting equipment to other teams in the Negro Leagues so that they, too, could host night games. The first regular-season night game in MLB was played at Cincinnati's Crosley Field in 1935.

The opener of the '42 Negro World Series was all Monarchs—they whitewashed Josh Gibson and the Grays, 8–0. The Grays were hurt by sloppy defense—they committed six errors, including two on one play. Paige started for the Monarchs and threw five shutout innings, allowing only two singles. Monarchs manager Frank Duncan replaced Paige in the sixth inning with Jack Matchett, who completed the shutout, retiring all twelve batters that he faced.

Two days later, the action moved to Forbes Field in Pittsburgh for Game 2. The Monarchs kept the Grays off the scoreboard until the eighth inning; by that time, the Monarchs had built a 5–0 lead. Tireless Satchel Paige relieved Hilton Smith after five innings. He pitched out of a two-out, bases-loaded jam in the seventh inning, when he fanned Josh Gibson on three pitches. The Grays touched Paige for four runs in the bottom of the eighth, but the Monarchs hung on to win, 8–4.

The venue switched to Yankee Stadium for Game 3. The famous mayor of New York City for whom the airport in Queens was later named, Fiorello La Guardia, threw out the first ball. The Grays, unable to find their dominant regular-season form under manager Vic Harris, lost their third game in a row. Paige, on two days' rest—more than he had when he appeared in Game 2—pitched again, allowing two runs in two innings before departing. The Monarchs coasted to a 9–3 victory.

The two teams were not finished playing that day. In accordance with the Negro Leagues' tradition of mixing exhibition games into the schedule, the Monarchs and the Grays played another game but agreed it would not be part of the World Series. In keeping with the custom in the Negro Leagues for the second game of a doubleheader, the Monarchs and the Grays' exhibition game following the World Series game was shortened to seven innings. The Monarchs recruited the Birmingham Black Barons pitcher Gready McKinnis to start the game. Because it was an exhibition game, the Grays did not object to his pitching for the Monarchs even though he had just been added to the roster. McKinnis, throwing a seven-inning shutout, led the Monarchs to a victory over the Grays.

Game 4 of the World Series would take place in the Monarchs' home park in Kansas City, Ruppert Stadium, sometimes known as Blues Stadium. But the game would have to wait. The Monarchs were the stadium's second tenant—the Kansas City Blues, a minor league affiliate of the New York Yankees in the American Association, were the first. The Blues made the playoffs and got first dibs on the stadium.

To stay sharp during the interlude in the World Series, both teams took to the road and played exhibition games. The day after their doubleheader against the Monarchs, the Grays played a doubleheader against the Newark Eagles in Hartford, Connecticut. The following day, they played the Philadelphia Stars in Philly in a game that went extra innings, and they then traveled down to Baltimore to face the Elite Giants. The Monarchs played exhibition games in Indianapolis and Louisville, Kentucky.

Cum Posey, the longtime owner of the Grays, had previously played for and managed the club. Because his team's roster was somewhat depleted by injuries and by the military draft, Posey picked up several players from the Eagles and the Stars before the exhibition game against the Elite Giants: pitcher Leon Day, outfielder Ed Stone, and first baseman Lennie Pearson from the Eagles; and shortstop Bus Clarkson and pitcher Edsall Walker from the Stars. Posey did not acquire benchwarmers, either—most of his recruits were ringers. Pearson won the Triple Crown in the NNL; Clarkson finished second (behind Pearson) in batting in the NNL; and Day led the NNL in ERA and strikeouts and also hit .341 as a part-time outfielder.

After a one-week delay, the stadium in Kansas City became available, and the World Series resumed. Down 3–0 in the Series and needing a win to stave off elimination, Cum Posey decided to keep his recently signed players, except for Edsall Walker, on the roster to give the Grays a boost. Before the game, the Monarchs lodged an objection to the Grays' use of the additional players but agreed to proceed with the game to avoid disappointing the fans who had showed up and paid admission to the game. The Monarchs, however, played the game under official protest.

Marquee pitcher Leon Day locked horns with Satchel Paige and came out on top, striking out twelve batters and leading the Grays to a 4–1 win. Day and the new signees also played a big part in the Grays' offense. Ed Stone doubled in a run, and Lennie Pearson doubled twice and came around to score both times. He scored the second run on a fly out by Day, who would have been credited with a sacrifice fly and an RBI under current MLB rules.

Then the shit hit the fan. Because the Monarchs lost the game, they followed through on their protest and sought to have the game disallowed. Posey called for the dismissal of the protest, arguing that the game should count because the Monarchs' co-owner, Tom Baird, had given him verbal permission at a meeting to use the extra players. Baird denied granting Posey permission, and J. L. Wilkinson, the Monarchs' other owner, insisted that he had no knowledge of any concession. The Monarchs' traveling secretary and business manager Dizzy Dismukes described the sentiments of the team: "We didn't [lose to] the Homestead Grays. We lost to the National League All-Stars." The Monarchs were so angry that initially they threatened to cancel the remainder of the Series, but they backed off on their threat.

Because of the seriousness of the situation, officials from the NNL and the Negro American League (NAL) as well as from both teams met the day after the game. At the meeting, it was determined that the Monarchs' protest would be upheld and the Grays' victory would be stricken, leaving intact the Monarchs' 3–0 lead in the Series. It was further agreed that the Grays would be prohibited from using the four extra players for the rest of the Series.

The Monarchs and the Grays each played another exhibition game against other teams before the World Series restarted. The next game was scheduled to be played at Wrigley Field in Chicago, but it was rained out, so the teams traveled to Philadelphia to face off at Shibe Park, home of the MLB's Phillies and the Athletics. Since Game 3 on September 13, there had been a slew of exhibition games and a disallowed contest, but this was the first World Series game that would count in sixteen days.

Without Leon Day, Lennie Pearson, and the other players from the Eagles and the Stars, and with Josh Gibson mired in a Series-long slump, the Grays lost, 9–5, and were swept in the Series. Jack Matchett started for the Monarchs and allowed five unearned runs in 3⅔ innings. Frank Morgan then gave the ball to his ace, Paige. While Satchel was mowing down the Grays' batters, the Monarchs scored twice in the seventh inning to take the lead and added three more runs in the eighth to ice the game. Paige tossed 5⅓ hitless innings in relief for the win.

Paige posted a 2.20 ERA in the Series, and second baseman Bonnie Serrell collected 10 hits; his biggest blow was a three-run triple in Game 2. The Grays batted just .206 in the Series; Josh Gibson hit only .077.

As World War II continued to rage overseas, the Grays came back to win the Negro World Series in 1943 and 1944, defeating the Birmingham Black Barons in both Series.

In 1945, Jackie Robinson, after playing baseball, football, and basketball, in addition to running track at UCLA, and serving two years in World War II, signed with the Monarchs. He was the starting shortstop for the West in the East-West Game. Branch Rickey, president and general manager of the Brooklyn Dodgers, began to scout the Negro Leagues for talent with the intention of signing a Black player and integrating MLB. He narrowed his list to Jackie Robinson, Baltimore Elite Giants catcher Roy Campanella, and Newark Eagles pitcher Don Newcombe. In October 1945, Rickey picked Robinson and signed him to a contract. J. L. Wilkinson and Tom Baird objected to the signing because the Monarchs had contractual rights to Robinson, but their objections were to no avail.

In his Ebbets Field office, Rickey told Robinson that he would be assigned to the Dodgers' Triple-A team, the Montreal Royals. Rickey warned his new player that he would be subjected to racial abuse if he broke the color barrier and took the field for the Dodgers. Robinson had endured such abuse before and had stood up for himself. A notable example occurred in 1944 when he boarded a US Army bus and was told to move to the back. Robinson refused, and the driver called the military police, who took him into custody. Robinson was later court-martialed and acquitted.

"Mr. Rickey, do you want a ballplayer who is afraid to fight back?" Robinson asked.

"I want a player with the guts *not* to fight back," Rickey replied.

Before the 1946 season started, Rickey signed Campanella and Newcombe and they were assigned to play for Nashua in the Dodgers' minor league system. Robinson had an outstanding season with the Royals in '46, paving the way for him to move up to the Dodgers in 1947.

Wilkinson, Baird, and the other owners of Negro League teams feared that the future of the Negro Leagues was in jeopardy if the major leagues integrated. Attendance of Negro League games held its own in 1946, and the Monarchs returned to their first World Series since 1942, losing to the Newark Eagles.

In January 1947, Josh Gibson collapsed and died of a stroke. He had been plagued by a variety of health problems over the previous few years. The most notable were a seizure, which sent him to the hospital, and depression, which landed him in a sanitarium. At times, he was said to drink and use drugs excessively. He was only thirty-five years old when he succumbed to the stroke.

Three months after Gibson's death, Robinson made his historic debut with the Dodgers. Robinson heeded Rickey's advice by gritting his teeth and remaining silent when Philadelphia Phillies manager Ben Chapman pelted him with racial slurs from the dugout during a game. While Robinson was hitting over .300 for the Dodgers, in July, Cleveland Indians owner Bill Veeck signed outfielder Larry Doby, who had been playing for the Newark Eagles. Doby bypassed the minors and made his first appearance for the Indians three days later.

Interest in the Negro Leagues dwindled considerably in 1947 as many fans turned their attention to Robinson and, later, Doby to see whether they could prove they were major-league-quality players. Coverage of the Negro Leagues by the Black press also dropped dramatically after Robinson entered into the majors. As Grays first baseman Buck Leonard later lamented, "After Jackie [started with the Dodgers], we couldn't draw flies." Despite the Negro Leagues' decline in popularity, they held a World Series in 1947, and the New York Cubans beat the Cleveland Buckeyes. Jackie Robinson helped the Dodgers win the National League pennant in 1947, but they lost to the Yankees in the World Series.

On his forty-second birthday, July 7, 1948, Satchel Paige signed a contract with the Indians. In view of Paige's age, some skeptics felt that the signing was a publicity stunt by Bill Veeck. To refute that notion and ensure that Paige still had the stuff to pitch in the major leagues, Veeck had the crafty hurler throw pitches to Lou Boudreau, the shortstop and manager of the Indians who went on to win the MVP in 1948. When Boudreau struggled to make solid contact against Paige, Veeck knew he had made a wise decision.

Paige did not disappoint Veeck, Boudreau, and the Indians fans who flocked to Municipal Stadium in Cleveland to watch the old pro pitch in the majors. Pitching as a starter and a reliever, Paige logged a 6–1 record and a 2.48 ERA; he threw back-to-back complete-game shutouts in August. Along with Larry Doby, the team's starting center fielder, he earned a World Series ring when the Indians won their first pennant since 1920 and beat the Boston Braves in the Series. Paige retired the two batters he faced in the Series, and Doby, who started all six games, hit .318.

That same fall, in what would be the final Negro World Series, the Grays beat the Birmingham Black Barons to win their third Series in six years. The game-winning hit in the Black Barons' only victory of the Series was delivered by seventeen-year-old Willie Mays, playing his first year of professional baseball. The NNL folded after the 1948 World Series. The Stars, the Elite Giants, the Cubans, and the Eagles (after relocating to Houston) joined the NAL. The New York Black Yankees dropped out. The Grays took a different tack, becoming a member of the minor-league Negro American Association; but the league dissolved after the 1949 season.

Over the next few years, the NAL struggled to stay afloat, though several Negro League players flourished in the majors. After he pitched another season with the Indians in 1949, Satchel Paige was released, and then in 1951 he signed with the St. Louis Browns. By that time, Bill Veeck had sold the Indians and bought the Browns. Paige compiled a 3.31 ERA during his five seasons with the Indians and the Browns, quite impressive for a pitcher in his forties. He was also named to the American League All-Star team in 1952 and 1953. Satchel pitched one more game in the majors, for the Kansas City Athletics in 1965 when he was fifty-nine. This time, the signing of Paige was a publicity stunt by the Kansas City owner, Charlie Finley. Remarkably, the crafty right-hander threw three shutout innings against the Red Sox.

After Campanella and Newcombe moved up the ladder in the minors, the Dodgers brought them up to the majors. Newcombe was named National League Rookie of the Year for the Dodgers in 1949, the same year that Jackie Robinson won the MVP. Newcombe won the Cy Young Award and MVP in 1956. Campanella won three National League MVPs for the Dodgers in the 1950s.

Willie Mays signed with the New York Giants in 1950 and was named National League Rookie of the Year in 1951. He followed it up by winning an MVP in 1954 and another in 1965. Hank Aaron played for the Indianapolis Clowns in the NAL and signed with the Boston Braves in 1952. By 1954, the Braves had moved from Boston to Milwaukee, and Aaron was in the team's starting lineup. He won the National League MVP in 1957. Ernie Banks played for the Monarchs in 1950 and 1953 before signing with the Chicago Cubs late in the '53 season. He won consecutive National League MVPs in 1958 and 1959. Elston Howard became the first Black player for the Yankees in 1955; he had played three years for the Monarchs before signing with the Yankees in 1950. He won the American League MVP in 1963.

For their achievements in the major leagues, Robinson, Mays, Aaron, and Banks were all voted into the Hall of Fame on the first ballot. Campanella was inducted into the Hall in his seventh year of eligibility;

had he not been involved in a career-ending car accident when he was thirty-six, Campy may have made it on the first ballot.

The NAL stumbled along until 1962 before finally closing its doors. The league went from having ten teams in 1950 to eight in '51, six in '52, and four in '53. It bounced among having four to six teams over the next several years but fell to having three teams—Birmingham, Kansas City, and Raleigh, North Carolina—during its last two years. The tradition of the East-West Game continued each year until the end, but the attendance at the games reflected the decreased interest in Negro League baseball. The game averaged fewer than ten thousand fans during the last ten years, a substantial drop from the glory years of the 1930s and 1940s when the game routinely attracted more than thirty thousand fans and twice surged past fifty thousand.

In 1971, Satchel Paige became the first superstar of the Negro Leagues to be enshrined in the Baseball Hall of Fame in Cooperstown. Satchel's induction was followed up the next year by Josh Gibson's and Buck Leonard's. The Grays' first baseman for fourteen years, Leonard drew comparisons to Yankees great Lou Gehrig for his quick and easy left-handed stroke that consistently delivered a high batting average and plenty of runs. Who knows what numbers these legends would have put together if they had played their entire careers in the major leagues alongside their white counterparts? It is likely that they would have reached major statistical milestones: 300 wins for Paige, 500 home runs for Gibson, and 3,000 hits for Leonard.

The walls of the Hall of Fame are lined with the plaques of eight players who participated in the 1942 Negro World Series. Paige's teammates on the Monarchs, pitcher Hilton Smith, outfielder Willard Brown, and first baseman and later ambassador of the Negro Leagues, Buck O'Neil, also were voted in. Pitcher Ray Brown and infielder Jud Wilson joined Gibson and Leonard from the Grays. Leon Day, who pitched the complete game for the Grays in the nullified game, also got the call from the Hall.

The 1942 Negro World Series stands out because it was the only time the two revered teams, the Monarchs and the Grays, played against each other in the Series. In contrast, two of MLB's most successful teams, the

Yankees and the Dodgers, have gone head-to-head in eleven World Series. The unusual sixteen-day interlude between Game 3 and Game 4 is attributable to a few factors specific to the Negro Leagues: Even though the Monarchs and Grays were *major*-league teams, they had to play second fiddle to a white *minor*-league team for the right to play in the Kansas City stadium; the teams played several exhibition games between the two final Series games—as Buck O'Neil noted, "It might seem odd, but that's the way it was done"; and the factious relationship between the teams' owners, an issue that began in the early days of Negro baseball, led to the protest by the Monarchs and the ruling that the original Game 4 would be thrown out.

When asked later about the strength of his 1942 Monarchs team that swept the Grays in the World Series, O'Neil responded, "I believe we could have given the New York Yankees a run for their money that year." It's a shame they did not get the chance.

Satchel Paige: racial pioneer, showman, barnstormer, and all-time great pitcher. He had two wins against the Homestead Grays in the 1942 Negro World Series and helped the Kansas City Monarchs capture the title in a Series that was marked by a sixteen-day hiatus, barnstorming tours, and allegations of ringers being used by the Grays. *National Baseball Hall of Fame and Museum*

3

The Missed Call and the Meltdown

SOME PEOPLE, BY VIRTUE OF THEIR LIFE CIRCUMSTANCES—GAMBLERS with debts to mobsters, wives of crazy ex-husbands—may receive death threats and arson threats. *But a Major League Baseball umpire who missed a call?* Incredibly, it happened after the 1985 World Series.

It was dubbed the "I-70 Showdown Series" because a 250-mile stretch of that highway connected St. Louis and Kansas City where the Cardinals and Royals met to determine which team would be crowned baseball's world champion in 1985.

The Cardinals were managed by Whitey Herzog, a Midwesterner himself from New Athens, Illinois, which is less than an hour's drive from St. Louis, where he had grown up a fan of the Redbirds. Before he managed the Cardinals, Herzog piloted the Royals to American League Western Division titles in 1976, 1977, and 1978, which included a 102-win season in '77. Each year, the New York Yankees beat the Royals in the best-of-five League Championship Series (LCS). The Royals parted ways with Herzog after the 1979 season, mainly because of friction between owner Ewing Kauffman and him. He was not out of a job long, though, because the Cardinals hired him as their manager in the middle of the 1980 season, and he also became the team's general manager shortly thereafter. Two years later, in 1982, Herzog took the Cardinals all the way, beating the Milwaukee Brewers in a hard-fought, seven-game World Series.

Herzog's Cardinals returned to the Fall Classic in 1985. Several key players from the '82 team were holdovers in '85: pitcher Joaquin Andujar, center fielder Willie McGee, shortstop Ozzie Smith, second baseman Tom Herr, and catcher Darrell Porter. There were three notable additions to the '85 squad: Jack Clark, the San Francisco Giants' right fielder for eight years, was acquired in a trade right before spring training; pitcher John Tudor came over in a deal from the Pittsburgh Pirates in the offseason; and left fielder Vince Coleman broke into the majors.

Herzog's style of play, which the media branded "Whiteyball," was built on speed, defense, and pitching. The Cardinals stole 314 bases—almost two per game—the highest single-season total in the National League since 1912. Coleman swiped 110 bases to lead the majors, his first of three straight 100-stolen-base seasons. McGee stole 56 bases, which along with his league-leading .353 batting average and 216 hits, 114 runs scored, and Gold Glove earned him the MVP Award. Smith (also a Gold Glove winner), Herr, and right fielder Andy Van Slyke each stole more than 30 bases. Herr also hit .302 and his 110 RBIs ranked third in the National League.

The Cardinals needed speed to score runs since they ranked second-to-last in the majors with just 87 home runs. Clark, whom Herzog shifted to first base because he had Coleman, McGee, and Van Slyke in the outfield, led the team with 22 homers. No other Cardinal hit as many as 15 home runs. Their pitching was strong—righty Andujar and lefty Tudor each won 21 games. Tudor led the majors with 10 shutouts.

St. Louis faced Tommy Lasorda's Los Angeles Dodgers in the League Championship Series, which had been expanded from five games to seven that season. Things did not look promising for the Cardinals when the Dodgers beat Tudor and Andujar in the first two games in Los Angeles. But the Cardinals bounced back to take the next three in St. Louis, winning Games 4 and 5 without one of their best players, who had been injured in a freak accident.

During pregame warm-ups before Game 4, Vince Coleman and his teammate, third baseman Terry Pendleton, were heading to the dugout to grab bats and take some batting practice swings. Rain began falling, and Cardinals coach Hal Lanier told Coleman and Pendleton to stay where they were; he would get their bats. The two players were standing between the first-base foul line and the pitcher's mound. The grounds crew started rolling out the automatic tarp to cover the field, and Coleman, caught off guard, was struck in his left leg by the tarp. His leg became trapped underneath. It took him a minute or two to pry it loose, and when he got up he had trouble walking. He was scratched from the lineup. Tito Landrum, who replaced Coleman in left field that night, contributed four hits to help the Cardinals win Game 4 and tie the Series. Coleman was initially diagnosed with a contusion, but later an MRI revealed that he had sustained a fractured tibia, ending his season.

In Game 5, Ozzie Smith, known for his wizardry with his glove at shortstop but not his power, hit a walk-off home run in the bottom of the ninth inning off Dodgers reliever Tom Niedenfuer to break a 2–2 tie.

Back in Los Angeles, the Dodgers needed a win to stay alive. Orel Hershiser took a 4–1 lead into the seventh inning for the Dodgers, but Willie McGee hit a two-run single to close the gap to 4–3, and Tommy Lasorda again went to Niedenfuer. The young right-hander had led the Dodgers in saves in each of the past two seasons. Smith continued to have Niedenfuer's number, smoking a game-tying triple. Lasorda intentionally walked the switch-hitting Tom Herr to set up a double play. Niedenfuer reared back and struck out Jack Clark and Andy Van Slyke to end the threat.

Jeff Lahti led the Cardinals in saves during the regular season, but Todd Worrell, brought up from the minors in late August, had quickly become the go-to guy out of the bullpen for Herzog. Worrell took over for Andujar in the bottom of the seventh, and in the eighth Mike Marshall hit a leadoff home run to give the Dodgers a 5–4 lead. With two outs, a runner on first, and the ninth spot in the order up next, Lasorda raised some eyebrows by electing not to send up a pinch-hitter to try to plate an insurance run. Instead he allowed Niedenfuer to bat so that he could stay in the game. The relief pitcher, who rarely batted, went down on strikes.

In the top of the ninth inning, McGee hit a one-out single off Niedenfuer and stole second. Smith walked and Herr grounded out to first, advancing the runners to second and third. The Dodger Stadium crowd rose to their feet, anticipating the third out and a Game 7.

Jack Clark was due up next. Lasorda was faced with the difficult decision—permit the righty Niedenfuer to pitch to the right-handed-hitting Clark or intentionally walk the slugger and allow his pitcher to go after the left-handed-hitting Andy Van Slyke, a third-year player who batted .259 during the season and was 1-for-10 in the League Championship Series. Lasorda declined to walk Clark. It was a costly mistake. Clark silenced the crowd by burying Niedenfuer's first pitch into the left-field bleachers for a three-run homer to put the Cardinals up 7–5. Southpaw Ken Dayley retired the Dodgers in order in the bottom of the ninth, and the Cardinals, losers of the first two games of the Series, were National League champions.

The Royals' road to the World Series was not easy either. Managed by Dick Howser, the Royals squeaked out the American League Western Division title by one game over the California Angels, having trailed the Angels by as many as 7½ games in July. Howser's first managerial job was with the Yankees in 1980. He led the Yanks to 103 wins and the American League Eastern Division title. However, when the Yankees were swept by the Royals in the League Championship Series, the impetuous owner George Steinbrenner gave him the axe. The Royals, managed by Herzog's replacement, Jim Frey, lost in six games to the Philadelphia Phillies in the 1980 World Series.

When the Royals struggled in the strike-shortened 1981 season, Frey was let go at the end of August and replaced by Howser. Because the Royals won the "second half" division title, they made the playoffs in the expanded format that was used that season because of the strike, but they were beaten 3–0 by the Oakland Athletics in the first round. Howser again guided the Royals to the postseason in 1984, but ghosts of playoffs past continued to haunt him as his team was swept by the Detroit Tigers in the League Championship Series.

When Howser's Royals met the Toronto Blue Jays in the 1985 League Championship Series, he was 0–9 in postseason play. Howser's roster included five veterans who had been with the Royals since the years when Whitey Herzog led them to three division titles: third baseman and future Hall of Famer George Brett, second baseman Frank White, center fielder Willie Wilson, outfielder/designated hitter Hal McRae, and catcher John Wathan. The Royals finished next-to-last in the American League in runs scored, though Brett hit .335 with 30 home runs and first baseman Steve Balboni socked 36 homers. Second-year pitcher Bret Saberhagen won the Cy Young Award on the strength of his 20–6 record, and sidearm funny man Dan Quisenberry led the American League in saves for the fourth straight year.

The Royals lost the first two games of the League Championship Series to the Blue Jays, extending Howser's postseason winless streak to 11. But they rebounded to win four of the last five games, giving them the opportunity to face the Cardinals and win their first World Series.

The Cardinals won 10 more games than the Royals in the regular season and were favored in the World Series. The Royals dug themselves an early hole by losing the first two games at their home ballpark. Tudor and Worrell combined to hold the Royals to one run in the opener. In Game 2, Kansas City was on the brink of tying the Series after Charlie Leibrandt, a 17–game winner during the season, took a 2–0 lead into the ninth inning. The Cardinals rallied, though, scoring four runs with two outs to pull out the game, 4–2; Terry Pendleton's three-run double was the big blow. Jeff Lahti picked up the save for St. Louis.

The Royals won Game 3 in St. Louis, 6–1, when Bret Saberhagen defeated Joaquin Andjuar. Herzog and Andujar were not happy with the ball-strike calls by home-plate umpire Jim McKean. "Saberhagen's zone that night was about 22 by 22 inches, Andujar's was six by six," Herzog later cracked.

Tudor threw a five-hit shutout in Game 4 for his second win of the Series to give St. Louis a commanding 3–1 lead and afterward made some disparaging comments about the media. Tudor, a seven-year veteran, had never pitched in the postseason before, and he was not accustomed to the enormous media coverage. When Tudor walked into the clubhouse after his shutout and saw the hordes of reporters gathered around his locker, he scoffed, "What's it take to get a media pass, a [driver's] license?"

For the second straight postseason series, the Royals had fallen behind, 3–1. With the Busch Memorial Stadium crowd behind them, the Cardinals expected that the corks would be flying after Game 5. When the players arrived at the clubhouse before the game, their lockers were covered with clear plastic to protect them from postgame champagne showers. But it was not to be. The Royals knocked out Cardinals starter Bob Forsch in the second inning and cruised to a 6–1 victory.

The home-field advantage shifted back in the Royals' favor when the teams returned to Kansas City for Game 6. Charlie Leibrandt and Danny Cox, a strong number-three starter behind Tudor and Andjuar, got the ball for the Cardinals. It was a pitchers' duel from the start. The Royals may have been robbed of the game's first run by an umpire's call in the bottom of the fourth inning. With one out, Frank White beat out a bunt. He tried to steal second, and umpire Billy Williams called him out. Replays showed that White beat the tag by Ozzie Smith. Pat Sheridan, at the plate when White was called out at second, grounded a single to right field. If White had been called safe, he probably would have scored on Sheridan's hit. But Sheridan was stranded at first when Cox retired Steve Balboni.

The game remained scoreless through seven innings. In the top of the eighth inning, Leibrandt allowed a single and a walk, and, with two outs, Herzog pulled Cox in favor of a pinch-hitter, Brian Harper. A utility infielder-outfielder who also served as a third-string catcher, Harper had only 52 at-bats in the regular season and was 0-for-4 in the postseason. Harper hit a 1-2 pitch into center field for a single, and Terry Pendleton sped around to score from second to give St. Louis a 1–0 lead. Ken Dayley replaced Cox and pitched a scoreless eighth. Howser sent in Quisenberry in a non-save situation in the ninth to keep the deficit at one run, which he did.

The Cardinals were three outs away from their second world championship in four years. Herzog and Howser engaged in a chess match before a pitch was thrown in the bottom of the ninth. Southpaw Dayley went back to the mound, and left-handed-hitting Sheridan was scheduled to lead off. Howser picked right-handed-hitting Darryl Motley to bat for Sheridan. Herzog countered by lifting Dayley for righty Todd Worrell. Howser responded by bringing in Jorge Orta, a left-handed batter, as a pinch-hitter to face Worrell.

Cardinals fans were confident that Worrell would hold the lead. After all, their team was 91–0 during the season in games in which they led after eight innings and had added six more wins in the post-season. Despite his inexperience, the rocket-armed Worrell, with a nasty fastball-and-slider combination, had tied a World Series record in Game 5 by striking out six consecutive batters. He pitched the sixth and seventh innings, faced six Royals, and struck out all six swinging.

Worrell, whose major-league debut had been just sixty days earlier, had the chance to notch a save in a World Series–clinching game. He surveyed the defense behind him: Pendleton, Smith, Herr, and Clark in the infield; Landrum, McGee, and Van Slyke in the outfield. He looked at Porter, his gritty catcher, behind the plate. Royals fans screamed at the tops of their lungs, trying to incite a rally by their team. Al Michaels, Tim McCarver, and Hall of Famer Jim Palmer were calling the game in the broadcast booth for ABC.

Orta, in his fourteenth major league season, stepped into the batter's box. The Royals, whom he had joined in 1984, were his fifth big-league club. At this point in his career, he was a part-time designated hitter. He batted .267 with four homers during the 1985 season. In the postseason, he was hitless in seven at-bats. Orta's best years were with the Chicago White Sox. Playing mostly second base, Orta was the hits leader of the Chisox in the 1970s.

Orta took a strike and then fouled two pitches off. What happened next would become one of the most controversial plays in World Series history. Orta hit a dribbler to the right of Clark and started sprinting down the line. The ball was hit slowly enough that Clark would not have been able to field the ball and beat Orta to the bag, so Worrell hustled over to cover first. Anticipating a close play, first-base umpire Don Denkinger, who had been an American League umpire for seventeen years and whose high grades by MLB had earned him two prior World Series and four League Championship Series assignments, moved closer to the base but remained in foul territory. Denkinger had been taught to assume that position, allowing him to listen for the ball smacking the pitcher's glove while eyeing whose foot touched the base first. Clark gloved the ball and made a sidearm toss to Worrell, who, with his outstretched glove, caught the ball on the bag. Orta then stepped on the bag and tumbled to the ground. Denkinger, about eight feet from the base, spread his arms three times rapidly to indicate Orta was safe.

Worrell, Clark, and Herr vigorously argued the call and were quickly joined by Herzog.

"Man, are you shitting me?" Herzog barked. "I know he didn't beat the throw. I could see that from the dugout. I thought maybe he missed the bag."

"No," Denkinger replied. "The runner beat him." Three decades before the advent of challenges and reviews, Herzog had no choice but to return to the dugout.

Meanwhile, Palmer and Michaels were watching the instant replay from the broadcast booth. "Looks like he was out," Palmer observed.

"Oh yes," Michaels agreed. "I don't think there's any doubt about it."

Denkinger was not sure whether his call was right or wrong, but secretly he began to hope the Cardinals would close out the inning and win the Series. If in fact he did get the call wrong but the Cardinals held on to win, his mistake would be forgotten because it would not have affected the outcome of the game.

With Orta at first base, burly right-handed-hitting Steve Balboni lifted a high pop in foul ground on the first-base side. Porter threw down his catcher's mask and headed for the ball; at the same time, Clark bolted from first toward the ball. The pop was similar to one Frank White hit against the Phillies in Game 6 of the 1980 World Series when Porter was with the Royals. The Phillies led the Series, 3–2, and took a 4–1 lead into the ninth inning at Philadelphia's Veterans Stadium. The Royals loaded the bases with one out against Tug McGraw, and, when White hit a foul pop, first baseman Pete Rose and catcher Bob Boone converged in front of the Phillies dugout. The ball bounced out of Boone's glove, and Rose alertly made the catch before the ball hit the ground. McGraw then struck out Willie Wilson to end the game and Series.

Porter initially called Balboni's pop and then exclaimed, "I don't have it!" Clark stumbled, lost track of the ball, and it bounced on the first step of the Royals dugout. Given a second chance, Balboni slapped a single to left, advancing Orta to second. Howser sent in Onix Concepción to run for the ultra-slow Balboni.

Worrell was frustrated. If Denkinger had made the correct call on Orta's ground ball, and Clark or Porter had caught Balboni's pop, there would have been two outs and nobody on. Instead, there were two on and no outs. Herzog went to the mound and talked things over with Worrell, Porter, and the infielders.

Veteran Jim Sundberg, known more for his defense than his offense, came up. Third-base coach Mike Ferraro flashed the bunt sign. Sundberg, a frequent bunter in his early years but not so much since, took two pitches outside the strike zone and, after bunting two pitches foul, bunted the 2-2 pitch back to Worrell, who fired to third to nail Orta.

Hal McRae pinch-hit for light-hitting shortstop Buddy Biancalana. Between 1976 and 1985, in even-numbered years, the designated hitter rule was used throughout the World Series; in odd-numbered years, there was no designated hitter, and pitchers batted. McRae, who was used exclusively as the designated hitter during the regular season and who started six of seven games as the DH in the League Championship Series, was limited to two pinch-hitting appearances in the Series before he headed to the plate. Worrell's 1-0 pitch was a slider that bounced off Porter's glove and rolled away, allowing Concepción and Sundberg each to move up a base. Porter had only five passed balls all season but made one in a crucial spot. McRae had a 2-0 count, and Herzog decided to walk him intentionally and set up a double play. John Wathan pinch-ran for McRae.

With the bases loaded and one out, Dane Iorg pinch-hit for Quisenberry. The Royals originally drafted Iorg in the sixteenth round of the 1968 draft, the year before they entered the American League as an expansion team. Iorg, in high school at the time, chose not to sign and instead played baseball at Brigham Young University. Three years later, he had developed into a top prospect, and the Phillies drafted him in the first round. This time Iorg signed and played in Philadelphia's minor league organization for six years before he cracked the majors for the Phillies in 1977. He played just 12 games for the Phils before he was traded to the Cardinals in a midseason deal. He spent the next seven seasons in St. Louis as a part-time outfielder and first baseman. He did not have much power, but he had two .300 seasons.

The Cardinals sold Iorg to the Royals in 1984, and Howser used him as a jack-of-all-trades, reserve outfielder, first baseman, and designated hitter. He hit only .223 in 1985, more than 50 points less than his career average. Because of his long tenure in St. Louis, Iorg remained friends with several players on the Cardinals. During batting practice before one of the World Series games, Iorg ribbed one of the Cardinals coaches, Dave Ricketts, "I'm gonna beat you guys with a pinch-hit."

Iorg made good on his promise when the left-handed swinger looped Worrell's second pitch into right field for a hit, scoring Concepción and Sundberg, whose headfirst slide just beat Andy Van Slyke's throw. The fans went bonkers, and the Royals bench poured onto the field to celebrate the win.

While Denkinger was on his way to the umpires' dressing room, he saw Peter Ueberroth, baseball's stern, second-year commissioner, at the door. "Did I get it right?" Denkinger asked.

Ueberroth shook his head. "No."

Denkinger was distressed, thinking that his bad call may have cost the Cardinals the World Series.

The mood was somber in the Cardinals clubhouse after the game—and had not improved the next day before Game 7. Whitey Herzog later lamented, "We had something taken from us the night before, and we all felt a sense of doom and gloom."

Years later, Tom Herr echoed Herzog's sentiments. "Our collective psyche was damaged; we had a feeling that we were robbed. That was hard to get over in 24 hours." Herr added that it was not easy to watch the World Series trophy get taken out of the Cardinals locker room after Game 6, knowing that it would have been presented by the commissioner to Herzog and his team if the Cardinals had won the game.

Herzog was not optimistic about his team's chances of winning Game 7. He knew, because of the rotation of the umpires, that Denkinger would be stationed behind the plate. "We have about as much chance of winning as a monkey," he snarled.

Both teams had their aces on the mound—Tudor for the Cardinals and Saberhagen for the Royals. It was all Kansas City from the start. Darryl Motley hit a two-run homer off Tudor in the second inning. In the third, Tudor became undone. When he walked Jim Sundberg with the bases loaded to force in a run, Herzog came out and yanked him. Tudor normally had great control—he walked just 1.6 batters every nine innings during the season—but issued four free passes in 2⅓ innings. Tudor was so angry that, when he got to the dugout, he punched an electric fan, slicing one of his fingers so deeply that the injury required stitches at the hospital. Things continued to go downhill for the Cardinals as Balboni greeted reliever Bill Campbell with a two-run single to make the score 5–0.

It all fell apart for the Redbirds in the fifth inning. The Royals scored four runs off three Cardinals relievers, and the side was still not retired. With runners on first and third and two outs, Herzog summoned Joaquin Andujar from the bullpen for a rare relief appearance. After Frank White greeted him with an RBI single, Andujar threw a 2-2 pitch that he thought was a strike, but Denkinger called it a ball. Andujar, still angry that Jim McKean had squeezed him in Game 3 and Denkinger had missed the call at first in Game 6, threw up his arms in disbelief. He walked to home plate and started jawing with Denkinger. Pendleton and Smith hurried in to restrain Andujar.

Herzog had been berating Denkinger most of the night from the dugout and went out to home plate to give the umpire a piece of his mind. "If you'd done your damn job last night, we wouldn't be here," he shouted.

"If your team was hitting better than .120, we wouldn't be here either," Denkinger retorted. (The Cardinals were not hitting .120, but it was below .200, and they had scored just 13 runs in the Series.) Herzog kept bickering and, when he called Denkinger an expletive, his night was over.

When play resumed, Denkinger called Andujar's next pitch ball four, and the pitcher exploded. He charged home plate, got in Denkinger's face, pointing his finger and shouting obscenities. Denkinger ejected Andujar, and several Cardinals players and coaches came over to restrain their pitcher and lead him off the field, where he went to the clubhouse to join Herzog. Al Michaels summed up things well: "I have never seen a team become so unraveled."

While Tudor had taken his frustration out on an electric fan, Andujar took his out on a clubhouse toilet, which he attacked with a bat. For his outburst on the field, Andujar was later suspended by the commissioner for the first 10 games of the following season; the suspension was eventually reduced to five.

Bob Forsch became the fifth pitcher for the Cardinals that inning, and he promptly threw a wild pitch, allowing another run to make the score 11–0. That's the way the game ended. Saberhagen went the distance and captured the Series MVP honors. For the second straight Series, the Royals rebounded from a 3–1 deficit to win in seven games.

For the Cardinals, Denkinger's missed call on Orta's ground ball triggered a meltdown. A missed pop and passed ball later in the inning contributed to the Game 6 loss. In Game 7, they allowed 11 runs, and managed only five singles while scoring no runs. Their manager as well as one of their pitchers were ejected. Havoc was wreaked on a dugout fan and a clubhouse toilet.

The fallout from Denkinger's call started before Game 7 ended and got worse than he could have envisioned. While the Cardinals were getting buried in Game 7, two St. Louis radio DJs obtained Denkinger's home address in Waterloo, Iowa, as well as his phone number, and announced them on the air. Angry Cardinals fans called the station accusing Denkinger of fixing the Series, while irate gamblers vilified the umpire for causing them to lose bets. A deranged caller threatened to burn down the Denkingers' house.

The day after the Series ended, Denkinger and his wife made the three-hundred-mile drive back to Iowa. When they reached their street, a police car blocked them from entering. An officer got out and gave them the frightening news about the arson threat. Denkinger and his wife and their two daughters were in fear for their lives.

Fortunately, the arson threat was not acted on, but, throughout the fall, Denkinger received obscene phone calls and letters. Two years later Denkinger received the most threatening letter, which the FBI traced to a St. Louis construction company. The letter read as follows:

I know what you do. I know where you go. And when I point my
.357 magnum at you, I'll blow you away.

This turned out to be an empty threat, and Denkinger was unharmed.
Still, the letter caused Denkinger and his family undue stress. Despite
receiving these nefarious threats, he went on to serve as a major-league
umpire for thirteen more years and umped his fourth World Series in
1991. Denkinger passed away in May 2023, at the age of eighty-six.

Instant replay was instituted by Major League Baseball in 2014, and,
as a result, many umpires' calls have been reversed; some of those over-
turned calls have changed the outcomes of games. The question arises—
would the Cardinals have won Game 6 and the World Series had instant
replay been used in 1985? Herzog, along with Herr and his teammates,
always maintained that if Denkinger had correctly called Orta out at first
base, the Cardinals would have won the World Series. There is no dispute
that would have been true if Orta had hit the ground ball with two outs.
It's not as clear, though, because he was the leadoff batter in the inning.
Even with the missed call, if Clark or Porter had caught Balboni's foul
pop, the Royals would have had a runner on first with one out—the same
scenario that would have occurred if Orta had been called out and Balboni's pop had been missed. Either way, Dick Howser almost certainly
would not have had Jim Sundberg bunt with a man on first and one out;
he would have let Sundberg swing away. The catcher did not run well and
could have grounded into a Series-ending double day. Furthermore, if
Porter had not let Worrell's second pitch to McRae get past him, Herzog
would not have intentionally walked McRae. Who knows what would
have happened?

And, if instant replay had been used in 1985, while Jorge Orta would
have been called safe at first in the ninth, Frank White would also have
been called safe at second in the fourth and the Royals likely would have
scored a run.

Denkinger's missed call got the Cardinals off on the wrong track in
the bottom of the ninth in Game 6 of the 1985 World Series. But was it
the team's collective meltdown that really did them in?

St. Louis Cardinals pitcher Todd Worrell (right) and second baseman Tom Herr (left), arguing with umpire Don Denkinger that Kansas City's Jorge Orta was out at first in the ninth inning of Game 6 in 1985. Denkinger blew the call, the Royals won, and the Cards never recovered, getting buried in Game 7 as Kansas City took the title. *Bettman/Bettman via Getty Image*

4

Shoe Polish and the Jones Boys

SMUDGES OF SHOE POLISH WERE AT THE CENTER OF PIVOTAL MOMENTS in two World Series twelve years apart in the second half of the twentieth century.

When the Milwaukee Braves, led by manager Charlie Grimm, broke camp at the end of spring training in 1956, they had high hopes of winning the National League pennant. The middle of the team's lineup featured sluggers Hank Aaron, Eddie Mathews, and Joe Adcock. Perennial 20-game winner Warren Spahn headed the pitching staff, and capable starters Lew Burdette and Bob Buhl followed Spahn in the rotation. The Braves were sluggish for the first seven weeks in '56, posting a 24–22 record and sitting in fifth place. General manager John Quinn fired Grimm and replaced him with one of the team's coaches, Fred Haney. Quinn did not make the switch because of Haney's exemplary track record as a manager. Haney had managed six years in the majors, three with the St. Louis Browns and three with the Pittsburgh Pirates. His winning percentage was a meager .354, and his teams lost 100 games in a season three times.

But Quinn liked Haney's fierce competitiveness and thought he could turn his struggling team around. With Haney calling the shots, the Braves caught fire and won 11 games in a row, lifting them from fifth place to first. They maintained the top spot for most of the remainder of the season, though the Brooklyn Dodgers and Cincinnati Redlegs were close on their heels. The Braves entered the final weekend of the season leading the Dodgers by one game and the Reds by 2½ games. But the Braves lost two out of three to the Cardinals in St. Louis, and the Dodgers swept the Pirates at Ebbets Field to win the pennant. It was heartbreaking for Haney and the Braves to let the pennant slip away.

In 1957, the Braves were determined to atone for their collapse and dethrone the Dodgers. They started strong, 12–2, but then slumped in May. Quinn pulled off a big trade on June 15, acquiring second baseman Red Schoendienst from the New York Giants, and the Braves went on to win the pennant by eight games. Aaron was the National League MVP, winning two legs of the Triple Crown (home runs and RBIs), Schoendienst led the league in hits, and Spahn notched his eighth 20-win season.

In the World Series, the Braves squared off against the venerable New York Yankees. The Braves had not won the World Series since 1914 when the team was based in Boston. Conversely, in the forty-three years since the Braves' last world championship, the Yankees had won 17 World Series. The "Old Professor" Casey Stengel had piloted the Yankees to six World Series victories in the previous eight years.

Game 1 at Yankee Stadium pitted the two best southpaw pitchers of the era, Whitey Ford for the Yankees and Spahn for the Braves, against each other. The Yankees got the better of the action, winning 3–1. The Braves, behind Burdette, a former Yankee farmhand, won Game 2.

Braves fans packed County Stadium for Game 3 to watch the first World Series game in Milwaukee history. The city had had a fifty-one-year drought without Major League Baseball. In the early 1950s, attendance sagged for the Boston Braves, and, a month before the start of the 1953 regular season, the team's owner, Lou Perini, decided to relocate the franchise to Milwaukee. It was the first time the city had featured a major league team since 1901, when the Brewers moved to St. Louis and became the Browns. Bill Veeck, who bought the Browns in 1951, had tried to move his club to Milwaukee, but the deal fell through, paving the way for Perini to take his Braves to Milwaukee. The team already had a stadium ready, because in 1950 the city had begun construction on a stadium slated for the Braves' Triple-A affiliate, with the hope of attracting a major-league team. When the parent team transferred from Boston to Milwaukee, the minor-league team relocated to Toledo, Ohio.

Milwaukee locals were thrilled to have a major-league team to cheer for, and attendance figures reflected their enthusiasm. After the Boston Braves drew fewer than three hundred thousand fans in 1952 to rank last in the majors, Milwaukeeans rang up the turnstiles in 1953 as the Braves led the majors in attendance with more than 1.8 million paying customers. In each of the next four seasons, the team drew more than two million fans and ranked first among the sixteen major-league teams, though Milwaukee was one of the least-populated cities with a major-league team. In 1957, the team not only paced the majors in attendance but also drew seven hundred thousand more fans than the second-place Yankees.

The Midwestern crowd was at a fever pitch when the Braves' public address announcer read the starting lineup. The Yankees, though, quickly silenced the crowd by scoring three runs in the top of the first on their way to a 12–3 trouncing of the home team. The American League Rookie of the Year, Tony Kubek, who had grown up in Milwaukee and graduated from one of the city's high schools just three years earlier, hit two home runs for the Yankees and Mickey Mantle added one. Hank Aaron hit a two-run homer in the fifth inning, which was about all Braves fans had to cheer about.

The loss did not dampen the fervor of the Braves faithful as their team tried to bounce back against the Yankees in Game 4 on a Sunday afternoon with temperatures in the mid-50s. At the same time, 120 miles north, the Green Bay Packers were going head-to-head with the Detroit Lions at New City Stadium. The Packers divided their home games between County Stadium in Milwaukee and New City Stadium (later renamed Lambeau Field) in Green Bay. In 1957, the Packers were still two years way from the start of the golden era in which Vince Lombardi coached the team and led them to five National Football League championships.

Spahn took the mound for the Braves, while Stengel gave Ford an extra day's rest and handed the ball to Tom Sturdivant. The right-handed Sturdivant had the best year of his career in 1957, compiling a 16–6 record. The Yankees scored a run off Spahn in the first, to take a 1–0 lead. Sturdivant held the Braves scoreless for three innings, but they broke through in the fourth with four runs. Aaron hit a three-run homer, and Frank Torre, the older brother of Hall of Famer Joe Torre, followed with a solo shot to make the score 4–1.

Meanwhile, Spahn mowed down the Yankees, allowing only four hits from the second inning to the eighth; three of those runners were erased on double plays. In the bottom of the eighth, with two outs and two Braves runners on, Stengel brought in his fourth pitcher of the game, Tommy Byrne, to face the dangerous Wes Covington.

Byrne was a left-handed pitcher who had spent most of his thirteen-year major-league career with the Yankees. Earlier in his career, when Byrne threw a hard fastball, control was his shortcoming—he led the American League in walks allowed for three seasons and hit batsmen five times. Though Byrne had been a starter for most of his career, Stengel used him mostly out of the bullpen during the last two years. By then, the veteran pitcher relied a lot on off-speed pitches. He did his job by striking out Covington looking, and the game went to the ninth with the Braves still leading, 4–1.

Spahn, in complete control, retired Hank Bauer and Mickey Mantle, and the vociferous Milwaukee fans rose to their feet, anticipating the third out and a tied Series. But then the unthinkable happened. Yogi Berra and Gil McDougald singled, and first baseman Elston Howard unloaded a three-run blast to left field to tie the game. Spahn maintained his composure and got the third out.

Byrne set down the side in the bottom of the ninth, and the game went into extra innings. Haney stuck with his horse Spahn, who picked up two quick outs in the top of the 10th, but then lightning struck again. Kubek singled and Hank Bauer tripled him home, to give the Yankees a 5–4 lead. Braves fans felt as though they had the wind knocked out of them.

Spahn was due up first for the Braves in the bottom of the 10th, and Haney sent up a pinch-hitter, Vernal "Nippy" Jones, a thirty-two-year-old, right-handed, reserve first baseman. Jones acquired his nickname while growing up on the south side of Los Angeles. His father had the moniker of "Nip," and father and son palled around a lot together. Family members would say, "There goes Nip and Nippy." So Vernal became Nippy.

***

Jones's road to the Braves was long and circuitous. Jones was only twenty years old when he broke in with the Cardinals in the middle of the 1946 season. He made a few pinch-hitting appearances and struck out as a pinch-hitter in the World Series, which the Cardinals won in seven games over the Boston Red Sox. By 1948, he was the Cardinals' starting first baseman in a lineup that included Stan Musial and Enos Slaughter. Jones hit .254 with 10 home runs and 81 RBIs that season.

In 1949, Jones was hitting .300, but in late September he sustained a season-ending and career-altering back injury. In a game against Brooklyn, he walked and Dodgers pitcher Joe Hatten tried to pick him off. When he slid back to the base, first baseman Gil Hodges slapped his glove on him. Jones felt a jolt of pain through his back. The game halted, as Jones was carried off the field on a stretcher. In the offseason, he underwent surgery for a herniated disc, and, for a time following the surgery, he was paralyzed from the waist down.

Remarkably, Jones made enough of a recovery from his back injury that he was able to return to the major leagues. But he was not the same player. And, though he played parts of the 1950 and 1951 seasons for the Cardinals, he was not as productive, and the Philadelphia Phillies picked him up in the Rule 5 draft in the offseason. In May 1952, after Jones had played eight games for the Phils, he was sent to the minors. It would be more than five years before he made it back to the big leagues. During that stretch he played in more than 800 minor-league games, mostly with the Sacramento Solons of the Pacific Coast League, a team not affiliated with a major-league team.

In late June 1957, the Braves' first baseman Joe Adcock broke his leg and was expected to be sidelined for about two months. It was a key injury because Adcock was one of the team's power threats; three years earlier, he had become the seventh player in major-league history to hit four home runs in a game. In need of another first baseman to back up Frank Torre while Adcock was on the disabled list, GM Quinn acquired Jones from Sacramento. Jones hit a respectable .266 in 79 at-bats for the Braves during the rest of the season; an 11th inning, walk-off home run at the end of July in a game against the New York Giants was his biggest highlight.

Adcock returned to the Braves in September, but Haney kept Jones on the team for the rest of the season and included him on the World Series roster. In Games 1 and 3, Jones grounded out as a pinch-hitter.

***

The pressure was on as Jones dug into the batter's box to lead off the bottom of the 10th inning. He remembered facing Byrne when the lefty was pitching for Seattle in the Pacific Coast League and expected a curveball on the first pitch. Jones guessed correctly—the pitch broke down and inside, and he felt a nick on his right foot. He dropped his bat and headed for first. Augie Donatelli, the home-plate umpire, called Jones back, saying the pitch was a ball. Jones argued that the ball had struck him on his foot, but Donatelli disagreed.

The ball had skipped past catcher Yogi Berra to the backstop and then rolled back toward home plate. Jones saw that the ball had a black smudge, picked it up, and stuck it in Donatelli's face. "Look," he barked. "There's shoe polish on the ball." Donatelli did what umpires rarely do—he reversed himself and awarded Jones first base. Berra argued against the reversal, and Stengel came out to join his catcher. But Donatelli would not budge. The shoe polish proved that the pitch had hit Jones in the foot.

As soon as Jones reached first, Haney replaced him with a faster runner, Felix Mantilla. Stengel replaced Byrne with right-hander Bob Grim. Red Schoendienst, Jones's teammate on the 1946 Cardinals World Series team, sacrificed Mantilla to second. Shortstop Johnny Logan laced a double to left, plating Mantilla to tie the game, 5–5. Mathews, who later became the first third baseman to hit 500 home runs, followed with a two-run homer to win the game and send Braves fans into a frenzy. Jones's hit-by-pitch had ignited the Braves' game-winning, three-run rally.

The Braves maintained their momentum by winning Game 5 at County Stadium, 1–0, behind Lew Burdette's complete game shutout, his second win of the Series. The Braves were a win away from capturing the World Series, but they would have to do it in front of a raucous New York crowd. The irrepressible Yankees won Game 6, 3–2.

The Series came down to Game 7. It was Spahn's turn to pitch, but he caught a bad case of the flu, so Haney went with his hot hand, Burdette, even though the righty had had only two days' rest. Don Larsen started for the Yankees. The year before, Larsen had pitched his historic perfect game in the World Series against the Dodgers.

The Braves knocked Larsen out in the third inning, scoring four runs, and Burdette did the rest, hurling his second straight shutout to defeat the vaunted Yankees and bring Milwaukee their first World Series title. Jones did not play in the Series after his pinch-hit hit-by-pitch in Game 4. That was his last plate appearance in the major leagues. He went back to the minors in 1958, playing two more seasons in Sacramento and one in Portland before calling it quits. All told, Jones had a much more stellar minor-league career than major-league career—he collected 1,678 hits and 119 homers in the minors but only 369 hits and 25 homers in the majors. He is most remembered for his rally-starting hit-by-pitch in Game 4 of the 1957 World Series.

Tommy Byrne's outing in Game 4 was his next-to-last appearance in the majors. He pitched two innings out of the bullpen in Game 7 and then chose to retire rather than accept a trade to the Cardinals. A few years later, in 1963, Byrne was working as a scout for the New York Mets. Early in the season, he was hired as manager of the Mets' Class A affiliate in Raleigh, North Carolina. One of Byrne's more promising players was a twenty-year-old outfielder from Mobile, Alabama, named Cleon Jones.

Jones was a September call-up for the Mets in '63, playing in six games. The Mets along with the Houston Colt .45s had joined the National League the year before as expansion teams. Casey Stengel, in his early seventies, initially declined but later reconsidered and accepted the managerial job for the Mets. After Stengel's Yankees lost the '57 World Series to the Braves, they won the rematch the following year but lost to the Pirates in the '60 Series on Bill Mazeroski's home run. Stengel and the Yankees parted ways after the Series.

In 1962, the Mets bumbled their way to a 40–120 record. They did not fare much better the next two years, losing 111 and 109 games.

Stengel went from finishing in first place in 10 out of 12 years with the Yankees to coming in dead last in his first three seasons with the Mets.

Cleon Jones had a strong season for the Mets' Triple-A affiliate Buffalo in '64, and he made Stengel's Opening Day roster in 1965. But he still had not learned to hit major-league pitching and was sent down to Buffalo in early May. He was recalled in September but hit only .149 in his stints with the Mets that season. Stengel stepped down as manager in July after suffering a broken hip, and Wes Westrum, one of the team's coaches, replaced him. The Mets recorded their fourth straight last-place, 109-plus loss season in 1965. In their first four years in the National League, the Mets' average record was 49–113.

With Westrum calling the shots in 1966, the Mets finally escaped the basement, finishing in ninth place and losing "only" 95 games. Cleon Jones earned the job as the Mets' starting center fielder and responded by hitting .275 and placing fourth in the Rookie of the Year vote. First baseman Ed Kranepool, who came up with the Mets in 1962 as a seventeen-year-old, led the team in home runs with a modest 16.

It was back to last place and triple-digit losses for the Mets in 1967. Wes Westrum, exasperated by all of the losing and doubtful that he would be brought back in 1968, resigned with eleven games left in the '67 season. The bright spot for the Mets that year was the emergence of Tom Seaver. The hard-throwing right-handed pitcher took home the Rookie of the Year trophy on the strength of his 16–13, 2.76-ERA maiden season.

The Mets made two moves in the offseason that shaped the team's destiny. In October 1967, they named Gil Hodges as the team's new manager, and, two months later, they acquired outfielder Tommie Agee and infielder Al Weis from the Chicago White Sox in a six-player trade. It is rare that a manager is involved in a trade, but the Washington Senators were willing to part with Hodges, who had managed the team for almost five years, in exchange for pitcher Bill Denehy and cash.

Hodges was an old favorite in New York, having started at first base for the Brooklyn Dodgers from the late 1940s until 1957 when the Dodgers moved to Los Angeles. He was a fixture in the Dodgers lineup, along with Roy Campanella, Duke Snider, Jackie Robinson, and the rest of the "Bums." Hodges's power, run production, and fine glove earned him regular selections to the National League All-Star team.

Hodges was winding down his playing career in Los Angeles in 1961 when the Dodgers declined to protect him in the expansion draft, and the Mets grabbed him. He hit the first homer in Mets history in the '62 opener but played infrequently, and in May 1963 he was traded to the Senators. Hodges, who had recently turned thirty-nine, opted to retire as a player following the trade and was picked to replace Mickey Vernon as manager of the floundering Senators. The Senators were an expansion team, joining the American League in 1961 along with the Los Angeles Angels. The "old" Senators team, which had been a member of the league since 1901, moved to Minnesota after the 1960 season and became the Twins.

While the Senators showed improvement with Hodges at the helm, progressing from 10th place to eighth to sixth and increasing their win total each season, he never fielded a winning team during his five years in Washington. Still, the Mets were confident that Hodges, with his quiet but firm leadership, was the right man for the job.

The trade for Agee and Weis did not garner big headlines at the time, but the Mets ended up reaping substantial dividends in the deal. Agee's 22 homers and 86 RBIs helped him secure the award as the American League's top rookie for the Chisox in 1966. When he tailed off his sophomore year, he became expendable. Agee already had a friendly face to greet him in the Mets clubhouse—he and Cleon Jones were childhood friends from Alabama. The two were teammates on the Mobile County High School baseball and football teams.

In 1968, Hodges moved Jones over to left field where he primarily played during the season, while Agee, the better defensive outfielder, usually manned center. The Mets played respectably during the first half of '68; they were just four games under .500 at the All-Star break. But they took a nosedive in the second half and finished at 73–89, in ninth place, one game ahead of Houston. Tom Seaver continued to shine, winning 16 games with a 2.20 ERA, and southpaw rookie Jerry Koosman did even better, falling a win short of 20 victories with an ERA of 2.08.

Gil Hodges had another young talented pitcher on his staff—Nolan Ryan. Poor control plagued Ryan during his rookie year with the Mets in '68; he walked five batters per nine innings and logged a 6–9 record. Tommie Agee took another step down from his Rookie of the Year season, hitting .217 with only five home runs. His pal Cleon Jones, however, had his best season yet, hitting .297.

Hodges had a scare during the final week of the season when he suffered a minor cardiac episode, which required that he be hospitalized. Coach Rube Walker managed the team for the last four games of the season.

Despite their team's dismal performance year after year, Mets fans supported their team with rabid enthusiasm. After they started playing at brand-new Shea Stadium in 1964 following two years at the Polo Grounds, the Mets finished at least third in attendance among National League teams each year. Many baseball fans in New York felt betrayed when the owners of the Dodgers and Giants moved the teams to California following the 1957 season, leaving them without a National League team to support. The Mets filled that void.

Major League Baseball expanded for the second time in a decade after the 1968 season. The National League added the Montreal Expos and San Diego Padres, and the American League added the Seattle Pilots and Kansas City Royals. There was also a change in the postseason format; each league was split into two six-team divisions, with the winners squaring off in a best-of-five League Championship Series. The winners of these Series would meet in the World Series.

The Mets were placed in the National League Eastern Division. The joke in New York was that, with the new divisional alignment, the worst the Mets could finish in 1969 was in sixth place. Even with a few good young arms on the pitching staff and some promising hitters in the lineup, baseball pundits predicted that another low finish was in store for the Mets. Oddsmakers set the chances of the Mets winning the '69 World Series at 100–1. Some think the odds should have been higher than that.

Through the first quarter of the season, the Mets were playing as expected—they had an 18–23 record and were nine games out of first place in the division behind the Chicago Cubs. Then, out of the blue, the Mets went on a binge and rattled off 11 wins in a row, catapulting them into second place, seven games out of first. Tom Seaver won three games during the streak, and the Mets notched three walk-off victories.

Soon after the winning streak ended, on June 15, the Mets made a deal before the trade deadline. Looking to add pop to their lineup, they picked up first baseman Donn Clendenon in a deal with the Expos.

Clendenon's history, personally and professionally, is eye-popping. He grew up in Atlanta; his father died when he was a baby, and his stepfather, Nish Williams, played for eleven years in the Negro Leagues. Clendenon attended Morehouse College, an all-male historically Black school in Atlanta. The tradition at Morehouse was for an upperclassman—called a "big brother"—to mentor an incoming freshman. Clendenon's big brother, however, was not an upperclassman; he was a family friend who had graduated from Morehouse years earlier and volunteered to serve as Clendenon's big brother. Clendenon never forgot the advice imparted to him by his mentor, Martin Luther King Jr.

Like his stepfather, Donn Clendenon was blessed with baseball talent, and he used it to break into the majors with the Pirates in 1961. Clendenon had a good bat for the Pirates in the early 1960s, but his glove at first base was his shortcoming. Clendenon worried that defense might jeopardize his starting job at first. Clendenon had met Jackie Robinson, who had high praise for his Dodgers teammate Gil Hodges—his character and his ability on the field, offensively and defensively.

Hodges's first spring training as manager of the Senators was in 1964. The first time the Pirates and Senators played each other that spring in an exhibition game, Clendenon took it upon himself to ask Hodges for some pointers to improve his defense. Hodges agreed, and, whenever the Senators and Pirates had a game that spring, the manager tutored the young player in the art of playing first base. From those meetings, the two men developed a friendship.

Hodges's tips helped Clendenon improve his game at first base. He also continued to put up solid offensive numbers. In 1968, Clendenon was deeply saddened by the assassination of King in April and the death of his stepfather in September, though still he managed to have a good year, driving in 87 runs. The Pirates, however, had a young, up-and-coming player, Al Oliver, whom they had pegged to play first base, so they left Clendenon unprotected in the expansion draft. The Expos picked him but traded him to the Houston Astros over the winter. (The team name changed from the Colt .45s when the team moved into the Astrodome in 1965.) The Astros were managed by Harry Walker, who had been Clendenon's manager for three years when he played for the Pirates. The two clashed often—Clendenon considered Walker a racist—and he refused to report to spring training for Houston.

Clendenon felt so strongly about the issue that, rather than play for Walker, he announced his retirement from baseball, even though he was only thirty-three, and took a job in Atlanta with a pen and lighter manufacturer. His job in business was short-lived. Clendenon missed baseball, and, as the regular season got under way, the Expos and Astros made a deal that allowed him to return to the diamond. The Expos sent two players and cash to the Astros as compensation for Clendenon's failure to report, and he was sent back to Montreal. With no spring training, Clendenon had a sluggish start, hitting .240 with four homers in 38 games, and, after just eight weeks, the Expos traded him to the Mets. Eager to play for Gil Hodges, Clendenon was happy about the trade.

Hodges was a big proponent of platooning; he used it somewhat in 1968 and even more in 1969. He often played the right-handed–hitting Clendenon at first base against left-handed starters and the left-handed Ed Kranepool against righty pitchers. Hodges also used a platoon at several other positions in '69—right field, third base, and second base.

Tom Seaver was establishing himself as a premier pitcher, and, in a game on July 9, he almost achieved perfection. Against the Cubs at Shea Stadium, he took a perfect game into the ninth inning. With one out, reserve outfielder Jim Qualls, who would total just 31 hits in his brief major-league career, singled to left-center field. Seaver retired the next two batters and had to settle for a one-hit shutout.

This game marked the halfway point of the season. The Mets were 47–34, 3½ games behind the Cubs, and Seaver was 14–3. Cleon Jones was tearing up National League pitching to the tune of a .352 batting average. Tommie Agee had bounced back from his disappointing '68 season;

he was hitting .281 with 12 home runs. Mets fans were excited that their team was within sniffing distance of first place in July.

The Mets then took a step back, losing three games in the standings between Seaver's masterpiece and the end of July. July 30 was a particularly unpleasant day for the Mets and Cleon Jones. They hosted the Astros for a Wednesday afternoon doubleheader at Shea. The Mets were crushed, 16–3, in the first game. In the second game, the Astros jumped on Gary Gentry, the Mets' number-three starter, for seven runs in the top of the third inning. Before he could record the third out, Gentry was lifted for Nolan Ryan. Johnny Edwards, the first batter Ryan faced, hit a ball in Cleon Jones's direction, which Hodges thought was catchable, but it fell in for a double. Hodges, apparently disturbed by the way Jones went after the ball, took a slow, deliberate walk out to left field, told his player he was coming out of the game, and walked him back to the dugout. Jones claimed years later that Hodges removed him not because of a lack of hustle but because the ground was wet and he was dealing with an ankle injury. The Mets lost the game, 11–5, and dropped the series finale to the Astros the next day.

The Mets' chances of staying in the pennant race continued to dwindle over the next two weeks. When they lost to the Astros again on August 13, the Mets dropped 10 games behind the Cubs in the National League East; the second-place Cardinals were nine games out. The Cubs were managed by Leo Durocher, who, ironically, was Gil Hodges's first manager for the Dodgers in the 1940s. Four players on Durocher's talent-laden team—Ernie Banks, Billy Williams, Fergie Jenkins, and Ron Santo—eventually made the Hall of Fame. It was going to take a miracle for the Mets to overcome a 10-game deficit with fewer than 50 games remaining.

Hodges would not let his team quit, though. Back-to-back doubleheader sweeps kicked off a 12–1 streak, and, by August 27, the Mets had trimmed the Cubs' lead to 2½ games. With the Mets breathing down the necks of the Cubs, Tom Seaver became the team's first 20-game winner in its history on September 5. They continued to surge and took over first place on September 10. The Mets were on such a roll that, in a game against the Cardinals at Busch Memorial Stadium on September

15, they struck out 19 times against Steve Carlton, a record at the time for a pitcher in a nine-inning game—but won the game, 4–3, on a pair of two-run homers by Ron Swoboda.

On September 24, in front of a nearly capacity crowd of close to fifty-five thousand at Shea, the Mets beat the Cardinals to clinch the National League Eastern Division. Donn Clendenon, who had proven to be a valuable addition to the Mets, hit two home runs, and Gary Gentry tossed a four-hit shutout. The Mets' final record was 100–62. They went a sizzling 38–11 after August 13 to finish eight games ahead of the Cubs. It was a monumental collapse by the Cubs—a 1–11 stretch in September, including two losses to the Mets, was their undoing. Seaver closed the season at 25–7 and won the Cy Young Award almost unanimously. Jones finished third in the National League in batting with a .340 average. Agee smacked 26 home runs.

The Mets faced the Atlanta Braves, winners of the Western Division, in the first-ever National League Championship Series. Of the twenty-four major-league teams, the Mets finished 17th in home runs. They averaged six homers every nine games during the season but hit six home runs in the three League Championship Series games, completing a sweep of the Braves, scoring 27 runs. Ken Boswell, Hodges's left-handed-hitting platoon at second base, who hit only three home runs in 362 at-bats in '69, blasted two homers in the LCS. Left-handed-swinging Wayne Garrett, whom Hodges platooned at third base, hit just one homer in 400 at-bats but homered in the LCS. Tommie Agee also hit two home runs against the Braves, and Cleon Jones added a homer. The Mets could do no wrong.

The Mets had a mighty opponent, the Baltimore Orioles, in their first World Series. Earl Weaver, in his first full year as manager, led the Orioles. Small in stature, Weaver had plenty of vim and vigor. The O's could do it all—hit, pitch, and field. They ranked third in the majors in runs scored; Frank Robinson and Boog Powell were their biggest run producers. The Orioles had the lowest team ERA in the majors, and two of their pitchers, Mike Cuellar and Dave McNally, were 20-game winners. They also led the majors in fielding percentage; four of their eight everyday players won the Gold Glove. The Orioles took out the

Minnesota Twins in three games in the American League Championship Series. They were a 4–1 favorite to beat the Mets in the World Series.

The Series opened at Memorial Stadium in Baltimore. The Orioles made a statement in the bottom of the first inning when the leadoff hitter, Don Buford, launched a home run over the right-field wall against Tom Seaver. With Mike Cuellar throwing a complete game, the Orioles cruised to a 4–1 victory.

Hodges did not panic, though, and his sedulous squad pulled out a hard-fought 2–1 victory in Game 2. Jerry Koosman threw no-hit ball for six innings. Donn Clendenon, who did not play in the LCS because Hodges played Ed Kranepool all three games at first base against the Braves' right-handed starters, swatted an opposite-field homer in the fourth inning to give the Mets a 1–0 lead. Paul Blair broke up Koosman's no-hitter in the seventh, stole second, and scored on a Brooks Robinson single. The Mets pieced together three consecutive hits in the top of the ninth to score the go-ahead run, and Ron Taylor came out of the bullpen to nail down the last out with two Orioles on base.

The Mets delivered a 5–0 win in Queens to their screaming, sign-waving fans in Game 3. Gary Gentry and Nolan Ryan teamed up to shut out the Orioles. Center fielder Tommie Agee was the star of the game as he hit a home run and made two fabulous, runs-saving, warning track catches. In the fourth inning, he ran down Elrod Hendricks's long drive to left-center with two on and two outs, catching the ball backhanded on the run. In the seventh, with the bases loaded and two outs, Paul Blair hit one to the gap in right-center that Agee corralled with a diving catch. Agee's catches prevented five Orioles runners from scoring.

In Game 4, another Mets outfielder, Ron Swoboda, also made a terrific catch, which played a big part in the Mets' third straight win in the Series. Donn Clendenon's solo home run in the second inning was the only scoring of the game as Tom Seaver rebounded from his subpar performance in the opener to carry a three-hit shutout into the ninth inning. With one out, Frank Robinson singled and advanced to third on a Boog Powell single. Brooks Robinson then hit a liner that looked like a gapper toward right-center. Swoboda, playing right field and not normally an elite defensive player, sprinted toward the gap at the crack of the bat and, with a full-extension dive, caught the ball for the second out. Frank Robinson tagged from third and scored the tying run. But, if Swoboda had not made the catch, it likely would have been an extra-base hit for Brooks Robinson, and Powell may have come across the plate from first with the go-ahead run. Elrod Hendricks made the third out by lining out to Swoboda.

The game stayed even, at 1–1, into extra innings. Earl Weaver brought in right-handed reliever Dick Hall in the 10th inning. Jerry Grote hit a pop fly double to left, and seldom-used reserve outfielder Rod Gaspar pinch-ran for the catcher. Weaver instructed Hall to walk Al Weis intentionally. Hodges sent up left-handed hitting backup catcher J. C. Martin to bat for Seaver, who had thrown 10 innings. It would be Martin's only appearance in the Series. Weaver countered with lefty Pete Richert. Hodges, looking to move the runners up, flashed the bunt sign. Martin dropped a nice bunt down the first-base line. Richert came in and fielded the ball; his only play was to first. He wheeled and fired, but the ball hit Martin in the wrist and ricocheted toward right field. Gaspar rounded third and scored the winning run. Replays showed that Martin illegally ran inside the first-base line and should have been called out. Gaspar would have been sent back to third. This was long before plays could be reviewed so the play stood, and the Mets were winners of Game 4.

Game 5 featured a rematch of the Game 2 pitchers: Dave McNally versus Jerry Koosman. Hodges, despite the magnitude of the game, remained calm as he drove to Shea with his brother that morning for the 1 p.m. start. Hodges made no mention of the game on the ride in. Adults called out of work and kids cut school to attend or watch the game on TV. If the Mets were going to win the World Series that day, these die-hard fans weren't going to miss it.

Koosman had a rough start. In the top of the third, McNally, a .085 batter with one home run during the season, hit a two-run homer. Three batters later, Frank Robinson added another run with a bases-empty dinger.

The game stayed 3–0, Orioles. With one out in the top of the sixth, Koosman threw a slider that appeared to hit Frank Robinson in the thigh. Umpire Lou DiMuro, in his first postseason game behind the plate, ruled that the ball had struck Robinson's bat and was therefore a foul ball. A lengthy argument ensued, with Earl Weaver and Robinson arguing that it was a hit by pitch, but DiMuro did not change his mind. Robinson got back in the box and struck out.

Cleon Jones led off the bottom of the sixth for the Mets. After a stellar LCS against the Braves in which he hit .429, Jones was batting just .111 in the World Series. McNally's first pitch was a curveball that darted down and in. Jones tried to get out of the way of the pitch and landed on his left knee. The ball took a crazy bounce and landed in the Mets dugout on the first-base side. Jones slowly rose and made his way to first base, but DiMuro stopped him. "The ball didn't hit you."

Jones held up and, with the bat still in his hand, put his left hand on his hip and smirked, as if to say, "Are you kidding? Of course, the ball hit me."

About twenty seconds after McNally's pitch, Gil Hodges emerged from the dugout. Wearing his royal-blue warm-up jacket over his uniform, Hodges walked purposefully toward home plate, holding a baseball in his right hand. Hodges had a reputation dating from his playing days of being respectful toward umpires. He was never thrown out of a game in his long playing career. He was ejected just twice in his five years as pilot of the Senators and had been tossed only once in his two seasons with the Mets.

He handed the ball to DiMuro. Mets broadcaster Lindsey Nelson, working the series for NBC alongside Curt Gowdy, commented, "We might have a shoe polish play here. Remember the Nippy Jones shoe polish play in the 1957 World Series in Milwaukee."

Sure enough, the ball that Hodges handed to DiMuro contained a black smudge. Hodges did not raise his voice but stated matter-of-factly, "Lou, the ball hit him."

DiMuro carefully inspected the ball, glanced at Hodges, and pointed Jones to first base. Weaver, still stewing about the call on Frank Robinson, tore out of the dugout. His view of umpires differed dramatically from Hodges's. He did not like them and was quick to scream in their faces if he disagreed with a call. He had been thrown out the day before for griping about balls and strikes; he would rack up more than ninety ejections in his seventeen years as the Baltimore manager.

Weaver complained to DiMuro that he did not consult with Lee Weyer, the first-base umpire, before making the call. Weaver also insisted that, when the ball bounced into the Mets dugout, Hodges had time to do what he wanted with it. Accounts varied significantly about what, if anything, Hodges did with the ball before he walked out of the dugout. Long after the World Series, Jerry Koosman claimed that McNally's ball rolled to him, and Hodges asked him to swipe it against his foot. Koosman obliged and gave the ball to his manager. Ed Kranepool later said he saw Hodges pull out a scuffed ball from a bag of discarded baseballs. Jerry Grote provided a third account—the ball rolled to him, and he flipped the ball to Hodges, who carried it with him to show DiMuro. While Cleon Jones did not have his eyes on the dugout at the time, he vouched for his manager's integrity. "Gil Hodges would never do anything dishonest."

Whether Hodges did something untoward or not in the dugout, the consensus was, even on the Orioles' side, that the ball had hit Jones. He took his lead off first, and Donn Clendenon stood in. McNally, flustered by the commotion, hung a 2-2 slider, which Clendenon deposited off the auxiliary scoreboard in left field for his third homer of the Series, bringing the Mets to within a run.

An inning later, Al Weis electrified the crowd with a game-tying home run. It was the first time in his eight-year career that Weis homered in his home ballpark. The Mets capitalized on the game's change in momentum. Cleon Jones and Ron Swoboda hit doubles in the bottom of the eighth to plate the go-ahead run, and the Mets added a run on errors by Boog Powell and pitcher Eddie Watt on the same play.

With a 5–3 lead, Koosman faced the heart of the Orioles order in the top of the ninth inning. Frank Robinson worked a leadoff walk, and Boog Powell grounded into a force out. Chico Salmon ran for Boog. Brooks Robinson flied out to right field, and then Dave Johnson's high flyball settled into left fielder Cleon Jones's glove at the edge of the warning track. The "impossible dream" had come true—the "Amazin' Mets," after failing to finish higher than next-to-last place in any of their first seven seasons, had ascended to the top of the baseball world by beating the high-powered Orioles in the World Series.

Jones took a knee briefly and then ran to center field to celebrate with Tommie Agee. Koosman ran into the arms of Jerry Grote. Mets fans poured onto the field from the stands and, as the *New York Times* columnist Arthur Daley put it, "whooped it up with unrestrained glee." Fans grabbed home plate, the bases, and pieces of the turf as souvenirs. Donn Clendenon was named World Series MVP for his three home runs, including the critical homer in Game 5.

The Mets did not repeat their magic in 1970. Tied for first place on September 14, they went 5–10 the rest of the way and finished in third place at 83–79. The Mets logged the same record and finish in 1971. After the '71 season, the Mets made what turned out to be one of their worst trades in history, sending Nolan Ryan and three players to the California Angels for Jim Fregosi. Ryan went on to win more than 300 games and hurl seven no-hitters.

Toward the end of spring training in 1972, Gil Hodges had just completed a round of golf in West Palm Beach, Florida, with three of his coaches when he collapsed on his way to his hotel room. He suffered a fatal heart attack, two days short of his forty-eighth birthday. Doctors concluded that Hodges's heavy smoking was a substantial cause of his heart attack. Yogi Berra took over as the team's manager. To pay tribute to Hodges, the Mets wore black armbands during the 1972 season. The club retired his number, 14, following season.

In the 1957 World Series and again in the 1969 Series, a player named Jones was awarded first base on a pitch that was initially called a ball and then changed to a hit-by-pitch when the umpire was shown shoe polish on the baseball. Both hit-by-pitch calls triggered key rallies. Yogi Berra was there for both plays—he was the catcher for the Nippy Jones play and the first-base coach for the Cleon Jones play.

In the clubhouse after the game, when reporters told Cleon Jones about the Nippy Jones play that had taken place years earlier, he joked, "Us Jones boys have to stick together."

Twelve years apart, the umpires took center stage with game-changing results. In Game 4 of the 1957 Series, umpire Augie Donatelli inspects the ball with shoe polish before awarding first base to the Braves' Nippy Jones. In Game 5 of the 1969 Series, umpire Lou DiMuro points Cleon Jones of the Mets to first base after manager Gil Hodges showed him the ball with shoe polish. *AP Photo*

5

Owner's Remorse

IT WAS THE ONLY TIME IN MAJOR LEAGUE BASEBALL HISTORY—AND maybe the only time in the history of United States sports—that a team owner declined to accept a world championship. The scene of this extraordinary occurrence was Game 7 of the 1925 World Series, which James Harrison of the *New York Times* described as the "wettest, weirdest, and wildest" baseball game ever played. Filled with questionable umpiring and botched plays, the game was played in dreadful weather.

For the better part of the first quarter of the twentieth century, the Washington Senators were the dregs of Major League Baseball. As the old joke went, Washington was first in war, first in peace—and last in the American League. From 1901 to 1923, the Senators never captured the pennant and they fielded just six winning teams. Worse yet, they finished within 10 games of first place just twice and ended the season in last or next-to-last place in the eight-team American League 11 out of the 23 years; in seven of those seasons, the Senators finished 35 or more games out of first.

Ironically, for much of that agonizing stretch, the Senators boasted one of the finest pitchers ever to toe the rubber, a tall, lanky right-hander named Walter Johnson. He grew up on a Kansas farm and did not take up baseball until he was sixteen—his family had moved to Southern California by then—but, in just three years, Johnson was on a major-league diamond for the Senators. He began to show his brilliance in his second season when he won 14 games, which, incredibly, included three complete game shutouts in four days in September. Somehow, in the early days of baseball, pitchers—their rotator cuffs be damned—could occa-sionally throw on one day's rest or no rest.

In his early years, with his sweeping sidearm delivery, Johnson relied mostly on his fastball. Later he added a terrific curveball to his repertoire and became downright dominating. In the 1910s, he averaged 26.5 wins per season, with a high of 36 in 1913. His *highest* ERA in a season during the decade was 2.21; every other year it was lower than 2.00. He led the league in shutouts six times in the 1910s. If it were not for Cy Young, the top pitchers in the National League and American League each season would win the Walter Johnson Award. Grantland Rice, a top sportswriter of the time, popularized the nickname the "Big Train" for Johnson at a time when trains were the fastest mode of transportation. Even the perennial American League batting titlist Ty Cobb, who issued compliments sparingly, praised Johnson's blazing fastball.

Despite Johnson's spectacular pitching year after year, the Senators did not have enough of a supporting cast to compete against the top American League teams, notably the Philadelphia Athletics and Boston Red Sox, each of which won four pennants in the 1910s.

For nine years at the height of Johnson's dominance, former pitcher Clark Griffith managed the Senators. At 5'6", Griffith was not hard-throwing but relied on an assortment of pitches as well as guile to get outs. He was a big winner for the Chicago Colts and Orphans (later renamed the Cubs) in the 1890s. He was hired as player-manager of the Chicago White Sox in 1901, the first year that the American League achieved major-league status. Griffith won 24 games that year, leading the White Sox to the pennant. They did not square off against the National League winner because the inception of the World Series was still two years away. Over the next decade, Griffith's innings pitched gradually decreased, but he continued to manage—two years with the White Sox, six with the New York Highlanders (later renamed the Yan-kees), and three with the Cincinnati Reds.

Griffith had ownership aspirations, and, in late 1911, he purchased a 10-percent interest in the Washington Senators, making him the club's largest stockholder. He took over as manager of the team in 1912 and quickly transformed the Senators into a competitive team, posting a winning record for four straight years, a vast improvement over past seasons but still not good enough to win the pennant. After the 1919 season, Griffith and a businessman from Philadelphia became majority owners of the Senators. Griffith stayed on to manage one more year—the team finished in sixth—and then relinquished his position as manager to focus on his ownership role.

Griffith changed managers every year between 1921 and 1923, moving from George McBride to Clyde Milan to Donie Bush, as his club languished in mediocrity. Even Walter Johnson, now in his midthirties, started to show his age. He was barely above .500 for the three years, with an ERA of 3.32, a big jump for him. The 1924 season would be Johnson's eighteenth. With his skills fading and accepting the realization that he would almost certainly not pitch in a World Series, he decided to make this season his last. He planned to become the owner of a minor league team in the Pacific Coast League following the season.

Griffith replaced Bush as manager with Bucky Harris, his hard-nosed, fundamentally solid twenty-seven-year-old second baseman. Another sub-.500 finish was predicted for the Senators, and they spent most of the first third of the season in the second division. Harris developed a good rapport with his players, commanding their respect despite his youth, and it paid off. Things came together in mid-June and the Senators went on a 17–2 tear to climb into first place. It was nip and tuck the rest of the season as the Senators, New York Yankees, and Detroit Tigers battled for the American League pennant. The Tigers faded, but the Senators showed their true colors, going 14–6 in their last 20 games—all on the road—to edge out the Yankees and clinch the pennant on the next-to-last day of the season.

Walter Johnson, rejuvenated by the Senators' strong season, had his best performance in five years, pacing the American League with 23 wins and finishing atop the league in ERA, strikeouts, and shutouts.

Bucky Harris received a big boost from a rookie right-handed pitcher named Frederick "Firpo" Marberry. Marberry's intimidating scowl on the mound had earned him the nickname because it reminded some people of an Argentine boxer of the time, Luis Firpo. Relief pitchers were not in vogue in the early years of baseball—teams did not use closers, and starting pitchers compiled high complete-game totals. Harris broke tradition and frequently used Marberry out of the bullpen, giving him 36 relief appearances to go with his 14 starts. Saves were not recorded at that time, but decades later, they were calculated retroactively, and it was determined that Marberry chalked up 15 saves in 1924 to lead the majors.

Harris teamed up with veteran shortstop Roger Peckinpaugh, who had spent nine years with the Yankees before coming over to Washington in 1922. They teamed up to become one of the game's best keystone combinations, especially defensively. Twenty-three-year-old outfielder Leon "Goose" Goslin carried the offense with a league-leading 129 RBIs; he also hit 12 of the team's 22 home runs.

In the World Series, the Senators faced the New York Giants, managed by John McGraw. The fiery McGraw, in his twenty-third season at the helm for the Giants, had led his team to eight World Series, winning three. In this World Series, the Senators' first, Walter Johnson felt intense pressure when he took the mound for the opening game at Griffith Stadium in Washington. First named Nationals Park, the stadium was renamed in 1920 in recognition of Clark Griffith's significant contributions as manager and owner of the franchise. President Calvin Coolidge was on hand to throw out the first ball. Johnson's mother, who had never watched her son pitch in a major-league game, traveled from California to attend the game. The "Big Train" pitched a twelve-inning complete game, but the Senators fell to the Giants, 4–3.

The Senators evened the Series in Game 2. Firpo Marberry came in to strike out Giants shortstop Travis Jackson with the game tied, two outs, and a runner on second in the top of the ninth, and Peckinpaugh won the game with an RBI double in the bottom of the ninth. The teams split the next two games at the Polo Grounds in New York. In Game 5, Johnson had an opportunity to give the Senators a 3–2 lead, but he didn't have his good stuff. He allowed six runs, and the Giants won, 6–2. Johnson had waited eighteen years to pitch in a World Series and was frustrated and disappointed to lose his first two starts. The Senators eked out a 2–1 win in Game 6 behind Tom Zachary, who, though he had a long and respectable career, is known best for allowing Babe Ruth's record-setting 60th home run in 1927. Peckinpaugh helped seal the Game 6 win with a brilliant play in the ninth.

It all came down to Game 7 in Washington—up to that point it was just the third winner-take-all seventh game. Johnson could start on little or no rest when he was in his twenties but not when he was a month away from his thirty-seventh birthday. He let Harris know, though, that he could pitch in relief if necessary.

With the Senators hanging on to a one-run lead and with two runners on in the top of the sixth, Harris brought in Marberry from the bullpen. The Giants scored three runs, but Marberry was not to blame because the Senators committed two costly errors. Marberry shut down the Giants in the next two innings, and, when the Senators came to bat in the bottom of the eighth, they were down to their last six outs. With the bases loaded and two outs, Harris hit a ground ball to eighteen-year-old Freddie Lindstrom at third base. It looked like the third out, but, remarkably, the ball hit a pebble in the infield and bounced high over Lindstrom's head into left field for a game-tying two-run single.

Marberry was pulled for a pinch-hitter in the eighth inning, and Harris handed the ball to his ace in the ninth. "You're the best we got, Walter. We've got to win or lose with you."

In the top of the ninth, Johnson allowed a one-out triple to future Hall of Famer Frankie Frisch but escaped the inning unscathed. In the bottom of the 10th, Harris let Johnson, a pitcher who hit well, bat for himself. He hit a fly ball to deep left-center field, but it stayed in the park for an out.

With two Giants on and two outs in the top of the 11th, Johnson struck out the major league's 1924 RBI leader, George "High Pockets" Kelly. Johnson threw his fourth shutout inning in the top of the 12th. Then, in the bottom of the inning, thanks to some good fortune, the Senators scored a run to bring Washington its first World Series title. Johnson's batterymate Muddy Ruel doubled after Giants catcher Hank Gowdy failed to catch Ruel's pop. Johnson followed by hitting a ground ball to shortstop Travis Jackson, who bobbled the ball for an error. Earl McNeely then hit a grounder to Freddie Lindstrom, and, as in the eighth inning, the ball took a bad hop and bounced over his head, allowing Ruel to scamper home from second with the winning run. "It probably hit the same pebble," Lindstrom later lamented. Fittingly, Walter Johnson picked up the win in the decisive game to nail down the Senators' first world championship and, in so doing, redeemed himself after losing Games 1 and 5.

In the offseason, Johnson's purchase of the Pacific Coast League team fell through, and, to the delight of everyone in the Senators organization and the team's fans, Johnson returned to Washington in 1925 for his nineteenth big-league campaign. Though the Senators were defending champions, the Yankees were the preseason favorite to win the American League pennant. Babe Ruth, who had won six of the seven previous home-run titles and more than doubled the home-run total of the entire Senators team in 1924 (from 22 to 46), missed the first two months of the season because of an intestinal disorder. But he returned to the lineup on June 1, the same day that Lou Gehrig started his 2,130-consecutive-games streak with a pinch-hitting appearance. Walter Johnson beat the Yankees that day for his eighth win of the season, pushing New York 13½ games behind the Philadelphia Athletics. The Senators trailed the Athletics by two games at that juncture but eventually overtook them and won the pennant by 8½ games. The Yankees finished in seventh place, 28½ games out of first. The Bronx Bombers would not finish in the second division again for forty years.

Johnson recorded his 12th 20-win season in 1925. Astonishingly, he also batted .433 in 97 at-bats. The Senators featured another 20-game winner, Stan Coveleski. Firpo Marberry's role as a reliever increased. He pitched in 55 games, all out of the bullpen, and, based on retroactive calculations, again led the majors in saves, with 16. Peckinpaugh and Harris remained strong in the middle infield, turning a lot of double plays. Goose Goslin repeated as team leader in home runs and RBIs, while outfielder Sam Rice hit .350.

After failing to reach the World Series in the first twenty years, Clark Griffith's Senators had made it to their second Series in a row. Their foe in the 1925 World Series was the Pittsburgh Pirates, managed by Bill McKechnie, who was a journeyman infielder in his playing days and who assumed the job as manager of the Pirates in 1922. It was the Bucs' first appearance in the Fall Classic since 1909.

McKechnie's team was loaded. Seven of the eight players in the starting lineup cracked the .300 mark during the season. The seven included three players who were eventually enshrined in Cooperstown: third baseman and career Pirate Pie Traynor and outfielders Kiki Cuyler and Max Carey. The team complemented their hitting with speed—Carey and Cuyler ranked one-two in the National League in stolen bases.

The Pirates had no 20-game winners, but they did have a well-balanced core of starting pitchers. Forty-three-year-old Babe Adams, a spot starter and reliever in 1925, was the longest-tenured Pirate. He was a rookie when the team last played in the World Series—and he was the star of the Series, as he hurled three complete game wins over the Detroit Tigers.

Walter Johnson, with a World Series title under his belt, felt more relaxed when he took the mound for the opening game at Forbes Field in Pittsburgh. The Senators breezed to a 4–1 win; only a solo homer by Pie Traynor in the fifth stood between Johnson and a shutout.

The players on both teams wore black armbands in Game 2, paying tribute to New York Giants great Christy Mathewson, a 373-game winner, who had died the day before of tuberculosis at the age of forty-five. Johnson had passed Mathewson on the career wins list in 1924 and trailed only Cy Young. The Pirates won the game, 3–2. Pittsburgh scored the go-ahead runs in the eighth inning when Eddie Moore reached on an error by Roger Peckinpaugh and, two batters later, Kiki Cuyler delivered a two-run homer to give the Pirates the lead.

The Senators won Game 3 in Washington but not without some controversy. The Senators plated two runs in the bottom of the seventh inning to take a 4–3 lead. Firpo Marberry took over on the hill; Earl McNeely, who had pinch-run and scored the tying run in the seventh, stayed in the game to play center field; and Sam Rice moved from center to right. Marberry struck out the first two Pirates in the eighth before left-handed-hitting Earl Smith lifted a long fly to right field. Rice went back, timed his jump, leaped above the nine-and-a-half-foot wall, and tumbled into the bleachers. After a tense fifteen seconds, with Smith running around the bases, Rice emerged with the ball, and the umpire ruled that Smith was out.

The Pirates made the game interesting in the ninth inning, loading the bases with one out. Marberry, who thrived on pressure, reared back and induced Clyde Barnhart to pop out to catcher Muddy Ruel and Pie Traynor to fly out to center, preserving the hard-fought win.

Pirates fans were furious, believing that Earl Smith had been robbed of a game-tying home run. Many of them wrote to Commissioner Kenesaw Mountain Landis, insisting that he overturn the umpire's call. The prevailing theory was that Rice had dropped the ball, and a friendly Senators fan had placed it in his glove. Landis let the call stand.

Walter Johnson, eyeing another world championship, tossed a shut-out in Game 4, allowing just six singles to the hard-hitting Pirates. The Senators won, 4–0, to take a commanding 3–1 lead in the Series, but Johnson suffered a minor injury in the game. In the bottom of the third, he lined a hit to left field and, while trying to stretch a single into a double, pulled a muscle in his leg and was easily thrown out at second. Johnson stayed in the game and completed his shutout, but his leg was sore after the game.

Harris hoped that he would not need Johnson again and that his team would close out the Series in Washington the next day. The Pirates showed they were worth their salt by banging out 13 hits and stealing two bases en route to a 6–3 win in Game 5. In front of the home crowd for Game 6, Pittsburgh evened the Series.

The seventh game was scheduled for the following afternoon in Pittsburgh, but heavy rains forced a postponement. The weather forecast called for more heavy rain the next day. The decision about whether to play the game or postpone it for the second straight day fell to Commissioner Landis. He became baseball's first commissioner in 1920. His background was in the law—he had practiced as a lawyer in Chicago for a few years and then had been appointed by President Teddy Roosevelt to become a federal judge in 1905.

Soon after his appointment as commissioner, he was compelled to respond to the now-infamous "Black Sox" scandal in which eight Chicago White Sox players, including Shoeless Joe Jackson, accepted money from gamblers to throw the 1919 World Series against the Cincinnati Reds. A Chicago grand jury handed down an indictment of the eight players in October 1920. In 1921, the indictments were dismissed, the players were re-indicted, and, in August of that year, a jury acquitted them of all charges. Despite the acquittals, Landis imposed lifetime bans on all eight players. Jackson, thirty-four years old and a .356 career hitter, would never play in another major-league game. Several months later, Landis fined Babe Ruth and his Yankees teammate Bob Meusel $3,362, the amount of their 1921 World Series shares, and suspended them for the first six weeks of the 1922 season for barnstorming after the 1921 season. Landis thought that the World Series was baseball's most prized event, and, when it ended, players should stay off the field until spring training the following year.

Landis became embroiled in a controversy between the Giants and the Yankees in the 1922 World Series. The two teams shared the Polo Grounds as their home field, so all games in the Series were played there. The Yankees were considered the home team in Game 2, which was tied after 10 innings. At 4:45 p.m., home-plate umpire George Hildebrand called the game because he thought that the impending darkness, coupled with the heavy haze that was already reducing visibility, would prevent the teams from completing another inning. As a result, the game was declared a tie and would have to be replayed in its entirety. Fans in attendance disagreed vociferously because at least forty-five minutes of light time remained. Furthermore, since the game was played at a much faster pace in those days and the average inning took only ten to fifteen minutes, there was still time to play another inning or two. Some fans also charged that the decision was designed to allow the teams to garner gate receipts for an additional game.

Commissioner Landis was seated in a box above the Yankees dugout. Though accounts differ about whether or not Hildebrand consulted with Landis before calling the game, fans held Landis, as commissioner, responsible. An angry mob chased the commissioner from his seat to his car in the parking lot, shouting profanities and making obscene gestures. When Babe Ruth, still harboring some anger toward Landis for suspending him, observed that the fans were enraged with the commissioner, he noted, "Well, I don't blame them." In an effort to refute the notion that the decision to call the game was motivated by a desire to lengthen the Series and increase revenue, Landis ordered that the gate receipts from Game 2 be donated to charities for disabled soldiers.

Landis was fifty-eight years old, diminutive, and white-haired. He usually wore a serious expression on his face. Opinions of Landis ran the gamut from "honest and dignified" to "cold and egotistical." On the morning of the day after the postponement of Game 7, Landis trudged through the rain to inspect the infield and outfield at Forbes Field. He found large puddles in the outfield and a wet and muddy infield, pitcher's mound, and home-plate area. As poor as the field conditions were—one sportswriter quipped, "It was a great day for water polo"—Landis did not want to disappoint the fans by postponing the game for a second day in a row, and so he announced that the game would proceed that afternoon. By the 2 p.m. game time, a capacity crowd of nearly forty-three thousand fans, dressed in rain gear and armed with umbrellas, packed Forbes Field to battle the elements and cheer on the Pirates. Shortly before the first pitch, Landis gave both teams a pep talk, emphasizing that he did not want to let down the fans who were eager to watch the deciding game of the World Series.

Walter Johnson, still battling a sore leg, was tasked with pitching for the Senators under the atrocious conditions. Vic Aldridge, who was a 15-game winner during the season and who had won Games 2 and 5 for the Pirates, got the start for the home team. An overly optimistic Bill McKechnie declared, "The Senators fear Aldridge as much as we fear Johnson."

The rain was light when the Pittsburgh fans gave Aldridge an ovation as he took the mound. It was hard for him to get his footing, and after allowing two runs in the top of the first on two hits, three walks, and two wild pitches, he was replaced by Johnny Morrison, who inherited a bases-loaded, one-out jam. Morrison allowed two more runs, and the Senators had a quick 4–0 advantage.

Johnson also had difficulty with the mound conditions, and he had trouble getting a firm grip on the ball. But he managed to throw two scoreless innings before getting touched for four hits and three runs in the bottom of the third. Between innings, the grounds crew brought in sand to try to soak up the puddles in the infield. Johnson put some sand in his cap, hoping it would absorb the water.

The rain picked up in the fourth inning. The Senators collected three hits off Morrison in the top of the inning to score two runs. Because it was a do-or-die game, Bill McKechnie was willing to pull out all the stops, so, in the fifth inning, he brought in Ray Kremer, who had thrown a complete game win for the Pirates in Game 6 two days earlier. Kremer blanked the Senators in his first inning of work, and then Max Carey and Kiki Cuyler hit back-to-back doubles off Johnson in the bottom of the fifth to close the gap to 6–4. With five innings in the books, it was considered an official game. The downpour was torrential, and Landis was faced with a difficult decision.

Bud Selig was in a similar predicament eighty-three years later during the 2008 World Series between the Philadelphia Phillies and Tampa Bay Rays. The Phillies took a 3–1 lead in the Series and were poised to clinch in Game 5 before a raucous Philadelphia crowd at Citizens Bank Park. When the game started at 8:30 p.m., a light rain was falling, and the temperature was 47 degrees. The rain was not forecast to become heavy until after midnight. But, as the game progressed, the rain picked up, the temperature dropped, and the wind kicked in. The Phillies led 2–1 through five innings. By then, it was an official game, and if it had been a regular season game, the umpires well might have called the game because of the nasty conditions and declared the Phillies the winner, or they might at least have delayed the game. But Commissioner Selig, who was entrusted with the responsibility of deciding whether to delay or postpone a World Series game, had informed management for both teams beforehand that he would not permit a team to win a World Series clincher in a rain-shortened game.

The Rays scored a run in the top of the sixth to even things up. The field had become so unplayable that Selig decided it was time to stop the game. But rather than waiting it out that night to see whether conditions would improve, Selig determined that the game would be resumed two nights later (not the following night because the rain was supposed to continue) in the bottom of the sixth inning. The Phillies won that night, 4–3, to capture the World Series.

Landis, seated next to the Washington dugout underneath an umbrella, had seen enough. There was no end in sight for the rain, and the field conditions had become more and more deplorable. Clark Griffith was sitting nearby, and Landis, without consulting with the umpires, told the Senators' owner, "You're world champions. I'm calling the game."

Griffith surprised Landis by not taking advantage of Landis's declaration. In a show of sportsmanship, Griffith replied, "Once you started in the rain, you've got to finish it." The game continued.

Play continued, and both Kremer and Johnson pitched a perfect sixth inning. By the seventh inning, a fog had enveloped the outfield, and it was difficult for outfielders to pick up the ball off the bat.

After Kremer dispatched the Senators in the top of the seventh, as rain continued to blanket the field, rabid Pirates fans stood and cheered wildly during the seventh-inning stretch. They remained on their feet, trying to spark a rally, as Eddie Moore led off the bottom of the seventh against Johnson. Moore hit what appeared to be a routine pop-up toward shortstop. Roger Peckinpaugh took a couple steps back, looked into the downpour, slipped while he tried to get his bearings, and dropped the ball for a two-base error. It was Peckinpaugh's seventh error of the Series.

Max Carey followed by lofting a fly ball down the left-field line. Left fielder Goose Goslin sloshed through the rain and mud but could not get to the ball. And, though the third-base umpire Brick Owens was closest to the play (umpires did not man the left-field and right-field lines in the World Series back then), the home-plate umpire, Barry McCormick, who could hardly track the ball through the fog, called it fair. Moore scored, and Carey made it to second for a double. Goslin ran in and insisted to Owens that the ball had landed in the mud in foul territory. Harris ran over from his position at second base to join his player in the argument. It was to no avail, though. Owens deferred to McCormick, and the ruling stood.

Johnson, soaked from head to toe, his ankles shackled in mud, retired the next two Pirates, but then Pie Traynor hit a shot to the gap in right-center field to score Carey and tie the game. Traynor never stopped running, rounded third, and barreled home, trying for an inside-the-park home run. Harris took the relay throw and fired a strike to catcher Muddy Ruel to nail Traynor at home and keep the game at 6–6.

Both runs were unearned because of Peckinpaugh's error. He was disgusted with himself when he returned to the Senators dugout. When he stepped into the batter's box with one out and no baserunners on in the top of the eighth, he was determined to atone for his miscue. He pounced on Ray Kremer's first pitch and hit a long fly through the fog that cleared the wall in left for a go-ahead home run. The emotional Peckinpaugh, in tears as he circled the bases, was carried from home plate to the dugout by his teammates.

Firpo Marberry, having pitched just 2⅓ innings in the Series, was well rested and ready to come into the game. A small but vocal throng of Senators fans sitting near the team's dugout urged Harris to bring in Marberry for Johnson, who had allowed 12 hits and six runs and was visibly exhausted. Harris stuck with the great Johnson, who got two outs on a foul pop and fly ball that Sam Rice managed to catch in center despite the fog. Catcher Earl Smith lined one into right-center for a double. McKechnie sent in one of his starting pitchers, Emil Yde, to run for the slow-footed Smith at second. Washington fans continued calling for Harris to turn things over to Marberry, but the manager ignored them, opting to sink or swim with his superstar.

Carson Bigbee, a reserve outfielder and ten-year Pirate, was called in to pinch-hit for Kremer. On a team replete with .300 hitters, Bisbee had batted just .238 during the season, but he smacked a 2-0 pitch over Goslin's head to score Yde. Johnson walked Eddie Moore on a 3-2 pitch. Johnson looked as though he was out of the inning when Max Carey—already 4-for-4 off Johnson on the day—hit a ground ball to shortstop. Peckinpaugh, fighting the field conditions and his confidence with the glove, juggled the ball and, while trying for the force out at second, threw high. Harris came down on the bag too late as Moore slid in safely. Peckinpaugh was charged with his eighth error, which remains an ignominious World Series record.

With the bases loaded and the game tied at 7–7, Kiki Cuyler got behind on the count 1-2, and Johnson fooled him with a curve. Ruel thought it was strike three and took off his mask; Johnson thought the same and started to walk off the mound. Barry McCormick called it a ball, though, and Cuyler took advantage by then hitting a fly ball down the right-field line. It dropped in and rolled into foul territory, underneath a tarp. All three runners scored, but it was ruled a ground rule double, and Carey was sent back to third. But the damage was done, and the Pirates took a 9–7 lead into the ninth inning.

With two left-handed hitters due up for the Senators in the top of the ninth, Sam Rice and Goose Goslin, McKechnie brought in lefty Red Oldham for his first appearance of the Series. Oldham caught Rice looking, retired Harris on a liner to second, and then Goslin was called out on strikes to give the Pirates the Series. After the game, the gentlemanly Johnson embraced his crestfallen shortstop and told him that he lost the game with his pitching; it was not Peckinpaugh's fault.

Bucky Harris was heavily second-guessed for leaving Johnson in, not only by Senators fans and writers but also by the American League president, Ban Johnson, who criticized the manager for letting sentimentality dictate his decision. "You run the American League," Harris retorted. "I'll manage the Washington baseball team."

Commissioner Landis was also widely criticized for forcing the teams to play in horrendous conditions. His detractors insisted that rain, mud, and fog, not the abilities of the players, decided the game and that Landis could have waited another day or two till the rain had stopped and the field was dry to play the critical seventh game.

Walter Johnson pitched two more seasons and then retired. He became manager of the Senators in 1929 and held the job for four seasons; his best year was a second-place finish in 1930. His 417 wins still ranks second to Cy Young's 511. He remains the career leader in shutouts with 110.

Clark Griffith stayed on as a majority owner of the Senators for another thirty years until his death in 1955. His team returned to the World Series just one more time after 1925, in 1933, but they lost to the Giants in five games. After 1933, the Senators reverted to their poor early-century play—during the last twenty-two seasons that Griffith owned the team, they fielded just four teams with a winning record.

If Griffith had simply accepted Landis's proclamation to call Game 7 after five innings, his club would have repeated as world champions in 1925. Walter Johnson would have been credited with his third win of the Series. Undoubtedly, Bill McKechnie would have put up a fierce argument. But Landis—as Shoeless Joe Jackson, Babe Ruth, and others learned the hard way—ruled as commissioner with an iron fist and likely would not have backed down.

Griffith's Senators could have done what several of the original sixteen major-league franchises have failed to do—win back-to-back World Series. Since the dawn of the Series, the Pirates, Phillies, Tigers, White Sox, Cleveland Indians/Guardians, St. Louis Cardinals, Brooklyn/Los Angeles Dodgers, Boston/Milwaukee/Atlanta Braves, and St. Louis Browns/Baltimore Orioles have never repeated as world champions. On a miserable afternoon in Pittsburgh in 1925, Clark Griffith had the opportunity to accomplish this rare feat but said in so many words: "No thanks. Let's keep playing."

One of baseball's all-time best pitchers, Walter Johnson ranks first in career shutouts and second in wins. But the Pirates beat Johnson and the Senators in a wild
Game 7 of the 1925 World Series that was marked by terrible weather conditions
and a curious decision by Senators owner Clark Griffith. *National Baseball Hall of
Fame and Museum*

PART II

WHO *ARE* THESE GUYS?

6

An Open Window

THE MODERN ERA OF MAJOR LEAGUE BASEBALL ARRIVED WITH THE turn of the twentieth century and was officially ushered in with the founding of the American League, which started play in 1901. For the next roughly fifty years, baseball was played by two competing eight-team leagues that sent their regular-season champions directly to the World Series. Before the late 1950s, there were no teams west of the Mississippi and the westernmost outpost was St. Louis. In 1944, with the nation deep into World War II, St. Louis became the center of the baseball universe when the Browns and Cardinals made it to an improbable World Series.

In those days, like today, there were the haves and the have-nots. But, unlike today, when struggling teams can retool quickly through strategic free-agency acquisitions, analytics, and the draft, in that era, teams often had long droughts between World Series appearances and even between seasons when they could field competitive teams.

The National League was dominated in the early part of the twentieth century by the Giants and then by the St. Louis Cardinals, who benefited from Branch Rickey's innovative player-development techniques and foresight in the creation of the minor-league system through which Rickey seemed to have a never-ending stream of prospects filling the Cardinals major-league pipeline. While most teams struggled at times, the Pirates, the Reds, the Cubs, the Phillies, and even the Dodgers made occasional appearances in the Series or, at least, had periods during which they were very competitive. The American League was less democratic.

Dominated by the Red Sox in the early part of the century and then by the Yankees, who built their early dynasty by looting the financially strapped Red Sox of the early 1920s, some teams spent long stretches in the second division with only occasional appearances in the pennant race, much less the World Series.

The Athletics had dominant teams off and on from 1902 through 1914 and again from 1929 through 1931, making eight appearances in the Fall Classic and winning five. Both, however, were dismantled prematurely by the chronically underfunded owner-manager Connie Mack, who sold his best players to pay his debts. In the aftermath of these events, the A's spent many years in the cellar losing 100 games or more ten times through 1950 and never really contended again in Philadelphia. When they left Philadelphia in 1955 to spend more than a decade in purgatory in Kansas City, the dynastic Oakland A's teams were not even a glint in Connie's eye.

The Washington Senators may have had a legacy of losing, but they had a number of great teams led first by Walter Johnson and then by Joe Cronin and a cast of others. They made appearances in the Series in 1924, 1925, and 1933 and won the Series in 1924 in an epic Series against John McGraw's Giants, fueled by the legendary Johnson's pitching heroics.

Then there were the St. Louis Browns. The Browns were an original American League franchise that made its American League debut as the Milwaukee Brewers in 1901 before moving to St. Louis for the 1902 season. For the next fifty years, the Browns were the epitome of futility. Enduring 41 losing seasons from 1902 to 1953, they were, in aggregate, more than an astounding 1,000 games under .500. In the era of a 154-game regular season, they lost 100 or more games eight times. It's hard to believe that this was the franchise that would go on to become the Baltimore Orioles, who had an extended period of greatness from the mid-1960s through the early part of the twenty-first century. However, it was indeed, and, over their fifty-year existence, only one Hall of Famer would enter Cooperstown as a Brown. That was the great George Sisler, who ended his career in 1930 with a .340 lifetime average and more than 2,800 hits but retired having never seen the promised land.

Though the Browns occasionally competed, nearly winning the American League crown in 1922, they were, more often than not, a hapless franchise that endured some very lean years. In 1935, during the height of the Great Depression, only 80,922 fans came to see the Browns at Sportsman's Park—throughout the entire year!

Not surprisingly, Don Barnes, the owner of the Browns in the early 1940s, had been working behind the scenes to move the Browns to Los Angeles. He had negotiated a deal with Phil Wrigley, owner of the Chicago Cubs, to buy Wrigley's Los Angeles Wrigley Field as part of his relocation strategy. The forward-thinking Barnes also knew that the cost of transportation to the West Coast might be an issue for some American League owners; such owners feared incurring the major travel expenses needed to accommodate road trips to a single West Coast franchise. To that end he entered into talks with the railroads and Trans World Airlines to address the travel and logistical issues that were sure to arise. His efforts were so successful that a draft of the 1942 American League schedule that included a Los Angeles edition of the Brownies was circulated. The league owners were set to vote on the move on December 8, 1941. On December 7, 1941, the Japanese bombed Pearl Harbor, and the United States formally entered into World War II.

The war impacted major-league baseball in a way that almost nothing before it had. Neither the Spanish flu pandemic of 1917–18 nor the Black Sox scandal in the aftermath of the 1919 World Series changed the face and makeup of major-league baseball the way the war did. For the Browns, the impact was immediate.

The owners held their meeting the day after the Pearl Harbor attack and unanimously rejected the proposal to move the Browns to Los Angeles. Even the Browns voted against their own proposed move. This was not done out of some sense of patriotism but out of recognition that, with the entrance into the war, governmental travel restrictions were sure to follow and anything related to West Coast travel could be problematic for the rest of the American League.

Though Barnes would sell the Browns after the 1944 World Series, he was going to be in St. Louis long enough to benefit from one of the consequences of the war. Having failed to relocate the Browns after the 1941 season, he decided to invest more in acquiring better players. Picking up the likes of Don Gutteridge from the Cardinals and signing a young Vern Stephens to solidify the infield, Barnes was going to take advantage of a small opening that was in the making and that would level the playing field around baseball during the years following the country's entrance into the war, an opening that uniquely affected the Browns.

Despite Commissioner Kenesaw Landis's offer in January 1942 to suspend major-league baseball in light of the growing conflict in Europe and Japan, President Franklin Roosevelt declared immediately that, in his opinion, baseball was a necessary distraction for the country and should continue to be played, though he left the final decision up to the commissioner and the league owners. The games did continue, but the war effort did not exempt players from military service, and, by the beginning of the 1944 season, through the draft and voluntary induction, 340 major leaguers were in the military and others were performing war-related services.

Roosevelt's opinion was not the final say in the matter, however. Critics continued to take issue with players who were active in the big leagues despite having 4-F draft status (a classification designating a person to be physically, psychologically, or morally unfit for military duty). Even J. Edgar Hoover weighed in, noting that, if players were trying to evade the draft, the FBI would be obligated to look into the matter. But it was the government's doctors and not the major leagues that declared those players to be unfit for service. In the end, the criticism faded away and it became clear that Roosevelt's faith in the game and its players was well founded—major-league players answered the call of duty with as many as five hundred enlisted from the ranks of the major leagues.

The war, however, gutted the major leagues. There were only sixteen teams at the time, and most teams suffered significant losses to their rosters. In the American League, virtually the entire starting lineup of the Yankees, including future Hall of Famers Joe DiMaggio, Phil Rizzuto, Red Ruffing, and even an aging Bill Dickey, was in the service. The Red Sox lost Ted Williams, Johnny Pesky, and Dom DiMaggio, among others. Tigers Hank Greenberg, Charlie Gehringer, and Birdie Tebbetts were all in the military by the beginning of that season, as was Bob

Feller of the Indians. The Browns, by contrast, lost center fielder Wally Judnich and pitcher Steve Sundra. The Yankees had won the 1943 Series by beating the Cardinals in five games, but their roster had already been depleted, and, though Joe Gordon, Bill Dickey, Charlie Keller, and the league MVP pitcher Spud Chandler were key contributors to that championship team, they were all gone by early 1944 as well.

The doors were now open to many players who would not otherwise have made it to the majors. In some instances, older players stayed on to play when they might otherwise have retired, but many roster slots were filled by players who, though called up to the majors, did not possess major-league talent. For the Browns it was, to a large degree, business as usual. Vern Stephens, their best player and a seven-time All-Star in his career with the Browns and Red Sox, failed his army physical, as did first baseman George McQuinn. Two of their top pitchers from 1943, Denny Galehouse and Bob Muncrief, returned for the 1944 season and were joined by Jack Kramer, who had had sporadic appearances with them since 1939. Nelson Potter was moved from the bullpen to the starting rotation, and rounding out the rotation was Sig Jakucki, who filled in for Denny Galehouse early in the year while Denny worked at a war plant in Ohio during the week.

Sig was a prime example of what a wartime roster might bring. He had pitched for the Browns in 1936. He was 0–3 with an ERA approaching 9.00, but more than anything he was a great source of agitation to the Browns front office. He was said to have a hundred-thousand-dollar arm and a million-dollar thirst. Jakucki, a native of Camden, New Jersey, was a hard man and already an army veteran. He had a ferocious temper and a bothersome habit of disappearing for days between pitching appearances.

By the end of 1936, Jakucki had managed to fight and drink himself right off the Browns team, beginning a seven-year odyssey through the minor leagues before general manager (and future team owner) Bill DeWitt, in an act of mild desperation, re-signed him for the 1944 season. Minor-league players and owners often conducted their operations independently in those days with predictable results. Sig, for instance, once found himself under contract to two minor-league teams at the same time.

Nonetheless, Sig found his way back into Dewitt's good graces and went 13–9 for St. Louis in 1944, winning several critical games down the stretch. He also continued his brawling ways, once reportedly disarming a gangster who had pulled a gun on him during an argument in a New York bar, knocking the man to the floor with his own gun and leaving him sprawled out on the floor as he made his exit.

Vern Stephens was another Brown who loved the night life and, in an era when most games were still played during the day, delighted in the possibilities the night might hold for him. Don Gutteridge was assigned to be Vern's roommate in the hope that he would slow down Stephens's nocturnal activities, but to no avail. Stealing a line used by Jimmie Reese of the Yankees, who briefly roomed with Babe Ruth in the 1930s, Don said that he actually roomed with Vern's suitcase.

Pitching propelled the Browns during the 1944 season. Their starters were not, for the most part, household names, but most of them would enjoy career years in 1944. Not one of their big four starters would retire from baseball with so much as a winning record, but that season Kramer was 17–13 with a 2.49 ERA, Potter went 19–7 with a 2.83 ERA, and Muncrief and Jakucki each won 13 games. Galehouse might have been their best pitcher overall, but he'd been working at a war plant in Ohio since before the season and was available only on weekends. On a typical Saturday night he'd board a train to whatever city the Browns were in and pitch the Sunday game—usually the front end of a doubleheader—and then return to Ohio for work on Monday. By midyear this routine began to take a toll on him, and, realizing that he was falling out of baseball condition, he contacted his draft board and asked how soon he would be inducted if he quit his job at the plant. Told he probably wouldn't be inducted until 1945, he took the gamble and rejoined the Browns full time. Denny didn't pitch in April and didn't win his first game until July 20, but he found his rhythm and closed strongly, winning nine games in the second half of the year.

The Browns got off to a fast start, winning their first nine games, and started to believe that they had a real shot at the pennant. After a brief slump, they regained their footing and, by early June, found themselves back in first place. The Red Sox were right behind them at the All-Star break but then lost several more key players to the war effort. While the Yankees remained competitive, it was becoming clear that the Red Sox, Yankees, and Tigers would be the teams that the Browns most needed to worry about. In early September, the Browns trailed New York and Detroit, but, by the last week of the season, they were a game back of the Tigers with the Yankees in their rearview mirror.

Though the Yankees were still mathematically in the race, it would come down to St. Louis and the Tigers, with the Browns hosting a four-game series with New York and the Tigers playing the Senators on the final weekend of the year. The Browns' pitching that weekend was excellent, and they beat the Yankees in the first three games of the series. The Thursday game had been rained out, and so a doubleheader was scheduled for that Friday. Kramer won the opener, 4–1, and Potter won the nightcap, 1–0. Galehouse won the third game on Saturday, 2–0, guaranteeing the Browns at least a tie for the pennant.

A coin toss was held to determine where an American League play-off would be held if the teams finished in a tie at the end of the season. The Browns lost the toss, but, with their bags packed for a potential trip to Detroit, they completed a four-game sweep of the Yanks on October 1, beating them, 5–2, before a crowd of more than thirty-five thousand fans (another estimated fifteen thousand were turned away at the gates) behind a complete game by Jakucki and two homers by Chet Laabs. The Senators finished off the Tigers, 4–1. By some accounts this was the first time in forty-two years that the Browns had sold out the stadium for a game, leaving the players to wonder where the fans had been all those years.

Along with very good pitching, the Browns did what most good teams do and compiled an outstanding 54–23 home record. In 1944, though, the Browns would not enjoy a home-field advantage in the World Series. For their great efforts they would face off with their cotenant at Sportsman's Park, the St. Louis Cardinals, who won 105 games and were finishing their third straight season with over 100 wins to become the first team in modern history to achieve that feat. After a more than forty-year, Moses-like journey through the baseball desert, the Browns would make their first Series appearance and wouldn't even need to leave home. In October 1944, the World Series would belong to St. Louis, and Sportsman's Park would play host to the entire Series.

In 1921 and 1922, the Giants squared off against their tenant, the New York Yankees, at the Polo Grounds as the Yanks awaited completion of their new home in the Bronx. This would be the last time one ballpark would be the site of every Series game until the pandemic-shortened 2020 season.

Sportsman's Park was already an aging stadium by 1944 and would be the last stadium to have segregated seating for its fans; the Cardinals and Browns agreed to that policy change before the beginning of the season. It was the home of the Browns from 1902 until their departure for Baltimore in 1954. In 1920, the Cardinals became the Browns' tenant at Sportsman's, an arrangement that continued until Bill Veeck sold the stadium to August Busch Jr. and the Anheuser-Busch Corporation in 1953 in an effort to raise cash and stay solvent. The teams shared the stadium for thirty-three years, much longer than the Giants and Yankees shared the Polo Grounds (ten years) and twice as long as the Phillies and A's shared Shibe Park in Philadelphia (sixteen years).

Over the years the park was remodeled a couple of times, and, by the time of the '44 World Series, it held about thirty-five thousand fans. The dimensions of the field were generally the same throughout the years, with the left-field line measuring out at 351 feet, 422 feet to straightaway center, and 310 feet down the right-field line.

As one can imagine, the arrangement between the two teams over all those years resulted in a number of intersections between the two organizations. One of the most significant, involving the services of Branch Rickey, predated the Cards' move to Sportsman's in 1920 and would profoundly affect the fortunes of the two teams and that of major-league baseball for the next thirty years.

Phil Ball, the owner of the Browns, had hired Branch Rickey to be the manager near the end of the 1913 season, and by 1916 Rickey was basically running the day-to-day operations of the club. Though the hard-drinking Ball recognized Rickey's talent, he was uncomfortable with Rickey's sympathetic views toward the growing temperance movement and his attitude toward alcohol in general.

After the 1916 season, the Cardinals offered Rickey the job of team president, and Ball saw a way out of their strained relationship. When Rickey explained the Cardinals' offer to him, Ball assured Rickey that he wouldn't stand in his way if this opportunity was as good as it sounded. In a generous gesture he even offered to help Rickey behind the scenes in getting the best deal and contract terms from the Cardinals. Rickey accepted the Cardinals' offer, but then some strange things began happening. The president of the American League, Ban Johnson, got wind of the arrangement and told Ball in no uncertain terms that it would be unacceptable to allow someone of Rickey's ability to jump to the National League and that Ball needed to put an end to the negotiations immediately. It's a little unclear why Ball seemed to be under Johnson's thumb, but he did as he was asked, telling Rickey that he needed to back out of the deal with the Cardinals. Rickey refused, saying that papers had already been signed and that the Cardinals were going to make the announcement of his hiring by the next day. Despite the threats by Ball, Rickey refused to renege and the deal was announced. Rickey wouldn't speak to Ball again for many years.

Ball would make one more strategic error in dealing with the rival Cardinals in 1920. The Cardinals had been struggling and were bleeding red ink. Sam Breadon, a self-made millionaire, had slowly bought up stock in the Cardinals and was now the de facto owner, but he needed operating funds for the team. He had the idea to sell the Cardinals' stadium (Robison Field) and the land around it, but he would then need a place for his team to play. He approached Phil Ball and begged Ball to help him out. Ball originally wanted no part of the Cardinals, saying he'd never sign a deal that would allow Branch Rickey to set foot back in Sportsman's Park.

Despite his wealth, Breadon pleaded poverty and agreed to sign any leasing deal Ball felt was fair if it would allow the Cardinals to play in Sportsman's Park. Breadon's appeal to the vanity of the man who controlled the fate of the Cardinals worked, and the Cardinals became the tenant of the Browns, beginning in 1920. The deal allowed Breadon to sell League Park and the land around it for about $275,000. With that money, Breadon and Branch Rickey proceeded to take over the St. Louis baseball market within just a few years. Though Branch Rickey would move on to the Brooklyn Dodgers before the 1943 season, his fingerprints were all over the 1944 National League champion Cardinals.

The Cardinals of 1944 were baseball royalty. They were defending National League champions. In 1942, they had won the World Series, beating the Yankees in five games. In 1943, the Yankees returned the favor, but from 1941 to 1949 the Cardinals never finished lower than second place and would also win the Series in 1946 against the Boston Red Sox.

The notorious Gashouse Gang of the early 1930s was mostly gone by then, with only forty-year-old Pepper Martin on the team in '44. Martin didn't play much but he was still in great shape. It was said he could still pile two steamer trunks on top of each other and then jump on top from a standing start.

The Cardinals were a well-balanced team, and though the future Hall of Famer Enos Slaughter was in the middle of a three-year stretch in the service, they still had Stan Musial, who was just entering his prime. Musial had received an exemption from the draft because he was the sole provider for his ailing father. Though just twenty-three that season, he was already the reigning MVP of the National League. Stan would eventually enter the service in 1945 and would return in 1946 to win another MVP Award on his way to the Hall of Fame. He played in an astounding 24 All-Star Games (two were played each season from 1959 to 1962).

All told, Musial would win three MVP Awards in all, finishing the 1944 season as the runner-up, and, when he retired, he had more hits (3,630) than anyone other than Ty Cobb and the most ever by a National League player. His accomplishments were many and legendary, but he was not alone on that team.

Marty Marion was their shortstop, and he would win the 1944 MVP Award and would wind up his career as an eight-time All-Star. Many felt Marion, even more than Musial, was the key to the Cardinals' success and maybe the best clutch hitter on the team.

Catcher Walker Cooper was another outstanding player, though he would go to the Giants by 1946 and would go on to make the National League All-Star team eight times. Walker's older brother, Mort, was the best pitcher on the team and won the MVP Award in 1942, and in 1944 he won 22 games and lost only seven, with an earned run average of 2.46.

Rounding out their pitching rotation were Max Lanier, at 17–12 with an ERA of 2.65; Ted Wilks, who had his best year ever by far at 17–4 with an ERA of 2.64; and Harry Brecheen, at 16–5 with an ERA of 2.85. Brecheen would go on to retire with a winning percentage of .591 and would have most of his best years after the war when the major-league rosters, filling up with returning war veterans, were much more competitive.

The Cardinals were about as loaded as a team could be in those years when rosters routinely included players who otherwise would never have seen an inning in the big leagues. They were managed by Bill Southworth, who would one day join Musial and Slaughter in the Hall of Fame. Southworth, who was a journeyman in many ways and a baseball lifer, played for John McGraw and once was traded for Casey Stengel.

Southworth's career managing statistics are pretty impressive. He managed more than 1,700 games with the Cardinals and the Boston Braves. He got off to an uneven start, however, when Branch Rickey named him as player-manager in 1929. In 1926, he had helped the Cardinals beat the Yankees for the title with a key home run in Game 2 of the World Series, but he struggled with the transition from being one of the guys to being the man in charge and was in over his head. Rickey saw leadership potential in him, though, and in July of that season rotated him back to the minor leagues, where he would languish for another ten years before returning for part of the 1940 season.

Southworth suffered multiple personal tragedies late in his playing career and during his years in the minors. His twin daughters died at birth; his young son, Billy, was shot in a hunting accident (he recovered); and his wife died of cancer in 1932. Sadly, Billy Jr., who by 1944 was a decorated major in the US Air Force, would die in a plane crash in February 1945, just four months after being photographed with his father at the World Series. These tragedies may have contributed to a long bout with alcohol; a report in the *St. Louis Dispatch* said that Southworth "hadn't ever been averse to burning a candle or two at both ends." By most accounts, he had overcome his drinking problems by the time he returned to the major leagues, though he backslid to the bottle after his son's death. Between 1941 and 1945, he won more than 100 games three times and 95 or more games five times before moving on to the Braves for the 1946 season, finishing the Cardinals part of his career with a .642 winning percentage.

In 1944, Southworth and the Browns manager, Luke Sewell, to save money, shared a room at a boarding house, each taking up residence when the other St. Louis team was on the road. For the Series, someone had to go, and, in the end, Southworth found another room that was to be vacant for a couple of weeks during the Series.

The Cardinals would be the home team for what would be known as the St. Louis Showdown or the Trolley Series, batting last in Games 1, 2, 6, and 7. The Browns would be the home team for Games 3, 4, and 5, with no off days during the Series. The Cardinals were certainly the betting favorites, at 1–2, having swept through the National League and having won 16 games more than the Browns. The Browns, however, had great faith in their pitching and had ridden their arms down the stretch to the pennant, including the final season-ending series sweep of the Yankees, and so they had a lot of momentum in their favor.

Game 1 was on October 4. Denny Galehouse got the ball for the Browns, facing off against Cardinals ace Mort Cooper. Cooper gave up only two hits that day, but one was a two-run homer by McQuinn following a single by right fielder Gene Moore in the fourth inning. Galehouse made it stand up with a seven-hit complete game, holding the Cards scoreless until the bottom of the ninth. Galehouse also gave up four walks but stranded nine baserunners, giving the Browns a big boost going into Game 2.

Nelson Potter was the starter for the Browns in Game 2. Many on his team considered him their best bet during the Series. He had shut out the Yanks, 1–0, in the last series of the regular season, and they felt that, if they could just get him a run or two early, he'd get them the win. He almost did, but some bad fielding by Potter cost the team an early run that would come back to haunt them. In the third inning, after a single by Emil Verban, Cards pitcher Max Lanier laid down a sacrifice bunt that Potter first mishandled then threw wide of first, letting Verban move to third as Lanier reached on what was scored as a sacrifice and an error. Verban scored on a ground out by Augie Bergamo, and the damage was done. The weak-hitting Browns would fall two runs behind in the fourth when another error, this one by third baseman Mark Christman, following a Whitey Kurowski single, would allow Verban to deliver the run with a sacrifice fly.

The Browns managed to string together a single, a double, and then another single by Frank Mancuso to tie the game at 2 in the seventh inning. They turned the ball over to Bob Muncrief, and he held the Cards scoreless through the seventh, eighth, ninth, and 10th innings. In the top of the 11th inning, George McQuinn led off with a double, and the Browns, sensing this might be their opportunity to take control of the Series, had Christman attempt to lay down a bunt to get McQuinn to third with one out. Blix Donnelly was pitching for the Cards, having come on in relief in the top of the eighth. Now in his fourth inning, he made the play that would be seen as the turning point of the Series. Fielding Christman's bunt cleanly on the third-base line, Donnelly wheeled and blindly fired to third, hoping to cut down the lead runner rather than take the sure out at first. The throw was right on the bag, and McQuinn slid into the tag for the first out. Some Browns were shocked that Donnelly even attempted the throw and even more surprised with the outcome, noting that, even if his snap throw to the third baseman had been just chest high, McQuinn would have been safe and the Browns in the driver's seat with two on and nobody out. The reality was that, with his momentum carrying him into foul territory, the throw to third was the only one Donnelly could make.

When the next batter, Gene Moore, hit a deep fly to right, it only confirmed the importance of the play at third. What would have been a sacrifice fly and a one-run lead was simply the second out of the inning. Donnelly struck out Red Hayworth to end the inning, and in quick fashion the Cardinals finished taking the wind out of the Browns' sails. Ray Sanders led off the bottom of the 11th with a single and was sacrificed to second by Kurowski. Following an intentional walk to Marty Marion, pinch-hitter Ken O'Dea, a backup catcher, singled to right and the Cards had tied the Series.

Over the course of what turned out to be a six-game Series, the Browns would score more than two runs in a single game only once and that was in Game 3. Appearing for the first time as the home team, the Brownies would win the game, 6–2, behind Jack Kramer, who, like Galehouse in Game 1, would pitch a seven-hitter. The game would underscore the importance of the Donnelly play in Game 2. What was then a 2–1 Series advantage could as easily have been 3–0 for the Browns, but it wasn't to be.

After giving up an unearned run in the first inning, Kramer settled down and cruised through the next five innings, relatively untouched. In the third inning, his teammates would give him all the run support he needed. Batting as the home team, the Browns mounted a two-out rally with five consecutive singles by Moore, Stephens, McQuinn, Al Zarilla, and Christman. Three runs scored before Southworth could even get a relief pitcher ready. When he finally replaced starter Ted Wilks with Freddy Schmidt, the change would cost the Cards further when, after an intentional walk to Red Hayworth, Schmidt unleashed his first wild pitch of the season, allowing the Browns' fourth run to score and giving Kramer a three-run lead. This was the only offensive outburst the Browns would enjoy in the entire Series. Both teams scored late, with the final score at 6–2, leaving the Browns to wonder, "What if?"

The bookmakers, however, weren't wondering, "What if?" They still had the Cardinals as 4–5 favorites to win the Series going into Game 4. Harry Brecheen took the mound for the Cardinals in Game 4, making his first appearance in the Series and, in not uncommon fashion, pitched a complete game, putting thirteen men on base but limiting the Browns to just one run on a double-play ball in the bottom of the eighth. Musial did early damage with a home run in the top of the first, hitting only the second homer for the two teams combined to that point. During the whole six-game Series, both teams would account for only four homers.

Sig Jakucki made his only start of the Series. But he didn't have his best stuff, lasting only three innings and yielding four runs on five hits. Though the Browns relievers held the Cards relatively quiet after the third inning, the lack of offense was now becoming a real problem. They would score a meaningless run in the eighth and only one more run over the final two games. The Browns had entered the Series with the worst winning percentage of any American League champion to that point and the difference in talent between the two teams, especially in hitting, was becoming readily apparent.

Though the fans were squarely on the side of the Browns, Game 5 wouldn't be much different. Galehouse and Cooper would again face each other. Galehouse pitched well again, throwing a complete-game six-hitter. But he gave up two homers and the Browns couldn't mount much of a counterattack against Cooper, who went the distance in a seven-hit shutout. Cooper and Galehouse combined for what was then a record 22 strikeouts in the game. One Browns player tried to explain the high number of strikeouts (for that era), noting that, during the regular season, with smaller crowds, the bleachers were usually closed but now were full of fans wearing white shirts. The sea of white made it difficult to see the ball when the pitcher released it. Ironically, the same would be said about the center-field bleachers in Baltimore's Memorial Stadium (the Browns' next home) about twenty-five years later when teams in the World Series facing the Orioles complained about the same situation.

Game 6 would prove to be a bit anticlimactic though once again well pitched. In a rematch of the Game 2 starters, Nelson Potter faced off against Max Lanier. This time, neither pitcher would make it deep into the game. Potter was taken out in the fourth, having given up three runs in that inning (though only one was earned), and Lanier was taken out in the sixth. Max had given up only a single run, but, in addition to yielding three hits, he walked five batters before Southworth gave him the hook and handed the ball to Ted Wilks. Wilks closed out the game with 3⅔ scoreless innings of no-hit shutout ball.

After George McQuinn singled in Chet Laabs in the top of the second, the Browns were essentially done. The Cards scored three runs in the fourth after Vern Stephens committed a one-out error on a potential inning-ending, double-play ball to extend the rally for the Cards. After back-to-back singles by Emil Verban and Lanier, the home team had their final margin of victory. The outcome really underscored the themes of the Series for the Browns—weak hitting and poor defense. In the end, the Browns as a team hit only .183, with one home run and nine RBIs over six games. McQuinn was the only starter to hit over .240, posting a sterling .438 average and knocking in five of the Browns' nine runs. Their defense failed them terribly, committing 10 errors to the Cardinals' one and sabotaging an excellent collective pitching effort by the Browns' pitching staff. Of the 16 runs scored by the Cardinals, only nine were earned. In contrast, all 12 of the Browns' runs were earned, negating the advantage the Browns held in team ERA (1.49 to 1.96 for the Cardinals).

While the Cardinals celebrated their victory, the Browns' window of opportunity was already closing and probably faster than most realized. The next ten years would be tumultuous ones for the Browns, and changes would come immediately. Right after the season, Don Barnes sold the team to Richard Muckerman, marking the first of four times they would be sold before moving to Baltimore in 1954.

Though most of the roster would be intact for 1945, Denny Galehouse did join the military and missed the entire season. Rosters would remain depleted for all of the major-league teams through that season. With the rest of their pitchers back, the Browns did make a run at another title but never got within fewer than five games of the lead after Labor Day. They finished with an 81–70 record and ended up in third place, six games behind the Tigers. Some players honestly thought that they should have won another title, but losing Galehouse definitely hurt. In addition, their anemic offense continued through the '45 season. Only one player, Vern Stephens, had more than eight home runs, and the team as a whole hit .249.

This was also the season of Pete Gray, the one-armed outfielder who was brought in as a publicity stunt. Though he could outrun a scalded dog, according to Browns teammate Ellis Clary, he was a weak hitter with no power. He managed a .217 average in his only season in the majors, with no homers and a handful of extra-base hits in 77 games. It was understood by many of the players that promotional events would be needed to generate attendance, and so they accepted Gray but some viewed him as a sideshow at best and a distracting problem at worse. Reasoning that Gray was taking away at-bats from better players at a time when they actually thought they could win, some players were less than understanding of his presence and some were openly hostile to and tormented Gray.

Sig Jakucki was one of those players. He ridiculed Gray constantly, playing vicious pranks on him and virtually isolating Gray, a loner by nature, from the rest of the team. Toward the end of August, this behavior, along with his constant fighting, drinking, and disappearances, led to Jakucki's release from the team, despite the team having won his last two starts and Jakucki having compiled a winning record. He never pitched in the majors again.

Muckerman began making wholesale changes to the team in an effort to come up with money to offset lagging attendance. Before he sold the team in 1949, virtually the entire starting lineup and pitching rotation from the '44 champs was gone. Catcher Red Hayworth was out of the majors by 1946, and first baseman George McQuinn was traded to the A's after the 1945 season. Outfielder Gene Moore retired after the '45 season, and Mike Kreevich was sold to the Senators that same season, and he retired at the end of the year. Outfielder Milt Byrnes was also gone after that season and never played in another major-league game.

The biggest buyer at the St. Louis Browns fire sale was the Red Sox. Between 1946 and the end of the '47 season, the Sox purchased Vern Stephens, Don Gutteridge, Jack Kramer, and Denny Galehouse, basically gutting the team before Nelson Potter was mercifully sent to the A's in early 1948. All of these moves along with the return of military veterans to their teams for the 1946 season quickly relegated the Browns to the second division, where they languished for the rest of their days in St. Louis, never finishing higher than sixth place again.

Stephens was the only Brown from the pennant winners of 1944 to ever play a game as a Baltimore Oriole. After spending his most productive years in Boston, he was traded to the White Sox and was subsequently picked up off of waivers by St. Louis in July 1953. He appeared in more than a hundred games for the Orioles in '54 and was released early in the 1955 season, finishing his career with the White Sox.

Muckerman made one last stab at keeping the team's fortunes afloat in 1947, when he purchased Sportsman's Park from the estate of the late Phil Ball. He poured about $750,000, which represented just about everything he had, into renovating the stadium before admitting to failure and selling the team and the park in 1949 to Bill DeWitt, who had been working for Muckerman as his general manager. DeWitt had come up in the Cardinals organization working for Branch Rickey. In the end, however, he was no more successful than Muckerman, and in 1951 he sold the team to Bill Veeck. As they say, that's a whole other story.

From 1912 to 1953, the major leagues were remarkably symmetrical and unchanging, remaining constant, with the same eight teams in each league playing in the same cities in each league. Through World War I, the 1917–18 Spanish flu pandemic, the Black Sox scandal, and World War II, not a single franchise shifted. Boston, Philadelphia, Chicago, New York, and St. Louis were all homes to more than one team.

In 1953, however, the Boston Braves moved to Milwaukee. In a related move, Bill Veeck, having failed to persuade Braves owner Lou Perini to sell him his "rights" to the Milwaukee market (through Perini's ownership of the minor-league Milwaukee Brewers), was forced to sell the Browns to an ownership group that promptly moved them to Baltimore and renamed them the Orioles. At the time of the sale, Veeck was staggering under about $300,000 of debt he inherited when he bought the Browns in 1951. Desperate for cash as always, he sold Sportsman's Park to Augie Busch to secure operating revenue and to get out from under a requirement from the city that he complete $250,000 worth of renovations to the park before the next season. That expense would have bankrupted him. In the end, Veeck himself estimated that the repairs cost Busch more than one million dollars. How the other American League owners managed to separate Veeck from the Browns before the move to Baltimore is a tale of palace intrigue requiring a more in-depth explanation than time permits here, but in a few short years he went from proclaiming his intentions to run the Cardinals out of town to selling all he had before being forced to back out of the newly formed ownership group that would take the team to Baltimore. In the end, the Browns were so forlorn that, when their last game in St. Louis at the end of the 1953 season went into extra innings, they literally ran out of new baseballs.

This completed a sort of circle of baseball life for Milwaukee and Baltimore, both of which were charter members of the American League in 1902, when the Milwaukee Brewers moved to St. Louis and became the Browns, and the Baltimore Orioles moved to New York and became first the Highlanders and later the Yankees. In short order, the Philadelphia Athletics would move to Kansas City, and the Dodgers and the Giants would pick up stakes and abandon New York for the West Coast. These moves triggered a forty-year period during which various events, including integration, would change the face of Major League Baseball forever.

Over the following ten years or so, the original Senators would move from Washington to Minnesota, and expansion teams would emerge in both leagues. By 1958, only Chicago would have two teams, and franchises such as the "new" Washington Senators, the Los Angeles Angels, the New York Metropolitans, and the Houston Colt .45s would appear on the horizon. Soon the Braves would move again—this time to Atlanta—and the Athletics would depart Kansas City for Oakland. Another round of expansion in 1969 brought the Seattle Pilots and the Kansas City Royals to the American League and the Montreal Expos and the San Diego Padres to the National League, marking the advent of divisional play and bringing down the curtain on the winner-take-all regular season.

The Browns of 1944 are gone now, and, though more teams than ever can qualify for the postseason and the emergence of analytics has done much to level the playing field between the haves and the have-nots, it's unlikely that we will ever see the likes of them again or witness the combination of circumstances that allowed the Browns to come ever so close to glory.

Camden, New Jersey, native Sig Jakucki, a pitcher with a checkered past, had
been out of the major leagues for seven years when he returned to the St. Louis
Browns in 1944 and helped them to an improbable American League pennant.
National Baseball Hall of Fame and Museum

7

The Strike and the Scrub

IN 1978, A CAREER .161 HITTER CAUGHT FIRE AND BATTED .438 IN THE Fall Classic to help his team win the world championship. His team probably would not have made it to the World Series but for a strike that shut down the city's newspapers for the last third of the season.

For those who loved baseball and soap operas, the late 1970s was a great time to be a New York Yankees fan. The Yankees were winners, and there was no shortage of clubhouse drama. In 1973, the egotistical shipbuilding magnate George Steinbrenner became the principal owner of the Yankees. When Steinbrenner hired Billy Martin as manager in August 1975, it was the fourth managerial job in six years for Martin. Previously, he had managed the Minnesota Twins, the Detroit Tigers, and the Texas Rangers and had developed a pattern. With his fiery, motivational style, Martin had transformed each team from a loser to either a division winner or a contender in one season. But then, each time, he had self-destructed—his volatile personality, his drinking, and his fighting were the main culprits—and had been fired within a year or two.

In 1976, with Martin at the helm, the Yankees won the American League pennant, their first in twelve years, but were swept by the Cincinnati Reds in the World Series. In the offseason, Steinbrenner, hungry to elevate his club to the next level, beefed up the Yankees offense by signing the prima donna slugging outfielder Reggie Jackson to a lucrative five-year contract, making him the highest-paid player in baseball at the time. Jackson already had three World Series rings on his fingers from his years with the Oakland A's. Martin opposed the signing, concerned that Jackson would become a clubhouse cancer.

Before long, Martin and Jackson clashed. In a June 1977 game at Fenway Park in Boston, Jim Rice of the Red Sox blooped a hit to right field. Jackson did not appear to hustle for the ball, and Rice stretched what should have been a single into a double. Martin was so incensed by Jackson's lackluster effort that he immediately pulled the outfielder out of the game and replaced him in right field with Paul Blair. When Jackson reached the dugout, he and Martin started arguing so heatedly that the two almost came to blows and had to be separated by coaches Elston Howard and Yogi Berra.

Other players, including catcher and team captain Thurman Munson and outfielder Lou Piniella, butted heads with Martin. Despite the infighting, the Yankees performed on the field, and Jackson proved his worth by hitting 32 home runs with 110 RBIs. They won 100 games, edging out the Red Sox and the Baltimore Orioles for the division title. After defeating the Kansas City Royals in the League Championship Series, the Yankees beat the Los Angeles Dodgers, led by first-year manager Tommy Lasorda, in the World Series. Jackson stole the show, blasting first-pitch home runs in three consecutive at-bats in the decisive sixth game; the last was a majestic 475-foot salvo over the center-field fence at Yankee Stadium.

Controversy started early in 1978 for the defending world champions. Sparky Lyle thought his closer role was secure after he won the Cy Young Award in 1977, but Steinbrenner signed another star reliever, Rich "Goose" Gossage, to a fat free-agent contract in the offseason. As third baseman Graig Nettles quipped, Lyle went from "Cy Young to sayonara." During spring training, Lyle asked Steinbrenner to trade him. Munson also requested a trade, preferably to the Cleveland Indians, so he could be closer to his home in Canton, Ohio, and escape the circus atmosphere in New York. Outfielder Mickey Rivers arrived late for workouts two days in a row and was hit with a fine. Rivers was told to meet with the team president, Al Rosen, to discuss the situation, but he showed up late for that meeting. Despite their disenchantment, Lyle, Munson, and Rivers remained with the Yankees.

On a team flight early in the 1978 season, Martin and Munson got into a shouting match, which started because the catcher was playing his music too loud. It escalated to the point that coach Elston Howard and Gossage had to intervene to prevent a fight. As the season progressed, other players, including pitcher Ed Figueroa, outfielder Roy White, and first baseman/designated hitter Jim Spencer complained that they wanted out.

Meanwhile, the New York media, notably beat writers Murray Chass of the *New York Times*, Henry Hecht of the *New York Post*, and Phil Pepe of the *New York Daily News*, were having a field day because the dissension provided splashy headlines that Yankees fans devoured.

The Yankees were not faring well on the field either. By June 26, the Red Sox, managed by Don Zimmer, had built an 8½ game lead over the Yankees. With Jackson stuck in a 5-for-31 slump and his defense in right field shaky, Martin dropped Jackson from fourth to sixth in the lineup and moved him to designated hitter. Jackson was irked by the demotion. Over the next three weeks, the Yankees continued to stumble, dropping 12 of 18 games and falling 13 games behind the surging Red Sox.

The low point came in a Monday-night home game against Kansas City in mid-July. The Yankees carried a 5–3 lead into the ninth inning, but the Royals scored two runs off Gossage to force extra innings. With the score tied in the bottom of the 10th inning, Munson led off with a single against hard-throwing lefty Al Hrabosky, and then Martin flashed the bunt sign to Jackson. It was a curious strategy because Reggie had not laid down a sacrifice bunt in six years. Hrabosky's first pitch was a fastball high and tight, and Billy took off the bunt sign. On the second pitch, Jackson tried to bunt but without success. Third-base coach Dick Howser walked to the plate to confer with his batter.

"Billy wants you to hit away," he said.

"I'm going to bunt," Jackson replied.

"He wants you to swing the bat," Howser persisted.

Jackson ignored the repeated directive and fouled off two more bunt attempts, the second of which was caught by catcher Darrell Porter. After the foul out, Martin snapped to coach Gene Michael, "Tell Jackson to get the hell out of the dugout and go into the clubhouse."

The Yankees failed to score in the 10th and lost, 9–7, in 11 innings. Jackson was due up in the 11th, but Cliff Johnson pinch-hit for him. It was the Yankees' seventh loss in eight games and, coupled with the Red Sox' win against the Twins, dropped them to 14 games out of first place.

After the game, Martin could not control his fury. In his office, he heaved a clock radio and a soda bottle against the wall. While Jackson insisted to reporters that his decision to continue bunting in the 10th inning was strategic, not defiant, Martin barked to general manager Cedric Tallis that he wanted Jackson suspended indefinitely. Steinbrenner backed the move. But because Major League Baseball rules required that a suspension be limited to a specific period, it was changed from indefinite to five days. "Reggie Jackson Penalized: 5 Days, $9,000," a front-page headline in the *Times* blared. Jackson flew home to Oakland; the rest of the team flew to Minnesota for a series. With Munson playing right field, Mike Heath behind the plate, and Cliff Johnson and Roy White sharing designated-hitter duty, the Yankees beat the Twins two straight and then swept the White Sox in Chicago three in a row. Jackson rejoined the team for the last game, but he missed the team bus to Comiskey Park, and Martin kept him out of the starting lineup.

Two hours after the game, at Chicago's O'Hare Airport to catch a flight with the team to Kansas City, Martin teed off on Jackson and Steinbrenner to Murray Chass of the *Times* and Henry Hecht of the *Post*. "The two of them deserve each other," he ranted. "One's a born liar and the other's convicted." Martin was alluding to Steinbrenner's 1974 guilty plea to two criminal charges for conspiring to make illegal corporate contributions to President Richard Nixon's 1972 reelection campaign and trying to influence and intimidate employees of his shipbuilding company to lie to a grand jury about the matter. Steinbrenner did not receive jail time, but he was fined. Commissioner Bowie Kuhn also suspended Steinbrenner for two years, which was later reduced to fifteen months.

It did not take long for Martin's comments to get relayed to Steinbrenner at his home in Tampa, Florida. Steinbrenner was incredulous. "Did he really say that?" Chass confirmed the quote. Steinbrenner called Al Rosen and told him to catch the next flight to Kansas City, along with the team's public relations director, Mickey Morabito, and fire Martin.

The headline, "Owner Stunned by Manager's Outburst," grabbed readers' attention the next day.

In the morning, Rosen called Martin at his room in the Kansas City hotel, but Billy hung up on him. Rosen told Morabito to round up Martin and bring him to their suite. Martin, fearing that Steinbrenner would fire him for his disparaging remarks, had already written a resignation letter. Morabito found Martin walking from the elevator, dark glasses concealing his tears. He went to the lobby and despondently read his resignation letter to the reporters.

Martin, in the middle of a three-year contract that Steinbrenner agreed to honor, remained with the Yankees organization as a consultant to Rosen. Dick Howser stepped in and managed the team that night in Kansas City, and the Yankees lost. The next day, Steinbrenner named Hall of Fame pitcher Bob Lemon as Martin's successor. Lemon was the Yankees' pitching coach in 1976, and he fared well in that role. Under his leadership, the team recorded the fourth-lowest ERA in the majors. White Sox owner Bill Veeck, looking to turn his team around after a last place finish in 1976, offered Lemon the managerial job in 1977, which he accepted. Lemon led the Chisox to a 90-win, third-place finish in 1977. But, when the team struggled in 1978, languishing in fifth place at the end of June with a 34–40 record, Veeck pulled the plug on his manager. Less than a month later, Steinbrenner hired his former pitching coach to take over for Martin.

Within a week, after the Yankees had started 3–2 under Lemon, another bombshell dropped. Saturday, July 29, was Old-Timers' Day at Yankee Stadium. A near-capacity crowd came out to cheer Joe DiMaggio, Mickey Mantle, Whitey Ford, and other retired Yankee greats. During the introductions of the players, Bob Sheppard, the longtime public address announcer, informed the crowd that, in 1980, Bob Lemon would become the Yankees' general manager and the manager would be Number 1—and Billy Martin trotted onto the field to a long, thunderous ovation by the fans. Murray Chass described the rehiring of Martin five days after his forced resignation as "one of the most bizarre developments in baseball history."

Bizarre developments continued to unfold. After Martin departed as manager, Steinbrenner urged his public relations man Mickey Morabito to keep Billy away from the press for the rest of the season lest he stick his foot in his mouth again. Morabito, twenty-six years old and Brooklyn born, had been fending off requests from the media to interview Martin. Morabito went to Rosen with an idea because he was concerned that the New York writers, who set the tone for baseball in the city, would be slighted if Martin would not speak with them but then decided to talk to writers from another city in the offseason. Morabito suggested that he arrange a lunch meeting for Martin and the beat writers—but not tell Steinbrenner. Rosen agreed with the risky proposal.

On August 9, Martin, along with Morabito, met at a Bronx restaurant with five beat writers for the team: Murray Chass, Henry Hecht, Phil Pepe, Moss Klein of the *Star-Ledger* in Newark, New Jersey, and Joe Donnelly of *Newsday* in Long Island, New York. When one of the writers brought up the line about Jackson and Steinbrenner, Billy, with a few drinks under his belt, unloaded. "I didn't mean what I said about George, but I did mean it about the other guy." Morabito whispered to Martin to stop, but to no avail. "I never looked at Reggie as a superstar. He never showed me he was a superstar." Billy added that he never put Jackson over the team's other top players—Thurman Munson, Chris Chambliss, Willie Randolph, Mickey Rivers, and others. Martin concluded his spiel with a derisive reference to light-hitting utility infielder Fred "Chicken" Stanley. "There were times I put Chicken ahead of Reggie."

No sooner was the lunch meeting over than the writers were on the phone with Steinbrenner to convey the latest bluster from Martin. Predictably, Steinbrenner was furious. He reamed out Morabito, telling him he would be canned if the newspapers published headlines about Martin's latest eruption. Morabito was a wreck for the rest of the day, fully expecting that he would be out of a job as soon as the papers hit the newsstands.

But then something remarkable happened that saved Morabito's job and impelled the Yankees to embark on a hot streak: the fifteen hundred pressmen for the three New York papers—the *News*, the *Post*, and the *Times*—went on strike when management, carrying out a threat, posted new work rules and cut staff. Though local papers in Newark and Long

Island carried stories about Martin's derogatory comments about Jackson, Steinbrenner didn't care because circulation of those papers paled in comparison to that of the three New York dailies.

Without Chass, Hecht, and Pepe in the players' faces every day, stirring things up and looking for the next juicy story, a calm fell over the clubhouse. And, with the low-key Bob Lemon leading the way, the Yankees went on a tear. They went on a 14–5 run and, by the end of August, they closed to within 6½ games of the Red Sox. A week later, they trailed the Sox by just four games. The Yankees then went into Boston for a crucial four-game series at Fenway. In what became known as the "Boston Massacre," the Yankees swept the series, outscoring the Red Sox 42–9. In the second game, which New York won, 13–2, Boston committed *seven* errors, which led to seven unearned runs.

The Yankees had come all the way back from 14 games behind to catch the Red Sox. Twenty games remained for both teams. The Yanks kept winning, and, by September 16, they held a 3½-game lead over the Bosox. But the Red Sox did not lie down. They won nine of their next eleven games and, heading into the final weekend of the season, trailed the Yankees by one game. Boston hosted the Toronto Blue Jays for a three-game series while the Yankees were at home for three against the Cleveland Indians.

In the first game of their series, the Indians led the Yankees, 1–0, into the bottom of the eighth inning. With one out and a man on second, second baseman Willie Randolph legged out an infield single, but in the process pulled a hamstring and had to leave the game. He was replaced by a pinch-runner, rookie Brian Doyle. The Yankees scored three runs in the eighth to win the game and preserve their one-game lead over the Red Sox, who beat the Blue Jays. Both the Yanks and the Sox won on Saturday, so, entering the final day of the regular season, one game still separated the teams. But the Yankees, with a chance to clinch, were thumped by the sixth-place Indians, 9–2, while the Red Sox completed a sweep of the Blue Jays to set up a one-game playoff the following afternoon. The Red Sox had won a coin toss a few weeks earlier to determine home-field advantage if such a game were necessary, so the game was played at Fenway Park.

On Sunday night, while the Yankees were on their way to Boston, negotiators for the *Post*, who had withdrawn from joint negotiations with the other two New York papers, reached a tentative deal with the pressmen. By the end of the week, Rupert Murdoch's *Post* was back in print, but the *News* and the *Times* remained on strike.

On Monday afternoon, Lemon sent his ace Ron Guidry to the mound on three days' rest. The lefty from Louisiana was having a terrific season, 24–3 (10–1 since the newspaper strike), with an ERA of 1.72. He would later win the Cy Young Award unanimously. Don Zimmer started the veteran Mike Torrez, who had collected a ring for the Yankees in 1977, winning two games in the World Series, before signing with the Red Sox as a free agent in the offseason. With Willie Randolph still hampered by his hamstring injury, Brian Doyle started at second base. There was a lot of pressure on the untested, twenty-four-year-old rookie—he had started only 13 major-league games. The Red Sox clung to a 2–0 lead through six innings. In the top of the seventh, with two outs and two on, shortstop Bucky Dent, one pitch after fouling a ball off his ankle, hit a three-run homer off Torrez over "the Green Monster" in left field to give the Yankees a 3–2 lead. For Dent, who choked up on the bat, it was just his fifth home run of the season. The Yanks tacked on another run in the seventh, and Reggie Jackson added a solo home run in the eighth. The Yankees hung on to win, 5–4, as Goose Gossage retired Carl Yastrzemski on a pop out to Graig Nettles, with two outs and runners on first and third in the ninth inning to seal the win.

The Yankees' comeback and the Red Sox' collapse was complete. The Sox' sixty-year drought of not winning a World Series would live on.

The Yankees had little time to celebrate because, on the following day, they were in Kansas City to begin a best-of-five League Championship Series against the Royals. Randolph remained unable to play, so Doyle started at second base in the first game.

Baseball was in the Doyle family's blood. Brian's older brother, Denny, had completed an eight-year major-league career the year before. Denny, also a slightly built second baseman and left-handed hitter, started all seven games in the 1975 World Series for the Red Sox, who lost to the Reds. The Doyles hailed from Glasgow, Kentucky. In 1961, Denny led his high-school team to the state championship. Brian and his twin brother, Blake, did the same in 1972. That year, Brian was drafted in the fourth round by the Texas Rangers; Blake was picked in the same round by the Baltimore Orioles. Blake played in the minors for nine years and, though he never made it to the majors as a player, he was the Colorado Rockies' hitting coach for three years in the 2010s. Brian played for five years in the Rangers minor-league organization and then was traded to the Yankees during spring training in 1977. He played for Triple-A Syracuse that season. In 1978, he began the season at Triple-A—the affiliate had moved to Tacoma, Washington—and was called up by the Yankees in April. He shuffled back and forth between Tacoma and the majors throughout the season. He hit .192 for the Yankees in 52 at-bats—all 10 of his hits were singles—and did not record a single RBI. But he was Bob Lemon's starting second baseman and number-eight hitter in Game 1 of the American League Championship Series. Doyle overcame his jitters to contribute two hits and his first major-league RBI in a 7–1 Yankees win.

Lemon platooned Doyle and Fred Stanley throughout the Series, playing Doyle against right-handed starting pitchers and Stanley, who swung from the right side, against lefties. The Yanks won the Series in four games and returned to the World Series for a rematch against the Dodgers.

Tommy Lasorda and his squad were looking to bounce back from their World Series loss the previous year. The Dodgers nucleus had changed little—first baseman Steve Garvey, third baseman Ron Cey, and outfielder Reggie Smith remained the team's offensive stars. Burt Hooton, Don Sutton, and Tommy John again anchored the starting rotation. A summer call-up, Bob Welch, had also made an impact. A starter and reliever with a 2.02 ERA during the regular season, Welch won the first game of the National League Championship Series against the Philadelphia Phillies with 4⅓ strong innings out of the bullpen.

Willie Randolph, determined to play in the World Series, worked with team trainers, but he was given the bad news on the day of the opener that his leg was still too unstable to play on. While riding in a taxi from the hotel to Dodger Stadium with Yogi Berra and Catfish Hunter, Brian Doyle learned from Yogi that he would be on the Yankees

World Series roster. For Doyle, playing in the World Series was a far cry from what he normally did in October—begin his offseason job selling shirts and fitting customers at a clothing store in Kentucky.

Bob Lemon kept using the platoon at second base, so Stanley started Game 1 against left-hander Tommy John. The Dodgers won, 11–5, as second baseman Davey Lopes hit two home runs.

With righty Burt Hooton on the mound for the Dodgers in Game 2, Doyle got the start and went 1-for-3. The game went down to the wire with the Dodgers leading, 4–3, through eight innings. Reggie Jackson had driven in all three Yankee runs, with a two-run double in the third and an RBI ground out in the seventh.

The Yankees put runners on first and second with one out in the top of the ninth. Lasorda pulled reliever Terry Forster in favor of the rookie sensation, Welch. Thurman Munson flied out to right field, setting the stage for a showdown between Welch and Jackson. With the count 1-1, Reggie fouled off three straight pitches and then looked at two pitches right off the plate sandwiched around another foul ball. On the ninth pitch, with the count full and the runners on the move, Welch struck out Jackson swinging on a blazing fastball to end the game and give the Dodgers a 2–0 lead in the Series.

The Yankees fought back, winning the next two games in New York to even the Series. Doyle went hitless in four at-bats in Game 3 against starter Don Sutton and reliever Charlie Hough. With John back on the mound for the Dodgers in Game 4, Stanley played second.

Doyle was back in the lineup in Game 5 against Hooton, and he came through big, delivering three hits and scoring two runs as the Yankees trounced the Dodgers, 12–2.

The Yankees still needed to win a game back in Los Angeles to take the Series. Two future Hall of Fame pitchers, Catfish Hunter and Don Sutton, received the starting assignments. Davey Lopes led off the bottom of the first with a home run off Hunter to stake the Dodgers to a quick 1–0 lead. The Yankees answered back in the top of the second. With Graig Nettles and Jim Spencer on base and one out, Doyle picked an opportune time to pick up his first major-league extra-base hit by drilling a double to deep left field, scoring Nettles and sending Spencer to third. Spencer and Doyle scored on a single by Bucky Dent, and the Yankees led, 3–1.

Doyle beat out an infield hit in the fourth, and, in the sixth, he again came through in the clutch, hitting a two-out single to center, scoring Lou Piniella from second. Bob Welch relieved Sutton, and Dent greeted him with a single to plate Doyle. The Yankees were up, 5–2, and Doyle had played a role in four of the runs, with two RBIs and two runs scored.

In the seventh, Jackson atoned for his game-ending strikeout in Game 2 by hitting a two-run homer off Welch to extend the Yankees' lead to 7–2. That's the way the game ended after Goose Gossage pitched the last two innings. The Yankees overcame a 14-game deficit and survived the suspension of Reggie Jackson, the resignation of Billy Martin, and other turmoil to win their second World Series in a row. Despite Doyle's strong Series, Bucky Dent was named MVP on the strength of his 10 hits and seven RBIs.

The newspaper strike may have been the turning point. Many who wore pinstripes thought so. The Yankees went 37–14, a clip of .725, after the strike, compared with 63–49 (.563) before the strike. For Bob Lemon, "The strike coming when it did, did more for us than if we picked up a 20-game winner." Willie Randolph added, "It got us back to being about the Yankees instead of about George or Billy or Reggie." Graig Nettles did not conceal his disdain for the press. "That was a lot of fun, not having those [reporters] in our face," he said. "A lot of them were there just to stir up shit. For two months, we didn't have to worry about what angle was being portrayed against us."

On November 2, a little more than two weeks after the last game of the World Series, the strike ended for the *News* and the *Times*. Four days later, the presses were rolling for both papers.

In the offseason, the Doyle brothers—Denny, Brian, and Blake—established the Doyle Baseball Academy in Davenport, Florida, to teach baseball to young, aspiring ballplayers. In the decades that followed, several future major leaguers, including Gary Sheffield, Paul Konerko, Tim Wakefield, and Trey Mancini received valuable instruction at the school.

Over the winter, the brass for the Yankees and Twins discussed a trade that would bring seven-time American League batting champion

Rod Carew to New York. Brian Doyle was one of a few Yankees players whose name was bandied about during the talks. But the teams could not work out a deal, and the Twins ended up trading Carew to the California Angels for four players.

The clubhouse fireworks started early for the Yankees in 1979. In April, Goose Gossage and Cliff Johnson got into a scuffle in the shower. Then, just 65 games into the 1979 season, with the team barely over .500, George Steinbrenner lowered the boom and fired Bob Lemon, though he had led the Yankees to the world championship the year before. Ironically, Steinbrenner replaced Lemon with Billy Martin, despite the announcement at the previous year's Old-Timers' Day that Billy would not return to the dugout until 1980. The Yankees improved under Martin, posting a 55–40 record. But the team finished in fourth place, and, after the season, the impulsive Steinbrenner fired him. In August 1979, tragedy struck the team when Thurman Munson, who had acquired his private pilot's license a year earlier, went home to Ohio on an off day to practice his takeoffs and landings and died when he crashed his plane.

In 1979 and 1980, Brian Doyle was on a roller coaster, shuttling between the majors and the minors. He hit .125 in 32 at-bats for the Yankees in '79 and .173 in 75 at-bats in '80. After the 1980 season, the Oakland A's acquired him in the Rule 5 draft. Billy Martin, picked up by the A's after Steinbrenner dumped him, was now managing the team. Doyle was in Oakland's starting lineup in three of the first four games in 1981, but then a hamstring injury sidelined him. A few weeks later, after he returned from the disabled list, he injured himself again in a collision at second base with Otto Velez of the Blue Jays, who was trying to break up a double play. Doyle never played in the majors again. He returned to the minors for the second half of the 1981 season and 1982 and then called it quits as a player.

Doyle's final major-league numbers were unimpressive: a .161 average in 199 at-bats with three doubles, one home run, and 13 RBIs. But, in the 1978 World Series, he was 7-for-16, for a sizzling .438 average. In both Game 5 and Game 6, when the Series was on the line, Doyle came through with three hits.

All-time greats Babe Ruth, Lou Gehrig, Joe DiMaggio, Mickey Mantle, Yogi Berra, and Derek Jeter collectively played in 57 World Series for the Yankees, a total of 299 games in the Fall Classic. None of the six ever collected three hits in two consecutive World Series games. Brian Doyle, who never got three hits in a regular-season game and never hit even .200 in a season, accomplished the feat and, for that, he will forever be a part of the glorious lore of the Yankees.

Brian Doyle delivers his first of three hits in Game 6 of the 1978 World Series. A late-season replacement for injured Wille Randolph, Doyle had the greatest week of his career in the Series, batting .438, with three hits in each of the last two games. *AP Photo*

8

The Surprise Starter

HEADING INTO THE 1929 WORLD SERIES AGAINST THE CHICAGO CUBS, Philadelphia Athletics manager Connie Mack had three strong choices for his Game 1 starter: 24-game-winner George Earnshaw, 20-game-winner Lefty Grove, and 18-game-winner Rube Walberg. Mack bypassed all three in favor of Howard Ehmke, an aging right-hander who had won only seven games for the Athletics that season. Did Mack make a brilliant tactical decision or a colossal blunder?

Mack completed his twenty-ninth season as manager—and part owner—of the Athletics in 1929. Mack played for eleven years in the major leagues, primarily as a catcher; during his last three seasons (1894–96), he was player-manager for the Pittsburgh Pirates. He then managed for four years in the minors before he was recruited to manage the Athletics in 1901, their first year in the American League. Mack also bought a 25 percent ownership interest in the club.

Mack's Athletics dominated the American League during the first decade and a half of the new league's existence. They won six pennants, including three World Series in a four-year span—in 1910, 1911, and 1913. The Philadelphia team in that era featured many future Hall of Famers, including pitchers Rube Waddell, Chief Bender, and Eddie Plank, as well as second baseman Eddie Collins.

After the Athletics lost the 1914 World Series to the Boston Braves, the team went into a lengthy tailspin. The rival Federal League began play in 1914, and they lured away Bender and Plank with lucrative offers. Rather than trying to match the offers by the owners of the upstart league, Mack chose to rebuild with younger and less-experienced players. In addition to losing Bender and Plank, Mack sold Collins to the Chicago White Sox and also got rid of some of his other top players. The results of the overhaul were disastrous and long-lasting—the team finished in last place for seven consecutive seasons, eclipsing the 100-loss mark in five of those years. The Athletics avoided the American League cellar for the next three years, but they still had losing records, making it ten years in a row without a winning season. By then Mack had turned sixty, and many baseball insiders thought the game had passed him by.

In 1925, the tide turned for the Athletics. By then Mack had acquired from minor-league teams four young players who would go on to become all-time greats: pitcher Lefty Grove (300 wins and nine ERA titles), catcher Mickey Cochrane (a .320 career batting average, the all-time leader among catchers), first baseman Jimmie Foxx (534 home runs, second to Babe Ruth when he retired), and outfielder Al Simmons (a .334 career batting average, nearly 3,000 hits). Mack's roster included a supporting cast of other solid players. The Athletics won 88 games in 1925, finishing in second place to the Washington Senators. On June 15, 1926, the Athletics were 10 games behind the New York Yankees, who were led by Ruth and Lou Gehrig. Hoping to make a run at the Yankees, Mack acquired Howard Ehmke in a trade from the Boston Red Sox. A tall, gangly thirty-two-year-old right-hander, Ehmke had proven himself to be one of the more durable pitchers in the American League for nearly a decade.

Ehmke started his professional career with the Los Angeles Angels of the Pacific Coast League in 1914, shortly before his twentieth birthday. The Washington Senators purchased Ehmke in August of '14, but he refused to sign with the Senators. Instead, he opted to sign with the Buffalo Blues of the rival Federal League and pitched for the Blues in 1915. When the Federal League folded after the 1915 season, Ehmke joined the Syracuse Stars of the New York State League and showed his great potential by winning 31 games that year. A dispute arose during the season regarding what major-league team had the rights to Ehmke. The Detroit Tigers purchased him from the Stars in July, but Clark Griffith, the owner of the Senators, insisted that Ehmke was the property of his team. American League president Ban Johnson intervened and ruled that Ehmke was in fact still the Senators' property. Nonetheless, Griffith ended up selling him to the Tigers in August. Ehmke came up to the majors in September and pitched in five games for the Tigers, which included three complete game wins.

Ehmke was a regular Tigers starter in 1917, winning 10 games. Ehmke missed the 1918 season because he was enlisted in the navy but he was discharged in March 1919. That season he became part of Detroit's rotation and won 17 games. A 15-win season followed in 1920. In 1921, Ty Cobb, who had won 12 batting titles in his 16 seasons with the Tigers, took over as the team's manager. Cobb continued to play center field while he managed the team.

Cobb and Ehmke had polar-opposite personalities, and they often butted heads. Cobb was ornery and vulgar; Ehmke was gentle and soft-spoken. Ehmke did not approve of Cobb's despotic managerial style. Cobb, in turn, criticized Ehmke, claiming he did not have the mental toughness to be a winner. Cobb dispatched Ehmke to the bull-pen for parts of the 1921 and 1922 seasons, which did not sit well with the right-hander. The two got into a shoving match in the dugout in a 1922 game. Still, Ehmke pitched respectably under Cobb, posting records of 13–14 and 17–17 for mediocre Tigers teams. After the 1922 season, Ehmke was traded to the Red Sox in a six-player deal.

The Red Sox were mired in a downward spiral when they traded for Ehmke. In 1922, they had taken over last place from the Athletics. Boston's manager, Frank Chance, of the famous Tinker-to-Evers-to-Chance double-play combination, named Ehmke as the team's Opening Day starter in 1923, giving him the honor of taking the mound for the first game at Yankee Stadium. More than seventy-four thousand fans filled "the House That Ruth Built," and, fittingly, Ruth's three-run homer in the third inning was the difference in a 4–1 Yankees win. Ehmke took the loss, allowing all four runs in seven innings of work.

In May, Ehmke faced the Tigers. He had a tendency to pitch inside and hit batters—he led the American League in that category five times. When he drilled Cobb in the knee with a fastball, it was no accident. Cobb made a gesture of throwing the bat at Ehmke but restrained himself and took first base. Cobb waited until after the game to unleash his fury. "When I went under the stands, he was waiting for me," Ehmke recalled later. "He took a shot at me, and we scuffled around."

Ehmke was the ace on the staff of the dismal Boston team. He had his finest moments in the final month of the season. On September 7, he threw a no-hitter against Mack's Athletics in Philadelphia. Four days later, he was back at Yankee Stadium for his next start. In the bottom of the first inning, Whitey Witt, the leadoff batter for the Yankees, hit a ground ball to third base. The ball caromed off the chest of Red Sox third baseman Howie Shanks, and Witt reached first safely. The official scorer ruled it a hit on the basis that Shanks could not have thrown Witt out if he had fielded the ball cleanly. Some observers thought the play should have been called an error. The ruling came under scrutiny when Ehmke did not allow the Yankees a hit for the rest of the game, and he finished with a one-hit shutout. Ehmke came within an official scorer's ruling of pitching back-to-back no-hitters—on the road, no less. Only one pitcher in baseball history, southpaw Johnny Vander Meer, has thrown consecutive no-hitters. Vander Meer accomplished the feat for the Cincinnati Reds in 1938.

Ehmke compiled a 20–17 record in 1923 for a Red Sox team that won only 61 games. Ehmke is one of just nine pitchers since 1900 to win 20 games for a last-place team. Ehmke almost did it again in 1924, winning 19 games for the Red Sox, who finished a half-game ahead of the last-place White Sox. The workhorse pitched more than 300 innings both seasons, leading the American League in 1924.

It was tough times for Ehmke in 1925. He contracted influenza, which slowed him down. He lost 20 games, winning only nine. Ehmke had another dust-up with Cobb in July of that season. Cobb pulled a ground ball that the Red Sox first baseman fielded to his right. Ehmke ran over to cover the bag, and Cobb slid into first base hard, nailing the pitcher with his spikes. Ehmke shoved Cobb, who shoved back before other players intervened and broke up the altercation.

Ehmke struggled mightily during the first two months of the 1926 season, going 3–10 with a 5.46 ERA. Mack recognized the right-hander's ability and picked him up at the June 15 trade deadline.

Ehmke and Mack hit it off right away. Mack was straitlaced, reserved, and respectful, which Ehmke admired. The new manager did wonders for Ehmke's game—Ehmke went 12–4 for the Athletics for the rest of the season, with a 2.81 ERA. Only Lefty Grove, with 13, won more games for the Athletics in 1926, and Grove pitched the entire season for the team. Despite Ehmke's stellar pitching for Philadelphia, the last three and a half months of the season, they could not catch the Yankees, falling six games short.

The Athletics acquired Cobb before the 1927 season. He had spent twenty-two seasons in Detroit, the last six as player-manager. With Mack as the peacemaker, Cobb and Ehmke had no skirmishes. Arm injuries nagged Ehmke in 1927, and his ERA jumped to 4.22 to go with a 12–10 record. The Athletics won 91 games, Mack's highest total since 1914, but his club was no match for the high-powered Yankees. Ruth blasted 60 home runs, Gehrig slugged 47, and the Yankees ran away with the American League, winning 110 games and then sweeping the Pittsburgh Pirates in the World Series.

The Athletics improved to 98 wins in 1928; Ehmke contributed, posting a 9–8 record. With three weeks left in the season, the Athletics won both games of a doubleheader and took over first place. But the Yankees finished strong, capturing the pennant by 2½ games. Ruth, Gehrig, and company made it two World Series sweeps in a row by bowling over the St. Louis Cardinals.

Mack went into the 1929 season determined to unseat the Yankees as world champions. The Athletics had not won the American League pennant in fifteen years. Cobb retired after the 1928 season, but the Athletics were still loaded. Grove, Foxx, Simmons, and Cochrane were in their prime, and Mack had other stars on his pitching staff and in his lineup. Ehmke, who turned thirty-five early in the season, was one of the oldest players on the team.

Philadelphia took over first place on May 14 and never looked back. At the end of July, they led the Yankees by 9½ games; their lead had increased to 12½ games by the end of August. It was a foregone conclusion that the Athletics would win the pennant and play in the World Series. Over in the National League, the Cubs had a commanding

11½-game lead on August 31, and Mack expected they would be the Athletics' opponent come October.

Mack used Ehmke sparingly during the season. Going into September, Ehmke had appeared in just nine games, seven as a starter. He had pitched a mere 43⅓ innings. A sore arm landed him on the disabled list for three weeks in the summer.

In the first week of September, Mack called Ehmke into his office at Shibe Park before a game. Mack was dapperly dressed, wearing a suit and tie and a straw hat atop his thinning gray hair. That was Mack's usual garb in the dugout—he did not wear the Athletics uniform. Mack broke the news to Ehmke that he would be released after the season.

Ehmke understood but implored his manager to let him pitch in his first World Series. "My arm is not what it once was, but I honestly feel there's one more good game left in it. I'd like a chance to prove it to you."

Mack considered the request. He was well aware that Ehmke had pitched in the majors for thirteen years and that none of his teams had won the pennant. This might be his last chance to pitch in the World Series. "Howard, here's what I'm going to do. After your next start, I'm going to shut you down for the rest of the season. You can study the Cubs lineup closely. When the World Series starts, we're going to give everybody a big surprise."

Ehmke started on September 13 and then Mack did not pitch him for the final three and a half weeks of the season. Ehmke scouted the Cubs for two weeks and learned that they had a predominantly right-handed hitting team. First baseman Charlie Grimm was the only left-handed swinger in the Cubs starting eight. Ehmke also found that the Cubs were a fastball-hitting squad and that their hitters struggled with off-speed pitches.

The Athletics finished the season 18 games ahead of the second-place Yankees. The Cubs also won the National League pennant handily, beating out the Pirates by 10½ games. The day before the World Series started, Mack made his bombshell announcement: his Game 1 starter against the Cubs was not Earnshaw, Grove, or Walberg but the wily Ehmke, who had toiled just 54⅔ innings during the season.

The Cubs' World Series drought was almost as long as the Athletics'—they had not won a National League pennant since 1918. Joe McCarthy managed the Cubbies; he went on to manage the Yankees to seven World Series titles in the 1930s and 1940s, six of which were during Joe DiMaggio's glory years.

Game 1 was a momentous occasion in Chicago—it was the first World Series game at Wrigley Field. Cubs fans packed the house, confident that their team would knock out Ehmke early. Ehmke faced a formidable Chicago lineup. One of the greatest hitters of all time, Rogers Hornsby, hit .380 during the season, with 39 home runs and 149 RBIs. Each of the Cubs' three outfielders, Riggs Stephenson, Kiki Cuyler, and Hack Wilson, hit .345 or higher. Wilson matched Hornsby's 39 home runs and bettered his RBI total, with 159. Stephenson and Cuyler each drove in more than 100 runs. All told, the Cubs scored 982 runs during the season (an average of 6.3 per game), the ninth-highest total for a team since 1900. The Cubs chalked up 10 or more runs in a game 34 times in 1929.

McCarthy gave Charlie Root the starting pitcher assignment. Root, who would become known for allowing Babe Ruth's "called shot" in the 1932 World Series, won 19 games for the Cubs in 1929.

After Root set down the Athletics in the top of the first, Ehmke went to work. Early in his career, he was thin, weighing in the 165-pound range while standing 6'3". Over the years, he had filled out, increasing his weight to about 190. As a younger pitcher, he had relied more on his fastball, but now, as a crafty veteran, he threw a heavy dose of off-speed pitches—curveballs and changeups. He sometimes threw overhand; other times, he came sidearm or submarine. Occasionally, he altered his delivery, hesitating after going into his windup in an effort to throw opposing batters off stride. Mickey Cochrane, known for being an outstanding pitch caller, was his batterymate.

Ehmke allowed an infield single to shortstop Woody English in the bottom of the first, but the Cubs did not score. In the second, he recorded his first two strikeouts, whiffing Cuyler and Stephenson. Ehmke ran into trouble in the third inning. After striking out Root, he allowed a single to leadoff batter Norm McMillan and a double to English, which put runners on second and third. Ehmke bore down and struck out the dangerous Hornsby and Wilson to end the threat.

The game remained scoreless through six innings. Root held the Athletics in check, while Ehmke did the same to the Cubs, racking up strikeouts along the way. In the sixth, Ehmke struck out the side for the second time, again fanning Hornsby and Wilson. Ehmke's strikeout total had ballooned to 11.

The Athletics broke the scoreless tie in the top of the seventh when Jimmie Foxx, who had smacked 33 home runs during the season, muscled a Root fastball into the left-center-field bleachers to give Mack's team a 1–0 lead. In the bottom of the seventh, after Cuyler and Stephenson singled and then were bunted over, Ehmke again escaped a second-and-third, one-out jam. McCarthy sent up left-handed Cliff Heathcote to bat for catcher Zack Taylor. Heathcote hit a fly ball to short left field, and Cuyler had to hold at third base. McCarthy called on Gabby Hartnett to pinch-hit for Root. A catcher who was in the middle of a twenty-year Hall of Fame career, in 1929 Hartnett battled a right-arm injury that impeded his ability to throw. His season was limited to 22 at-bats, almost all as a pinch-hitter. Ehmke struck out Hartnett to end the inning and, in so doing, tied the record of 12 for the most strikeouts in a World Series game, which was set by Ed Walsh of the White Sox in 1906 and duplicated by two pitchers since.

Guy Bush replaced Root and retired the Athletics in the top of the eighth inning, though Ehmke slapped a single to right field. Ehmke retired the Cubs in order in the bottom of the inning but did not record any strikeouts. The Athletics scored two insurance runs off Bush in the top of the ninth, aided by some sloppy fielding by Woody English at short. Cochrane led off with a single, and then English booted back-to-back ground balls by Simmons and Foxx. With the bases loaded, right fielder Bing Miller singled to center, driving in Cochrane and Simmons. Bush averted further trouble, and Ehmke, the beneficiary of two unearned runs, took the mound in the bottom of the ninth inning with a 3–0 lead, three outs away from a shutout.

Wilson led off with a line drive that struck Ehmke in the groin area. He recovered quickly and threw out the slow-moving Wilson at first.

Ehmke should have had the second out when Stephenson hit a routine ground ball to third, but Jimmy Dykes threw the ball away. Stephenson ended up at second, and Cuyler promptly brought him home with a single to center. Grimm followed with a single to right, and suddenly the Cubs had the tying run on first base and brought the winning run to the plate.

Mack had action in the bullpen but stuck with Ehmke. Catcher Mike Gonzalez was due up next. He had taken over for Taylor behind the plate after Heathcote pinch-hit in the seventh. McCarthy opted to pinch-hit left-handed Clarence "Footsie" Blair for the right-handed Gonzalez. Blair was a rookie who hit .319 with one home run in 72 at-bats. A blast into the bleachers would have made Blair a hero, but he rolled a grounder to Dykes, who fielded this one cleanly and fired to second baseman Max Bishop for the force out.

The Cubs were down to their last out. The pitcher's spot in the lineup was up next, and McCarthy went with Charles "Chick" Tolson, a right-handed-hitting, back-up first baseman. Like Blair, Tolson had little power—he hit a lone home run in 109 at-bats during the season and batted .257. Still, with one swing of the bat, Tolson could send the Chicago fans into pandemonium. The count ran full. Cuyler took his lead off third, and Blair broke for second with the pitch. Ehmke threw a nasty curveball, and Tolson swung and missed.

Mack and Ehmke had pulled off the improbable. Ehmke held the Cubs to one unearned run and set the World Series record by striking out 13 batters. Ehmke averaged only 3.3 strikeouts per nine innings in his career, yet racked up 13 Ks against the hard-hitting Cubs, including Hornsby, Wilson, and Cuyler, twice each. His record of 13 strikeouts in a World Series game stood for twenty-four years, until 1953.

Ehmke's masterful performance in Game 1 set the tone for the World Series. The Athletics took a 3–1 lead in the Series after a dramatic win in Game 4 at Shibe Park. The Cubs took an 8–0 lead into the bottom of the seventh inning when the Athletics exploded for 10 hits and 10 runs to take the lead. Home runs by Al Simmons and center fielder Mule Haas were the big blows. Mack brought Lefty Grove in from the bullpen, and he pitched two scoreless innings to preserve the win.

It was a demoralizing loss for the Cubs, who had appeared to be on the verge of tying the Series but now trailed, 3–1. Mack sent Ehmke back to the hill for Game 5 in front of the home crowd. McCarthy, with his team's backs against the wall, gave the ball to Pat Malone, a 22-game winner during the season. Malone had been hit hard by the Athletics in the Cubs' Game 2 loss.

Ehmke held the Cubs scoreless for 3⅔ innings and then allowed two runs on three hits and a walk in the fourth. Feeling his veteran right-hander was out of gas, Mack brought in Rube Walberg. Though Walberg had won 18 games during the season, he had pitched just one inning in the Series. He worked out of the jam in the fourth and kept the Athletics in the game with five scoreless innings after that. The Cubs held on to their 2–0 lead as Malone took the mound for the bottom of the ninth inning. If Malone could complete the win, the Cubs would take the Series back to Chicago for Game 6.

Haas again came through in the clutch by hitting a two-run homer with one out to tie the game. Then, one out later, Miller doubled home Simmons to stun the Cubs and give the Athletics their first world championship in sixteen years. Though Ehmke did not get the win in Game 5, he kept the Athletics in the game. His ERA for his two starts in the series was 1.42.

Ehmke's strong performance in the World Series earned him an invitation by Mack to return to the Athletics for the 1930 season. Ehmke lasted only three games. He allowed 13 runs in 10 innings, and, in May, Mack reluctantly released him. This time Ehmke decided to call it a career, finishing with 166 wins and 166 losses. Mack's squad won the World Series again in 1930 and made it back to the Fall Classic in 1931 but lost to the St. Louis Cardinals in seven games.

Unfortunately, the Great Depression devastated the economy of Philadelphia, and attendance at Athletics games dropped dramatically. Just as Mack had dismantled the Athletics roster after the team's run earlier in the century, he did the same not long after they won three pennants and two World Series in the years 1929 through 1931. They came in second place in 1932, finished third in 1933, but then suffered through thirteen straight losing seasons. Mack got rid of Simmons, Dykes, and

Haas after the 1932 season; Grove, Cochrane, Walberg, and Earnshaw after the 1933 season; and Foxx after the 1935 season.

Mack managed the Athletics until 1950. By then, he was eighty-seven years old and had been at the helm of the team for fifty years. He described Ehmke's performance in Game 1 of the 1929 World Series as his "greatest thrill" as a manager.

It was also Ehmke's greatest thrill as a pitcher. By making good on his promise to Mack that he had one good game left in his arm, Ehmke fulfilled his dream of pitching in a World Series and throwing a gem to help his team win the Series.

Howard Ehmke was a journeyman pitcher for the Philadelphia A's when he was named the surprise starter in Game 1 of the 1929 Series, featuring the A's against Chicago. Ehmke (shown here demonstrating his unique delivery) went on to win the game and strike out a record 13 Cubs, a mark that stood until 1953. *National Baseball Hall of Fame and Museum*

9

Giant Upset

WILLIE MAYS MADE "THE CATCH" IN THE 1954 WORLD SERIES—ONE of the greatest defensive plays in the history of the Fall Classic—but a much less well-known player provided most of the heroics.

Manager Leo Durocher's New York Giants were a strong, well-balanced team. They won 97 games during the regular season, finishing five games ahead of the Brooklyn Dodgers, the team that Durocher had previously managed. Mays, back after serving nearly two years in the army during the Korean War, tore up National League pitching as he won the MVP Award on the strength of a league-leading .345 average, along with 41 home runs and 110 RBIs. Johnny Antonelli, a young lefty acquired from the Milwaukee Braves in a trade before the season, led the staff with 21 wins.

The Giants' World Series opponent, the Cleveland Indians, however, were in a whole different category. They dethroned the five-time defending world champions, the New York Yankees, by winning 111 games against just 43 losses. Cleveland's .721 winning percentage in 1954 is the best ever for an American League team.

All facets of the Indians' game were superb. Defensively, they ranked tied for second in the league in fielding percentage. Catcher Jim Hegan was considered one of the top backstops in the game; he was especially adept at handling the Indians' pitchers. George Strickland was a slick-fielding shortstop. Dave Philley had an excellent glove in right field.

Offensively, Cleveland led the junior circuit in home runs and ranked second in runs scored. Second baseman Bobby Avila won the batting title with a .341 mark. Center fielder Larry Doby, the American League's first Black player (his entry into the majors in 1947 was three months after Jackie Robinson's), led the league in home runs and RBIs. Third baseman Al Rosen, who came within a whisker of winning the Triple Crown in 1953, was hampered by injuries in 1954 but still hit .300, with 24 home runs and 102 RBIs.

It was the Indians' pitching, though, that set them apart from the pack. Bob Lemon and Early Wynn were two of the finest pitchers of their time. They tied for the league lead with 23 wins, and each finished in the top five in ERA. Both were later inducted into the Hall of Fame. Mike Garcia won 19 games, and his 2.64 ERA was the lowest in the American League, slightly lower than Lemon's and Wynn's. The Cy Young Award had not yet been instituted, but, if it had been, it's possible that Lemon, Wynn, and Garcia would have finished 1-2-3 in the American League. The Indians' staff was so deep that Bob Feller, who was the author of three no-hitters and who later would become a first-ballot Hall of Famer, was relegated to a spot starter. Nearing retirement, the thirty-five-year-old Feller pitched well in this role, recording a 13–3 record and a 3.09 ERA. The Indians' bullpen was outstanding as well—Ray Narleski, Don Mossi, and Hal Newhouser combined for a 16–6 record, 27 saves, and a 2.16 ERA.

The Indians rattled off two 11-game winning streaks during the regular season, becoming the first team to accomplish the feat; no team would do it again until 2015. The Yankees and Chicago White Sox each split their 22 meetings with the Indians. Against the five other American League teams, Cleveland was 89–21, a scorching .809 percentage. If the Indians' 154 games were separated into 22 sets of seven games, they lost the "best of seven" only twice, both 4–3. Every other team, even the National League champion Giants, found the prospect of beating the Indians in a seven-game series daunting.

Another big key to the Indians' success was manager Al Lopez. He had a solid nineteen-year major-league career as a catcher. He caught mostly for second-division teams and never played in a World Series. As a manager, Lopez was overshadowed by Casey Stengel but nevertheless was a top-notch skipper. The 1954 season marked the fourth of

15 straight in which Lopez's team compiled a winning record—the first six were with the Indians, followed by nine with the White Sox.

This was Lopez's first taste of the World Series, and, with the 14-win differential between his squad and the Giants, history was very much in favor of his team coming out on top. Of the previous 13 Series in which one team won at least 10 more games than its opponent during the regular season, the team with the better record prevailed 11 times.

Durocher had piloted the Dodgers to the World Series in 1941 and the Giants to the World Series in 1951, but his teams had lost to the Yankees both times. He didn't want to lose a third straight Series, though he knew the cards were heavily stacked against his club. It helped that the Series opened in the Giants' home ballpark. The Polo Grounds, situated in upper Manhattan, was also home to the Yankees for a decade before they moved to Yankee Stadium in the Bronx, less than two miles away, in 1923.

The baseball field at the Polo Grounds was oddly shaped, like a bathtub—very short down the lines (279 feet to the left-field foul pole, 258 feet to the right-field foul pole), yet 483 feet to dead center and 450 feet to the alleys in left-center and right-center fields. As demonstrated in the '54 Series, a short poke down the line could be a home run, while a blast to center field could be an out.

Lopez picked Bob Lemon from his arsenal of star pitchers to start the first game. Durocher passed up his ace, Johnny Antonelli, in favor of right-hander Sal Maglie, even though his 1954 stats (14–6, 3.26 ERA) paled in comparison to Antonelli's (21–7, 2.30 ERA). Durocher chose Maglie because the Indians lineup was predominantly right-handed and Maglie was a wily veteran.

Maglie had an unusual and inspiring backstory. He pitched for five years in the minors but became disgusted when he did not get the call to the majors. He quit baseball after the 1942 season when he was twenty-five and returned to his hometown, where he worked in a defense plant during World War II in 1943 and 1944. (A sinus condition prevented him from being drafted.) In 1945, at the age of twenty-eight, he decided to give baseball another shot and played in the minor leagues, for the Jersey City Giants. He was called up to the majors in August and showed promise by throwing three shutouts in the final seven weeks of the season.

Maglie went to spring training for the Giants in 1946 but did not see eye-to-eye with manager Mel Ott, so he decided to accept a generous offer to play in the Mexican League. The commissioner of baseball, Happy Chandler, banned Maglie and four other players who "jumped" to Mexico for five years on the grounds that they violated baseball's reserve clause. Maglie pitched for two years in Mexico, then spent two years barnstorming in the United States and Canada. When the ban was lifted in 1950, he returned to the Giants and went east with the team from Arizona after spring training. When the season started, he was just shy of his thirty-third birthday and had pitched just 13 games in the majors. He began the season in the bullpen but worked his way into the starting rotation, where he shone, winning 18 games, leading the National League in ERA, and at one point throwing four straight shutouts. He won a league-leading 23 games for the pennant-winning Giants in 1951 and 18 more the following season. A back injury slowed him down in 1953, limiting him to eight wins, but he bounced back in 1954 to win 14.

Maglie was known as an intimidating pitcher—he acquired the memorable moniker "the Barber" because his high fastballs sometimes came so close to batters' heads, the pitches nearly "shaved" their chins. Maglie had the confidence and experience not to be unnerved facing Avila, Doby, Rosen, and the rest of the Indians lineup in the opening game of the World Series.

Things did not start well for Maglie. He hit leadoff batter Al Smith, and Avila followed with a single. Maglie retired Doby and Rosen, but then Vic Wertz drilled a 420-foot triple to right-center field, scoring both runners. Wertz had come over to the Indians in a trade with the Baltimore Orioles in early June. Rosen played for the first two months of the season at first base, but when Wertz took over first following the trade, Rosen moved back to third base. Maglie got the third out but was already behind, 2–0. The Giants tied the score off Lemon in the bottom of the third on an RBI ground out by Don Mueller and an RBI single by Hank Thompson.

Maglie and Lemon did not allow any other runs through the first seven innings. The Indians put runners in scoring position in the fourth, fifth, and sixth innings, but Maglie worked out of each of the jams. In the top of the eighth inning, Doby led off with a walk, and Rosen followed with an infield single to put runners on first and second with no outs. Wertz was due up next—he was 3-for-3 off Maglie with the long triple in the first inning and two line-drive singles. Durocher went to the bullpen and brought in southpaw Don Liddle to face the left-handed-hitting Wertz. Liddle had come over with Antonelli in the offseason trade. The runners took their leads. Wertz, locked in at the plate, launched a long fly ball over center fielder Willie Mays's head. Mays turned and sprinted with his back to the plate, reached out, and miraculously caught the ball with his outstretched glove, robbing Wertz of what seemed like a sure extra-base hit that would have scored both runners. After making the catch, Mays had the wherewithal to wheel quickly and fire the ball to the cutoff man in short center field. Doby tagged and advanced to third, but Rosen had to hold at first.

Right-handed hitter Hank Majeski was sent in to pinch-hit for switch-hitter Dave Philley. Durocher pulled Liddle for righty Marv Grissom. Liddle later cracked, "Well, at least I got my man." So what if the batter hit the ball more than 400 feet? Lopez countered Durocher's move by pinch-hitting left-handed-hitter Dale Mitchell for Majeski. Mitchell drew a walk to load the bases. Grissom escaped the bases-loaded, one-out pickle by striking out another pinch-hitter, Dave Pope, and retiring Jim Hegan on a fly out.

The game went into extra innings, tied at 2–2. In the top of the 10th, Wertz led off by hitting another shot, a 400-foot double to left-center field. It was a golden opportunity for the Indians to take the lead, but they failed to deliver a clutch hit, and the game stayed tied, heading into the bottom of the 10th. Lemon, the workhorse, was still on the mound for Cleveland. With one out, Mays walked and stole second. With Monte Irvin on deck, Lopez walked Hank Thompson intentionally. Irvin and Thompson had joined the Giants in 1949, having played in the Negro Leagues. The right-handed-hitting Irvin led the National League in RBIs in 1951 and finished third in the MVP vote. An ankle injury sidelined him for most of the 1952 season, but he rebounded in 1953 by hitting .329 with 97 RBIs. Irvin had a mediocre season in 1954, hitting .262 with 64 RBIs. Because of Irvin's struggles, Durocher sometimes used a pinch-hitter for him during the season, and, in this pivotal moment, he called his right-handed hitter back to the dugout and sent in left-handed-hitting reserve outfielder, James "Dusty" Rhodes.

Growing up, Rhodes was called "Jim" until a scout gave him the nickname "Dusty," which stuck. After he served in the navy during World War II, Rhodes played five and a half years in the minors and developed a reputation for being a good hitter, a poor fielder, and a hard drinker. One of his minor-league managers urged him to scale back his partying. "I cut down 50 percent," Rhodes later quipped. "I stopped drinking chasers."

In July 1952, with Rhodes tearing up the Southern Association for Double-A Nashville, Irvin on the disabled list with his ankle injury, and Mays drafted by the army to serve during the Korean War, the Giants brought Dusty up to the big leagues. Durocher put him in the lineup in left field, and he held down the position until Irvin came off the disabled list. Rhodes batted .250 but displayed good power, hitting 10 homers in 176 at-bats. His defense was shoddy; he committed nine errors in 56 games. In 1953, he was used as an occasional starter in left field and as a pinch-hitter. His average dropped to .233, but his power numbers were similar: 11 home runs in 163 at-bats. In one game against the Cardinals at the Polo Grounds that season, Rhodes homered in three consecutive at-bats.

Though Rhodes provided some power off the bench for the Giants, Durocher wanted to trade him after the 1953 season because of his bad glove and drinking habits. Horace Stoneham, the owner of the Giants and no stranger to the bottle himself, liked Rhodes, so he stayed. In 1954, Rhodes proved to Stoneham and Durocher that he was worth having on the roster. In the first three months of the season, he was used mostly as a pinch-hitter and hit only one home run with seven RBIs. He started more in July and responded by hitting seven home runs; for the second straight season, he hit three homers in a game. In an August doubleheader against the Cardinals, he tied a major-league record with *six* extra-base hits in a day—two home runs, two triples, and two doubles. The next day, with the Giants leading, 2–1, in the top of the ninth inning, runners on second and third with two outs, Cardinals manager Eddie Stanky walked Hank Thompson intentionally to get to Rhodes. Dusty gave the Giants insurance runs by lining a two-run single to center, and, when he reached first base, he gave Stanky a sarcastic tip of the hat.

His final stats in 1954 were impressive: a .341 average with 15 home runs and 50 RBIs in 164 at-bats. Rhodes also ramped up his game as a pinch-hitter in '54. In 1952–53, he was just 6-for-39 (.154) as a pinch-hitter, but that changed considerably in 1954 when he went 15-for-46 (.326).

While Rhodes preferred to be in the starting lineup, he also thrived in his role as a pinch-hitter. After Lopez intentionally walked Thompson in the bottom of the 10th, Durocher looked Rhodes's way, and he already had a bat in his hands. At 6'0" and 178 pounds, Rhodes was tall and lean. Lemon's first pitch was a curve ball that hung, and Rhodes swatted a fly ball down the line that that barely cleared the right-field wall. It was not a long shot—about 260 feet—but it was a game-winning, three-run homer. Lemon flung his glove in disgust as he stormed off the mound.

Durocher started Johnny Antonelli in Game 2, and Lopez went with Early Wynn, his other 23-game winner. When Wynn retired in 1963, he was one of only 14 pitchers with 300 wins. Intense on the mound, Wynn did not hesitate to knock down a batter that he thought was crowding the plate or acting cocky.

Al Smith led off the game against Antonelli by homering into the left-field bleachers. The Indians then loaded the bases with two outs, but George Strickland, with a chance to add to their lead, popped out to first. The Indians wasted a leadoff double by Jim Hegan in the second. After Wynn bunted him over to third, Smith struck out and Avila fouled out.

Wynn mowed down the Giants in the early innings, retiring the first 12 batters and striking out three. In the bottom of the fifth, with the Indians still ahead, 1–0, Mays became the Giants' first baserunner when he walked. Thompson collected New York's first hit by singling, which advanced Mays to third base. Irvin was due up next; Wynn had struck him out looking in the second. Though it was still early in the game,

Durocher called on Rhodes to pinch-hit. Wynn gave Rhodes a wake-up call by brushing him back with an inside fastball. He then got two strikes before Rhodes stroked one into center field for an RBI single to tie the game. Thompson later scored on a ground out by Antonelli to give the Giants a 2–1 lead.

Rhodes remained in the game to play left field, and the score was the same when he faced Wynn a second time in the bottom of the seventh. Again, Wynn knocked down Rhodes. And again, Rhodes answered the call, this time blasting a home run off the facade of the Polo Grounds' right-field roof. Antonelli went the distance to beat the Indians, 3–1. Though he surrendered eight hits and walked six batters, the leadoff home run was the only run he allowed. The Indians' struggles with runners on base continued, as they left 13 men on base, including two in the ninth after Smith and Avila each singled to start the inning.

Down 2–0, Lopez was looking forward to heading back to the Indians' home field, Municipal Stadium. If the Indians could sweep the Giants at home, or win two out of three, they still had a chance to win the Series. More than seventy-one thousand fans attended Game 3, eager to watch their team turn things around. Lopez started Mike "the Big Bear" Garcia, who narrowly missed joining Lemon and Wynn as 20-game winners. On the last day of the season, with 19 wins, Garcia pitched 12 innings but did not get a decision. His American League ERA title in 1954 was his second. Ruben Gomez, a 17-game winner, took the mound for the Giants.

The Giants wasted no time getting on the scoreboard, as Mays lined a two-out RBI single in the top of the first. Thompson walked, but Irvin, still in a funk, fouled out to catcher Jim Hegan to end the inning. With the score still 1–0, Alvin Dark and Don Mueller led off the top of the third with singles off Garcia, giving the Giants runners on first and third with nobody out. Mays hit a grounder to third; Dark, caught in a rundown, was tagged out by Hegan, while Mueller hustled over to third and Mays made it to second. Lopez intentionally walked Thompson to load the bases. Durocher did not hesitate—for the third straight game, he pinch-hit Rhodes for Irvin. Rhodes, exuding confidence at the plate, lined a two-run single to right, increasing the Giants' lead to 3–0.

Rhodes had three pinch-hitting appearances against three outstanding pitchers—two future Hall of Famers and a two-time ERA champion. He delivered a game-winning, three-run homer in Game 1, a game-tying RBI single in Game 2, and in Game 3 a two-run single that padded the Giants' lead. He also hit a solo home run in Game 2 to give his team an insurance run. Four at-bats, four hits, seven RBIs.

After Rhodes's hit, Davey Williams dropped down a bunt, and Garcia made an errant throw to first, which allowed Thompson to score. Rhodes stayed in the game, taking over left field for Irvin. Lopez, concerned that Garcia did not have his good stuff and that the game was slipping away, pinch-hit for him in the bottom of the third and went to the bullpen. In the top of the fifth, with one out, Thompson doubled off reliever Art Houtteman, and Lopez showed respect for Rhodes by intentionally walking him. One out later, Wes Westrum singled Thompson home. Indians pitchers finally found a way to get out Rhodes in the seventh and ninth, but by then the Giants had the game in hand and won, 6–2. Hoyt Wilhelm, whose specialty pitch was the knuckleball, relieved Gomez in the eighth and recorded the last five outs.

The Indians' backs were against the wall. No team had ever lost the first three games of a World Series and rebounded to win it. Bob Feller had not yet pitched in the Series, but Lopez bypassed him as starter and went with Bob Lemon in Game 4. Durocher saved Maglie for Game 5, in case the game was necessary, and went with Don Liddle, who had faced only one batter in the Series, Vic Wertz, in Game 1.

The Giants appeared to be a team of destiny. Sloppy fielding by the Indians contributed to the Giants scoring two runs in the top of the second. Monte Irvin picked up his first hit of the Series in the inning by following Thompson's leadoff walk with a double to left-center. Davey Williams hit a line drive to first that Wertz snared, but, when he tried to double Irvin off second, he threw the ball away. Thompson scored, and Irvin advanced to third. Wes Westrum lifted a fly ball to right field that Wally Westlake dropped for an error, allowing Irvin to trot home on what was scored a sacrifice fly. The Giants added a run in the third and broke it open with four in the fifth, knocking out Lemon in the process—Irvin's two-run single was the big hit of the inning.

Trailing, 7–0, the Indians needed a huge comeback to win the game and stay alive in the Series. Pinch-hitter Hank Majeski helped the cause by socking a three-run homer in the bottom of the fifth to close the gap to 7–3. The Indians put another run on the board in the seventh, and, when they brought the tying run to the plate in the bottom of the eighth with one out, Durocher brought in his stud, Game 2 winner Johnny Antonelli. The lefty struck out Wertz and Westlake to end the threat. Antonelli shut down the Indians in the ninth, and the Giants were world champions. It was the only game of the Series in which Durocher did not call on Rhodes to pinch-hit.

The Indians played .721 ball during the season yet were swept in the World Series. Their defense was shaky, and they failed miserably at the plate and on the mound. As a team, they hit .190 and a measly .100 (4-for-40) with runners in scoring position. They left 37 men on base, an average of a runner an inning, in the four games. Aside from Wertz, who hit .500 with two doubles, a triple, and a homer, the bats of the Indians' hitters were silent. Avila hit .133; Doby, .125; and Rosen, .250. None of the three drove in a run.

As for the pitchers, Cleveland's "Big Three" (Lemon, Wynn, and Garcia) had a combined 65–26 with a 2.70 ERA during the season and floundered in the Fall Classic, losing all four starts and getting shelled to the tune of a 5.68 ERA.

In retrospect, the Indians' propensity to dominate the weak teams in the American League during the regular season (better than .800 ball against teams with losing records) but to play mediocre baseball (.500 against teams with winning records) proved telling. Though the Giants won 14 fewer games than the Indians, they were still a strong team, and some think that Cleveland showed their true colors by struggling in the World Series against a tough foe.

After the Series, Rhodes, the unlikely hero, was honored with parades in his hometown of Montgomery, Alabama, and in his offseason home of Rock Hill, South Carolina.

In 1955, the Giants never got on track and finished in third place, 18½ games behind the Dodgers. Rhodes lost some of his power, hitting only six home runs in 187 at-bats, but he had another .300 year, finishing at .305. After the season, Durocher stepped down as manager of the Giants to pursue interests in broadcasting as well as show business, which were fueled by his marriage to the actress Laraine Day.

Bill Rigney succeeded Durocher as manager in 1956. Rigney's style differed drastically from Durocher's. The new manager's efforts to wield his authority didn't sit well with a lot of the players, including Mays and Rhodes. During the next two years under Rigney, Rhodes hit just .212. He later lamented, "When Durocher left the Giants, baseball wasn't fun anymore." In 1958, the Giants moved to San Francisco, but Rhodes spent the entire 1958 season with Triple-A Phoenix. In 1959 he returned to the Giants, and there his big-league career ended with a whimper—48 at-bats, all as a pinch-hitter, just nine hits for a .188 average, and not a single home run. He played his last game in the majors at the age of thirty-two.

Giants fans remember Dusty Rhodes for his heroics in the 1954 World Series. But his greatest legacy was the way in which he bonded with the Black players on the team, notably Mays, Irvin, and Thompson. After Jackie Robinson broke the color barrier in 1947 and in the years to follow, some white players treated the Black players with disrespect. Not Rhodes. Irvin, whom Rhodes pinch-hit for in the first three games of the '54 Series, extolled his teammate: "He was a brother to all Black players."

Pinch-hitter Dusty Rhodes approaches the plate after his Game 1 walk-off homer against the heavily favored Cleveland Indians in the 1954 Series. Rhodes went on to hit .667 with two homers and seven RBIs in the Giants' sweep of The Tribe. *AP Photo*

10

Down to the Last Strike

The hero of the 2011 World Series lifted his team to victory when it was down to its last strike. At times over the previous few years, that player had been down to his last strike in life as he battled the demons of depression and drinking.

When spring training broke for the St. Louis Cardinals in 2011, a big storyline surrounding the team was whether baseball's best player, Albert Pujols, in the last year of his contract, would leave St. Louis after the season for the riches of free agency. Pujols's accomplishments in the first ten years of his major-league career for the Cardinals were staggering. He was drafted in 1999 by St. Louis in the thirteenth round out of a community college in Missouri, but, after just a year in the minors, he became an everyday player for the Cardinals in 2001. All he did over the next ten years was hit .331 and average 41 home runs and 123 RBIs per season. For good measure, he won two Gold Gloves. He was named MVP three times and finished second four times. His Cardinals made it to the World Series twice, losing in 2004 and winning in 2006. During his first three seasons in the majors, Pujols played mostly in the outfield, but he also saw time at third base and first base. In 2004, he became the Redbirds' regular first baseman and remained a fixture at that position for the years to come.

The Cardinals brass quickly recognized Pujols's greatness and, after his third season, locked him into a seven-year, $100 million contract (about $14 million per season) that extended through 2010, with a club option for $16 million in the eighth season, which was picked up. Pujols's value increased in January 2010, when the Cardinals inked free-agent outfielder Matt Holliday, whom they had acquired in a trade in 2009, to a seven-year, $120 million deal ($17 million and change per year). Thus, in 2010 and 2011, Holliday, a very good player but not nearly in Pujols's class, was the Cardinals' highest-paid player. Pujols and his agent, Dan Lozano, took further note during the 2010 season when two players signed contracts worth more than $20 million per season: Minnesota Twins catcher Joe Mauer signed an eight-year, $184 million extension, and Philadelphia Phillies first baseman Ryan Howard received a five-year, $125 million extension. Pujols kept his focus on the field in 2010 and won his third MVP.

Tony La Russa had been Pujols's manager throughout his career in St. Louis—2011 was his sixteenth year as pilot of the Cardinals. He had previously managed the Chicago White Sox for seven seasons and the Oakland A's for nine and a half seasons. There were rumors that the sixty-six-year-old La Russa might retire after the 2011 season.

With the contract issue and the possibility that he might leave St. Louis, where he was adored by the fans, both hanging over his head, Pujols started the season tepidly. On May 22, Albert was hitting only .269 and had not homered in 26 games. He began to hit, but then, in a June 19 game, while reaching for a throw at first base, he collided with Wilson Betemit of the Kansas City Royals and fractured his left wrist. Though he had been expected to miss four to six weeks, he came back ahead of schedule, missing only 14 games. By late July, the Cardinals, while playing little more than .500 ball, were nip and tuck with the Milwaukee Brewers at the top of the Central Division. Before the July 31 deadline, the Cardinals made an eight-player trade with the Toronto Blue Jays, acquiring pitcher Edwin Jackson and three other players, as well as a deal with the Los Angeles Dodgers in which they picked up shortstop Rafael Furcal.

In early August, the Cardinals were right in the thick of things—2½ games behind the Brewers in the Central Division and 5½ games behind the Atlanta Braves for the National League's lone wild-card spot. When the Cardinals were swept in a three-game series by the Los Angeles Dodgers in the fourth week of August, they fell

10 games behind the Brewers and 10½ games behind the Braves in the wild-card race. With only 32 games left on the schedule, their chances of securing a postseason berth were slim.

La Russa had decided a few weeks earlier that he would retire after the season but had not told his players. He did not want to go out with a whimper. To that end, he exhorted his players to ramp up their game, impressing upon them the urgency of their predicament, which left little room for error. The players took La Russa's words to heart; after the thumping by the Dodgers, the Redbirds went 23–9 the rest of the way and lost no more than two games in a row. Though they did not catch the Brewers in the division, they overtook the Braves on the last day of the regular season to capture the wild-card spot.

The Cardinals would have their hands full in the Division Series. They were paired up against the Philadelphia Phillies, who led the majors with 102 wins. The Phillies boasted a starting rotation for the ages. Roy Halladay and Cliff Lee were previous Cy Young Award winners, Roy Oswalt frequently finished in the top five in the Cy Young voting, and Cole Hamels was a steady starter who won the World Series MVP for the Phillies in 2008. Despite La Russa's managerial genius and the team's torrid end-of-the-year run to make the playoffs, the Cardinals were not given much of a chance to beat the Phils in a best-of-five.

The Cardinals trailed in the Series, 2–1, but, in a do-or-die Game 4 at Busch Stadium, third baseman David Freese came up big. He started the Series 2-for-12 with six strikeouts, all of which were against Halladay, Lee, and Hamels. But, when he faced Oswalt, he hit a two-run double in the fourth inning and a two-run homer in the sixth to lead the Redbirds to a 5–3 Series-tying win.

***

That David Freese, a twenty-eight-year-old, third-year player, was in the majors—that he was even alive—was a wonder. Freese battled depression while growing up in Wildwood, Missouri, a St. Louis suburb. In an effort to escape the pain, he played baseball during all four of his years at Lafayette High School. In his senior year, he hit 23 home runs and was named the best high-school shortstop in the state. The University of Missouri offered him a scholarship, but, citing burnout, Freese turned it down and quit baseball. He enrolled at Missouri as a computer science major and joined a fraternity where drinking became too much of a priority for him.

During the summer after his freshman year at Mizzou, Freese worked at a maintenance job for the school district in Wildwood. One day, after a visit to his old high school, he felt the urge to play baseball again. He sought out Tony Dattoli, the baseball coach at St. Louis Community College-Meramec, and Dattoli told Freese he would offer him a spot on the team.

That November, however, before he stepped on the diamond for Meramec, Freese was busted for driving under the influence. The judge sentenced him to probation. Freese moved past the arrest and hit .396 with 10 home runs for Meramec in the spring. Dattoli recommended Freese to the coach at Division I University of South Alabama, and he upgraded to that college. Freese started as a sophomore, playing third base, and, in his senior year in 2006, he was voted the Sun Belt Conference Player of the Year. The San Diego Padres picked Freese in the ninth round of the '06 draft. Freese promptly signed a pro contract, and he suited up that year for two Single-A teams in the Padres organization.

Freese had an eventful year in 2007—some good, some bad. He moved up to High-A Lake Elsinore in the California League and had strong numbers on the field—a .302 batting average and 96 RBIs—but his drinking landed him in trouble again; he was arrested for public intoxication and resisting arrest in California. After the season, the general manager for the Padres, Kevin Towers, reached out to the Cardinals' new general manager, John Mozeliak, expressing interest in veteran outfielder Jim Edmonds, who had 362 career homers. Mozeliak had eyed Freese in 2006 when he was St. Louis's scouting director and asked for the minor-league third baseman in exchange for Edmonds. Towers agreed, and the deal was finalized. Freese picked up Mozeliak's phone message when he was eating at a Burger King. For Freese, it was a whopper of a trade because it paved the way for him to fulfill his childhood dream of playing for the Cardinals.

Freese's progression for the Cardinals' Triple-A Memphis affiliate in 2008, along with the additional experience he gained playing winter ball in Venezuela in the offseason, earned him an invitation to spring training for the Cardinals in 2009. He made the twenty-five-man roster and, on Opening Day, he entered the game in the seventh inning. In his second major-league plate appearance in the bottom of the eighth, he delivered a sacrifice fly to give the Cardinals a two-run lead, only for his team to lose the game in the ninth. Freese got some starts at third base over the next two weeks but then was sent down to the minors. In what would become the first of many operations, he underwent surgery to his left ankle in May, which sidelined him for two months. He spent most of the remainder of the season playing for Memphis; a late September call-up to the Cards allowed him to play a few more games in the majors at the tail end of the season.

Though Freese experienced the thrill of reaching the majors in 2009, depression still had its grip on him, and he continued to use alcohol as a coping mechanism. In December '09, after a night of partying, Freese was pulled over by a Missouri police officer who had observed his vehicle weaving. His blood alcohol level was high, and he was slapped with another DUI. Freese was humiliated and upset about his arrest and the state of his life.

Freese managed to pull himself together and return to the field in 2010. Teammate Matt Holliday took Freese under his wing and exerted a positive influence on his younger teammate, helping him to stop drinking. Freese held down the Cardinals' third-base job and he thrived, hitting .296. But then, at the end of June, Freese sustained a bone bruise to his right ankle and was placed on the disabled list. In a rehab assignment in the Texas League three weeks later, he rolled his ankle rounding third base. The injury required two surgeries and took him out of commission until spring training the following year.

Freese was resilient, though, and, after rehabbing his ankle injury, he regained the Cards' starting third-base position in 2011 and through the first month of the season was batting a blistering .365. But the injury bug got him again—he suffered a fracture to his left hand on May 1 when he was drilled with a pitch. He underwent another surgery and was on the shelf for almost two months. He played third the rest of the season and, though he could not maintain his early season pace, he still finished the year with a .297 average.

***

Freese's clutch performance in Game 4 of the Division Series gave the Cardinals life, and it came down to a Game 5 showdown in Philadelphia. Roy Halladay and Chris Carpenter, old friends from their years as teammates with the Toronto Blue Jays, drew the starting assignments. The two aces locked horns in a classic pitchers' duel, with the Cardinals ending up on the long end of the stick. Halladay allowed only one run, but Carpenter was better, throwing a three-hit shutout. The game ended with Ryan Howard in a heap on the ground between home plate and first base after he tore his Achilles tendon while grounding out to the second baseman for the last out in the bottom of the ninth.

The League Championship Series, which pitted the Cardinals against the Brewers, turned out to be the David Freese and Albert Pujols show. Each player racked up nine RBIs in the six games. Pujols hit .478 with two home runs while Freese smacked the ball at a .545 clip, which included three home runs. In the decisive Game 6, Freese went 3-for-4 with a homer, three runs, and three RBIs. He beat out Pujols for the MVP of the Series.

Meanwhile, in the junior circuit, the Texas Rangers were trying to win their first world championship in the franchise's beleaguered fifty-one-year history. The club moved to Arlington, Texas, in 1972 after 11 straight second-division finishes in Washington. Things did not get much better when they moved to Texas. Not until 1996, the franchise's thirty-sixth season, did the Rangers, led by manager Johnny Oates, first make the postseason. Oates's predecessors as skipper of the Senators and Rangers included some big-name managers: Gil Hodges, Whitey Herzog, Billy Martin, Don Zimmer, and Bobby Valentine. Hodges, Herzog, and Martin later managed a World Series winner, and Valentine took the Mets to the World Series. At the helm for Washington and Texas, though, none of the five finished higher than second place. Ted Williams, one of the game's all-time greatest hitters, also managed the Washington and Texas franchise but had only one winning season out of four.

Starting in 1996, Oates took the Rangers to three American League Western Division titles over a four-year period, but each year they were hastily eliminated in the first round, winning a total of just one game in the three LCSs.

In 2007, Ron Washington, with no managerial experience, took over the seemingly thankless job as pilot of the Rangers. A journeyman and a reserve middle infielder for ten years and an Oakland A's coach for eleven years, Washington had never been part of a World Series team (he played 10 games for the 1977 Los Angeles Dodgers when he was first called up to the majors that September but wasn't eligible to play in the World Series). Washington's Rangers team steadily improved under his leadership, and they reached the World Series for the first time in 2010. Bruce Bochy's San Francisco Giants knocked off Washington's squad in five games.

Nolan Ryan, the president of the Rangers since 2008, was also hungry for a World Series ring. After his New York Mets team won it all in 1969, Ryan did not appear in another World Series during his last twenty-four years as a player. Ryan and Washington felt confident that their well-balanced team (third in the American League in runs scored, fifth in team ERA) could take out the Cardinals in the World Series.

For the third straight series in the postseason, the Cardinals were not favored to win. The National League's victory in the All-Star Game over the summer gave the Cardinals home-field advantage in the World Series even though the Rangers won six more games during the regular season. The teams split the first two games at Busch Stadium in low-scoring games. The Cards won the opener, 3–2; the Rangers bounced back to win the second game, 2–1, rallying for two runs in the top of the ninth inning.

In Game 3, Albert Pujols made it clear that, if these were his final games in a St. Louis uniform, he was going out with a bang. He accomplished something that only Babe Ruth and Reggie Jackson had previously done—he slugged three home runs in a World Series game. (Pablo Sandoval has done it since.) After singling in the fourth and fifth innings, Pujols unloaded a three-run homer in the sixth, a two-run blast in the seventh, and a solo shot in the ninth to lead the Cardinals to a 16–7 rout of the Rangers. In addition to tying Ruth and Jackson's record for most home runs in a World Series game, Pujols set a record with 14 total bases in a game as well as hits in four straight innings.

The Cardinals should have saved some of those runs for the next two games because they were shut out in the fourth game and scored only two runs in a 4–2 loss in the fifth game. The Cardinals were one loss away from elimination.

Rain in St. Louis delayed Game 6 by a day. Play resumed the following night, and, anticipating that this might be Albert Pujols's last game as a Cardinal, many fans displayed signs paying tribute to the superstar. It would be an epic game to rival famous World Series Game 6s, such as the 1975 tilt between the Cincinnati Reds and the Boston Red Sox, which Carlton Fisk won with a 12th inning walk-off home run, and the 1986 battle between the New York Mets and the Boston Red Sox, which ended with a ball trickling between Bill Buckner's legs.

Colby Lewis started for the Rangers; Jaime Garcia, for the Cardinals. Both hurlers had started and pitched well in Game 2. The sixth game was rife with lead changes and errors in the early going. Through four innings, it was 3–3; the Rangers had held two leads, but the Cardinals caught up both times. Each team had scored an unearned run.

David Freese made a gaffe in the top of the fifth, which led to another unearned run. Josh Hamilton, the reigning American League MVP, hit a lazy pop-up that Freese settled under, but the ball bounced out of his glove and grazed the back of his cap before falling to the ground. Freese's blunder was the third error of the game for the Cardinals. First baseman Michael Young made up for his miscue in the fourth by doubling home Hamilton to put the Rangers back on top, 4–3. Freese was worried that he would be branded the goat by committing an error that led to the winning run in the World Series clincher.

The Cardinals evened things up with a run in the bottom of the sixth, but they wasted a chance to score more. Three Rangers pitchers threw 38 pitches, but the Cardinals managed to plate only one run. With one out, Lance Berkman singled, Matt Holliday reached on Michael Young's second error of the game, and David Freese walked to load the bases. Ron Washington pulled Colby Lewis and went to Alexi Ogando. Yadier Molina, the Cardinals' All-Star catcher, drew a walk to bring in a run.

Holliday then suffered the embarrassment of getting picked off third base on a laser by catcher Mike Napoli while Nick Punto was batting. To add to Holliday's frustration, he hurt his right wrist while diving back into third base and was replaced the next inning in the lineup by Allen Craig.

Ogando uncorked a wild pitch that allowed Freese and Molina to move up, then walked Punto on a full-count pitch, so again each base was occupied by a Cardinal. Washington had seen enough of Ogando and took him out in favor of Derek Holland, who had tossed 8⅓ shutout innings in Game 4. Jon Jay, who was a pinch-hitter during the inning before and who stayed in the game to play center field, hit a comebacker to Holland to end the threat.

Lance Lynn, Tony La Russa's third pitcher of the game, allowed back-to-back homers by Adrian Beltre and Nelson Cruz to lead off the seventh. Later in the inning, after Octavio Dotel had taken over for Lynn, Ian Kinsler singled in a run to stretch the Rangers' lead to 7–4.

The game stayed that way until there was one out in the bottom of the eighth when Allen Craig, batting for the first time since taking over for Matt Holliday, touched Holland for a home run to reduce the deficit to two runs. The Cardinals loaded the bases with two outs for Rafael Furcal; by this time, Mike Adams was on in relief for Holland. For the second time in three innings, a bases-loaded rally for the Cardinals was thwarted with a groundout to the pitcher.

Nolan Ryan, wearing a black overcoat on this chilly late October evening, was seated with his wife near the Rangers dugout. Ryan's outward calm belied his churning stomach. The Rangers were three outs away from winning the World Series.

Ron Washington brought in his closer, Neftali Feliz, to try to hold the Rangers' two-run lead. The stocky twenty-three-year-old righty from the Dominican Republic saved 40 games and won the Rookie of the Year Award in 2010, then followed it up with another banner season when he saved 32 games with a 2.74 ERA. His arsenal of pitches included a fastball whose speed sometimes exceeded 100 mph and a nasty slider. He was "lights out" in the 2011 postseason: 6-for-6 in save opportunities, including two straight in the World Series.

Feliz struck out Ryan Theriot to start the frame. Albert Pujols, hit-less in the Series since his monster Game 3, laced a double. Feliz walked Lance Berkman on four pitches. Allen Craig walked to the plate, representing the winning run. David Freese stood at the on-deck circle. Feliz froze Craig with a wicked slider on a 2-2 count for the second out.

Freese headed to the plate, anxious but awed by the spot he found himself in: two on, two outs, his team down by two, bottom of the ninth inning, the World Series hanging in the balance. He looked at two sliders, a ball and a strike, then swung through a fastball. The Rangers were one strike away from finally, finally winning the World Series for themselves and their long-suffering fans. Freese stepped out of the box to collect himself. Feliz's next pitch was a 98-mph fastball slightly above the knees, and Freese connected, hitting a long fly ball to right field. Nelson Cruz, not a particularly graceful right fielder who had been hampered by a hamstring injury during the season, raced back and appeared to have a bead on the ball. The baseball writer Jayson Stark later opined that eight out of ten major-league right fielders would have caught Freese's ball. Cruz was in the minority. The ball sailed out of his reach, struck the bottom of the right-field wall, and caromed away from him in the direction of the infield. Pujols and Berkman scored easily to tie the game, and, by the time Cruz corralled the ball and fired it into the infield, Freese was on third base, on his knees, after his headfirst slide. While the ball was catchable, it was ruled a triple.

It was an amazing turn of events. The St. Louis crowd went bonkers. Nolan Ryan and Ron Washington were speechless. Feliz looked dazed as well, but he retired Yadier Molina on a line out to Cruz to end the ninth and then walked off the mound with his head hung.

Jason Motte, a capable reliever who had come into the game in the ninth inning, went out for the 10th. With one out, Elvis Andrus grounded a single up the middle, and Josh Hamilton, who had hit 25 home runs during the regular season but was homerless in his first 65 postseason at-bats, followed with a first-pitch, two-run homer to right-center field to give the Rangers a 9–7 lead.

With left-handed hitters Daniel Descalso and Jon Jay slated to lead off the bottom of the 10th, Washington brought in southpaw Darren

Oliver, the winning pitcher in Game 5, an eighteen-year veteran who had turned forty-one three weeks earlier. Descalso and Jay both delivered singles, and pitcher Kyle Lohse was sent up by La Russa to lay down a sacrifice bunt, which he did successfully.

Out went Oliver, and in came Scott Feldman, a 6'6" righty who had split his seven-year career with the Rangers between starting and relieving. He had never recorded a save in the majors. Washington thought this would be a good time for his first. Feldman got Ryan Theriot to ground out to third for the second out. Descalso scored on the play to make it 9–8; Jay remained at second. Washington took no chances with Pujols and walked him intentionally.

Lance Berkman, a born-and-bred Texan, came up with runners on first and second and two outs. A switch-hitter batting left-handed against Feldman, Berkman had spent more than a decade with the Houston Astros, where he was an RBI machine, driving in 100 runs six times. The New York Yankees had acquired him at the trade deadline the previous July, and he had an unproductive two months in pinstripes. The Cardinals signed him as a free agent after the season, and he paid dividends by totaling 94 RBIs, second on the team to Pujols.

Rangers pitching coach Mike Maddux went out to the mound to discuss with Feldman and Mike Napoli how to pitch Berkman. The count went to 1-2, and, for the second time in two innings, the Rangers needed one strike to become world champions. It was not to be. After Feldman threw a ball inside, Berkman stroked a liner to center to score Jay and knot the game at 9–9. After Berkman took second on defensive indifference, Allen Craig grounded out to Adrian Beltre at third base to end the inning.

La Russa's seventh hurler, Jake Westbrook, disposed of the Rangers in the top of the 11th. Mark Lowe, who had pitched only one inning in the 2011 postseason, became Texas's eighth pitcher of the game in the bottom of the inning. David Freese stood in, and the count went to 3-0. The fourth pitch appeared to be out of the strike zone, but home-plate umpire Gary Cederstrom called it a strike. Freese swung at and missed the next pitch. Freese then boomed Lowe's full-count pitch to deep center. Center fielder Josh Hamilton went back and back until he ran out of room. As the ball passed over the center-field wall and landed in a grassy area twenty feet beyond the wall, fans scrambled out of the center-field bleachers for the ball. Broadcaster Joe Buck summed up what Freese's blast meant: "We will see you tomorrow night," a tribute to his father Jack's call of Kirby Puckett's Game 6 home run against the Atlanta Braves twenty years earlier. The Cardinals dugout emptied and greeted Freese with a joyous reception at home plate.

The Rangers failed to hold two-run leads in the ninth and 10th innings, coming within a mere strike in both innings of closing out the Series. They were ahead in the game five separate times but squandered each lead. It was an agonizing loss for the Rangers. And the odds of winning Game 7 were not in their favor. In the last seven World Series in which the home team won the sixth game to force a seventh game, they had gone on to win the seventh game every time.

Washington gave the ball to Matt Harrison, who was a 14-game winner for Texas during the regular season and who had been shelled in Game 3. La Russa went with Chris Carpenter, who started and pitched well in Games 1 and 5 for St. Louis. The rainout between the fifth and sixth games gave Carpenter an opportunity to pitch the seventh game, although it would be on three days' rest rather than his normal four.

On the heels of the riveting, nail-biting Game 6, Game 7 was anticlimactic. Josh Hamilton and Michael Young hit back-to-back RBI doubles off Carpenter in the top of the first to give the Rangers a quick 2–0 lead. David Freese, playing out of his mind, lined a two-run double to left with two outs in the bottom of the first to tie the score. Allen Craig, playing for the injured Matt Holliday, homered for the second consecutive game, a solo shot in the third, to put the Cardinals up, 3–2. Washington showed Freese respect by putting him on in the bottom of the fifth with runners on second and third and two outs. It was the first intentional walk of Freese's three-year major-league career. In contrast, the free pass that Pujols received in the 10th inning of Game 6 was his 271st. Washington's move backfired—Yadier Molina walked and Rafael Furcal was hit by a pitch to extend the Cardinals' lead to 5–2.

The Rangers hardly threatened the rest of the game, and the Cardinals won, 6–2, to take the Series. David Freese—who else?—was named MVP of the World Series. His 21 RBIs in the postseason set a major-league record.

Freese's World Series heroics made him an instant celebrity. Four days after the Cardinals won the World Series, he appeared on *The Tonight Show* with the host Jay Leno and a seventeen-year-old singing sensation named Justin Bieber. When Freese went out in St. Louis in the offseason, he was mobbed by fans, who asked him to scribble his autograph and pose for a picture.

Tony La Russa followed through on the pledge he made to himself over the summer and announced he was retiring from managing. His achievements were impressive. He ranked third on the all-time wins list among managers, trailing Connie Mack and John McGraw. Only he and Sparky Anderson had won World Series in both leagues. La Russa's successor, Mike Matheny, was named two weeks later.

With Albert Pujols's contract now expired, the monumental question remained whether he would re-sign with the Cardinals or take his considerable talents elsewhere. The Cardinals offered him a ten-year, $210 million deal, with significant deferred money, but the Los Angeles Angels won the sweepstakes, outbidding the Cardinals and two other teams by offering Pujols a guaranteed $254 million over ten years. On December 8, 2011, six weeks after the championship parade in St. Louis, Pujols bade farewell to the Cardinals and signed with the Angels.

In 2012, Freese enjoyed what would be the most productive regular season of his career, hitting 20 home runs with 79 RBIs and earning his only All-Star Game selection. Not long after the season ended, however, while out driving in his hometown, Freese swerved to avoid hitting a deer and ran his SUV into a tree. Alcohol was not a factor, and he was uninjured. Still, Freese was shaken up by the accident, and depression took hold of him for a time afterward.

With Mike Matheny at the helm, the Cardinals returned to the World Series in 2013, losing to the Red Sox in six games. Freese had a career-best 20-game hitting streak during the season, but he hit only .158 in the World Series. After the season, the Cardinals traded him to the Angels, where he reunited with Albert Pujols. Freese later had stops with the Pittsburgh Pirates and the Dodgers. He played in one more

World Series, for the Dodgers in 2018, and he flashed his October magic again, hitting .417 with a homer, but his team fell to the Red Sox.

Freese retired after the 2019 season. He played eleven seasons and compiled an unspectacular but respectable .277 batting average with 113 home runs. Tony La Russa, at the age of seventy-six, got the itch to manage again, and he was hired by the Chicago White Sox—the first team that hired him as skipper in 1979—to manage the team in 2021. He led the White Sox to the American League Central Division title before losing in the Division Series. During the season, La Russa passed John McGraw, becoming the second-winningest manager in history. Albert Pujols played nine and a half years with the Angels but was released in 2021, halfway through the tenth year of his contract. While he did not rack up the behemoth numbers that he had with the Cardinals, still, Pujols joined the 100-RBI club four times while with the Angels. Fittingly, he closed out his career on a strong note by returning to the Cardinals in 2022 and hitting 24 home runs in just 307 at-bats. Ron Washington finally got himself a World Series ring as a coach for the Atlanta Braves in 2021, his thirty-sixth year in Major League Baseball.

As for David Freese, he will always be fondly remembered in St. Louis for his phenomenal performance in the 2011 postseason, notably his game-tying triple and game-winning home run in Game 6. Remarkable for a man who often woke up in the morning and pensively mused, "I can't believe I'm still here."

David Freese of the Cardinals slides into third base headfirst with a game-tying two-run triple in the ninth inning of Game 6 of the 2011 World Series vs. Texas. Freese's 11th-inning homer, which forced a Game 7, capped off a roller coaster of a game in which the Rangers lost five different leads. *Scott Rovak/St. Louis Cardinals*

PART III
MEANWHILE . . . OFF THE FIELD

11

Say It Ain't So, Rube

MANY MAJOR LEAGUE BASEBALL PLAYERS HAVE RUN AFOUL OF THE LAW
over the years, but the story of the pitcher Rube Marquard's transgression
during the 1920 World Series might be the craziest. He got arrested on
the morning of one of the Series games—but was released in time to
pitch in the game that afternoon.

He was born Richard Marquard on the west side of Cleveland, and,
as a boy, much to the dismay of his strict, practical father, he dreamed of
becoming a professional baseball player. As a teenager, he was a batboy
for the Cleveland Bronchos and the Cleveland Naps (later renamed
the Indians) and developed into a highly touted sandlot pitcher. Locals
hoped the lefty would pitch on the big-league diamond in his hometown. He pitched for a Class-B minor-league team in Canton, outside
of Cleveland, in 1907 when he was twenty. The next year, he progressed
to a Class-A team in Indianapolis, where he thrived. It was there that
a sportswriter christened Marquard with the nickname "Rube" because
his pitching style resembled that of Rube Waddell, who was a southpaw
for the Philadelphia Athletics and who had just won his sixth straight
American League strikeout title. The New York Giants' brass considered
Marquard a peach and signed him to a bonus of $11,000, a substantial
sum for the times.

The going was slow for Marquard as he took his lumps in his first
two major-league seasons. His manager, John McGraw, saw a lot of
potential in his young pitcher and worked with Marquard on his motion,
and Wilbert Robinson, one of the team's coaches, taught the lefty the

importance of mixing up his pitches. Marquard also benefited from the tutelage of his teammate, ace pitcher Christy Mathewson, who showed him how to throw a screwball.

In 1911, during his third season, Marquard put it all together, winning 24 games and leading the National League in K's. Mathewson racked up 26 victories, about his average for a season, and the Giants won the pennant before losing to Connie Mack's Athletics in the World Series. In 1912, Marquard stepped up his game. With improved control and more finesse, he opened the season with an astounding 19–0 record and a 1.63 ERA. More than a century later, Rube still holds the record for most consecutive wins by a pitcher to start a season. He finally lost on July 8, and though he was not as sharp during the rest of the year, Marquard still finished with 26 wins and again helped the Giants to the pennant. He pitched brilliantly in the World Series, but the Boston Red Sox knocked off the Giants, four games to three.

Marquard was also making news off the field. In that era, it was common for baseball players to appear in vaudeville shows written especially for them. Following the 1912 season, Marquard's pitching exploits, coupled with his charisma, earned him an invitation to appear in a show in New York called *Breaking the Record*. The skit was created for Marquard, who was paired with a vaudeville star whose stage name was Blossom Seeley. Marquard fell for his costar. Seeley was married to another man at the time, and Marquard became entangled in a love triangle.

As the 1913 season approached, with 24- and 26-win seasons under his belt, Marquard made noise that he might stop pitching to become a full-time actor. Some thought he used the threat as a ploy to induce the Giants to bump up his salary. Whether it was a ploy or not, Marquard received an increase. He earned his pay raise by turning out another fine season, winning 23 games in 1913, and the Giants took their third straight pennant. After pitching well in the previous two World Series, Marquard was lit up in the 1913 Series, and the Giants fell to the Athletics for the second time in three years. That year also marked Seeley's divorce from her husband and her marriage to Marquard.

The bottom fell out for Marquard in 1914 as he found himself on the wrong end of a streak; he lost 12 consecutive games en route to a frustrating 12–22 season. Marquard did not pile up as many losses in 1915, but still he did not regain his top form. By August, relations had soured between John McGraw and him. Marquard helped orchestrate his release and selection off waivers by the Brooklyn Dodgers, who were managed by Wilbert Robinson, his old coach from the Giants, the team that helped turn him into a winning pitcher. It was Robinson's second season at the helm of Brooklyn. The jovial Robinson, affectionately known as "Uncle Robbie," was so revered by his players and the Brooklyn fans that, though the team's official name was the Dodgers, they were also referred to as the Robins.

Under Robinson's leadership, Brooklyn won the pennant in 1916 and advanced to their first World Series. Marquard, while not logging the innings he had in past years, recaptured some of his magic by winning 13 games and posting his career-best ERA of 1.58. His performance earned him the Game 1 start in the World Series, which he lost to the Red Sox. Marquard was also shaky in his Game 4 start, and his team went down in defeat in October for the fourth straight time.

Over the next three seasons, Marquard was up and down for Brooklyn; during this period, he was about a .500 pitcher overall. A leg injury in 1919 sidelined him for most of the season. The Dodgers posted losing records in all three years.

In 1920, though, Uncle Robbie led Brooklyn back to the World Series. The Dodgers, whose offense was pedestrian, relied on their strong pitching. Righties Burleigh Grimes, Leon Cadore, and Jeff Pfeffer were the team's big winners. Marquard, who was semi-regular in the rotation, contributed with a 10–7, 3.23 season, which was respectable but still a far cry from his dominating years with the Giants and his 1916 campaign for the Dodgers. A 20–4 streak to close the season propelled Brooklyn to the pennant, seven games up on the Giants.

Their foe in the World Series, the Cleveland Indians, endured a tragedy on their road to the pennant—and a first Series berth. The tragedy involved one of the team's leaders, Ray Chapman. Chapman played a solid shortstop and was a scrappy hitter and outstanding bunter who had a good eye at the plate. On August 16, the Indians were locked in a three-horse race with the Chicago White Sox and New York Yankees. They played the Yanks at the Polo Grounds on a dark, overcast day. Carl Mays, a submarine-throwing right-hander, pitched for the Yankees. Known as a headhunter, the surly Mays did not mesh well with his fellow players, even his own teammates. In the fifth inning, Chapman, a right-handed hitter, dug into the batter's box. With a 1-1 count, Mays's next pitch sailed inside. Babe Ruth, from right field, heard the sound of the ball striking Chapman on the left side of his head. In 1920, batters were still decades away from wearing helmets for protection. It was also common for balls to become discolored with dirt, spit, licorice, and tobacco juice, as well as being cut and scuffed, causing them to fly erratically. The ball caromed off Chapman's head and rolled back to the mound. Initially, Mays thought the ball hit Chapman's bat, and he fielded the ball and threw to first base. He then saw Chapman on the ground, unconscious, with blood gushing out of his left ear. Two doctors on hand rushed to home plate and were able to revive Chapman and get him on his feet. He shuffled toward the clubhouse beyond the center-field wall, but his knees buckled near second base and two teammates carried him the rest of the way. He was transported to a hospital, where he died the next morning before his pregnant wife arrived from Cleveland.

A police report was filed concerning Chapman's death, but Mays was not charged with any crimes. Mays insisted that he was not trying to bean Chapman; the pitch just got away from him, and Chapman never picked up the ball. The Indians managed to win the game in which Chapman was hit—Mays stayed in the game and pitched eight innings. But then the club, shocked by their teammate's death, went into a tailspin and lost seven of their next nine games. Tris Speaker, however, the team's center fielder and manager, rallied the troops and got them to snap out of their funk and start winning games again. Speaker, one of baseball's preeminent early-century players, went on to amass more than 3,500 hits and a .345 lifetime batting average. Two key personnel moves helped get the team winning again: the Indians acquired from unaffiliated minor-league teams pitcher Duster Mails and shortstop Joe Sewell. Both were impressive down the stretch—Mails went 7–0 and Sewell hit .329.

On September 28, five days away from the end of the regular season, with Cleveland clinging to a half-game lead over the White Sox and a three-game lead over the Yankees, an announcement sent shock waves through the baseball world. A grand jury had convened to investigate whether the 1919 World Series was fixed. Four White Sox players, including Shoeless Joe Jackson, admitted to the grand jury that they had accepted bribes from gamblers to throw the 1919 World Series, which they lost to the Cincinnati Reds. Four other players were also implicated. Chick Gandil, one of the ringleaders of the fix, had retired from the majors before the 1920 season, but the other seven players were still on the White Sox. Charles Comiskey, the president of the Chisox, immediately suspended the seven players, and the team was forced to play its last three games with a skeleton crew. They lost two of the three games, and Cleveland won the pennant by two games. Speaker, in addition to uniting the team after Chapman's death, hit .388 for the season.

As in 1919, the 1920 World Series was a best-of-nine. For the opener at Ebbets Field in Brooklyn, Wilbert Robinson had a well-rested pitching staff. Burleigh Grimes, a 23-game winner, seemed like the clear-cut choice, but Robinson was concerned that the Indians' usual starting eight included six left-handed hitters, five of whom hit over .300. To combat the Indians' strength, Robinson bypassed Grimes as well as his two other top righties, Leon Cadore and Jeff Pfeffer, in favor of lefty Rube Marquard. Robinson's decision was also based on Marquard's experience in pitching in four World Series, though he had not fared well in his last two.

Speaker countered Robinson's choice of Marquard by replacing three of his left-handed swingers with right-handers. One of the three substitutions was Smoky Joe Wood in right field for Elmer Smith. Wood had an interesting backstory—he broke into the majors as a pitcher for the Red Sox, and he was spectacular, winning 34 games in 1912. Wood fractured the thumb on his pitching hand in 1913, and, by 1916, the injury prevented him from effectively pitching ever again. In 1917, he salvaged his baseball career by connecting with Tris Speaker, his teammate for eight years on the Red Sox, and by converting from pitching to being an outfielder. For the next few years, he was a serviceable, part-time outfielder for the Indians—he hit .270 in 1920.

Speaker's Game 1 starter was the 24-game winner Stan Coveleski. Jim Bagby was actually the big gun on the Indians' pitching staff. He won 31 games during the season, but he threw a complete-game win to clinch the pennant three days before the start of the World Series, while Coveleski had not pitched in nearly a week.

Game 1 started well for Marquard. He retired the side in order in the first, catching Speaker looking to end the frame. The Indians countered by pushing across a pair of runs in the second; both were scored by right-handed hitters that Speaker had inserted into the lineup. Backup first baseman George Burns, acquired by the Indians from the Athletics in May, hit a blooper into short right field for a hit. Burns rounded first and headed for second. Brooklyn first baseman Ed Konetchy overthrew shortstop Ivy Olson, and by the time left fielder Zack Wheat tracked the ball down, Burns had circled the bases. It was a fluky run, but it gave the Indians a 1–0 lead. The Indians added a run in the inning on a walk to Smoky Joe Wood, a single by Joe Sewell, and a double by catcher Steve O'Neill. In the fourth, doubles by Wood and O'Neill off Marquard made the score 3–0.

The Dodgers could not do much with Coveleski, collecting just two singles through five innings. In the bottom of the sixth, Robinson, trying to spark a rally, pinch-hit utility outfielder Bill Lamar for Marquard, and he lined out. Brooklyn finally scored a run in the bottom of the seventh off Coveleski on a double and two ground outs, but that's all they would get. Coveleski went the distance, leading Cleveland to a 3–1 opening-game win. Marquard pitched adequately, allowing three runs in six innings, but the southpaw lost his fourth World Series game in a row, dating from 1913.

In Game 2, Robinson sent his stopper Burleigh Grimes to the mound. Usual starters Charlie Jamieson, Elmer Smith, and Doc Johnston were back in Speaker's starting lineup. Grimes shut out the Indians, 3–0, on seven hits. Grimes's defense came up big as left fielder Zack Wheat robbed Johnston of a homer with a runner on in the fourth inning. The next day, Brooklyn won their second straight game at home in another low-scoring game as Sherry Smith beat the Indians, 2–1.

After a travel day, the Series moved to Cleveland's League Park for Game 4. It was a Saturday afternoon game, and Clevelanders were buzzing with excitement, elated to host their first World Series game. The park's normal capacity was twenty-one thousand, but team owner Jim Dunn added temporary bleachers in center field and right field so that as many as six thousand more crazed fans could attend the Series games. The face value of box seats was in the $6.00 to $7.00 range, while reserved seats went for $3.50 to $5.50. In those days there was no Stubhub or the like, so the primary source for the sale of tickets on the secondary market was scalping—selling tickets at an inflated price. It was an illegal practice, and Cleveland police were on high alert for scalpers at the Hollenden Hotel in downtown Cleveland where the Dodgers were staying.

On the morning of Game 4, which fell on Marquard's thirty-fourth birthday, the pitcher, back in his hometown, was waiting in the hotel's lavish lobby for his brother to arrive from Youngstown, Ohio, to pick up tickets. About three thousand rabid Dodgers fans made the nearly 500-mile trip from Brooklyn to Cleveland, salivating at the opportunity to get their hands on tickets. A man from Brooklyn approached Marquard in the lobby and asked him surreptitiously, "Selling any tickets to today's game?"

Rube casually pulled from his pocket eight box-seat tickets, with a face value of $52.80, and said he wanted—depending on the source—$350 or $400 for them.

"That's too high," the man replied and walked away.

An undercover detective for the Cleveland Police, Detective Soukops, overheard the conversation and asked Marquard if he had any tickets for sale. Marquard again pulled out the eight tickets and offered them for $350 or $400.

"That's a violation of law," Detective Soukops said. "You're going to have to come with me."

Marquard insisted that he was not serious when he offered the tickets for sale. Nevertheless, he was transported by the detective to police headquarters. Marquard was not alone—at least half a dozen other people were arrested for scalping that day.

The chief of police, to avoid any accusations of being unsportsman-like, released Marquard on his own recognizance so that he would be available to pitch in that afternoon's game. He was ordered to appear in court on Monday, two days later, to answer to the scalping charges.

That afternoon, more than twenty-five thousand fans crammed into League Park, a concrete and steel structure in the shadow of Lake Erie. The ballpark was oddly configured, measuring 375 feet down the left-field line, 460 feet to deep left-center field, 420 feet to dead center, and a mere 290 feet down the right-field line. Rube Marquard was in uniform at the start of the game, still rattled by his brush with the law that morning. Stan Coveleski was on the mound for Cleveland. Robinson started Leon Cadore, a 15-game winner during the season. Cadore did not last long. The Indians scored two runs in the first, and when Cadore allowed back-to-back singles to start the bottom of the second, Robinson lifted Cadore and brought in Al Mamaux. He halted the rally with a strikeout and a double play.

The script for Mamaux in the third was similar to that for Cadore in the second. After allowing consecutive singles to Bill Wambsganss and Tris Speaker, Mamaux was taken out by Robbie. Elmer Smith was due up, and Marquard, three hours after being questioned at a police station, got the call to relieve Mamaux. The runners had each moved up a base on the throw in from the outfield on Speaker's hit, so Marquard inherited a second-and-third, no outs jam. George Burns pinch-hit for Elmer Smith and greeted Marquard with a two-run single to left. Both runs were charged to Mamaux. Marquard allowed another hit and intentionally walked a batter but got out of the inning with no further damage.

Marquard retired the side in order in the fourth and fifth, but, with Brooklyn down, 4–1, in the top of the sixth, Robinson, as he did in Game 1, sent up Bill Lamar to pinch-hit. Marquard's final numbers on the day were three innings, two hits, one walk, two strikeouts, no runs, and one arrest. The Indians breezed to a 5–1 victory; Coveleski again went the distance.

Despite the bad publicity Marquard's arrest created for him and for the Dodgers, just a week and a half after the indictments of the White Sox players, the Series continued the next afternoon with Game 5, and even more fans packed into League Park than had the day before. Those fans witnessed several World Series firsts.

It had been a low-scoring Series up to that point, with an average of only four runs scored in each of the first four games. More of the same was expected with the two teams' aces, Jim Bagby and Burleigh Grimes, pitted against each other. However, Bagby had his good stuff, and Grimes did not.

In the bottom of the first, the Indians loaded the bases on three singles out of the gate and then cleanup batter Elmer Smith blasted a ball over the right-field wall into the temporary bleachers for a grand slam. It was the first slam in the seventeen-year history of the World Series. In the bottom of the fourth, with the Indians up, 4–0, Bagby came up with two on and two outs. Robinson had elected to walk Steve O'Neill intentionally to face Babgy. He had hit only two home runs in his career, but he connected for a three-run shot over the center-field wall. It marked the first time that a pitcher had hit a home run in World Series play. A hit later, Robbie yanked Grimes and brought in Clarence Mitchell.

The fifth inning featured another first—and this one was a bigger rarity than the grand slam and the homer by a pitcher. Pete Kilduff and Otto Miller led off for the Dodgers with singles. The pitcher's spot was due up next. Even with Brooklyn trailing, 7–0, Robinson allowed Mitchell to bat because he had just come into the game and he was a good enough hitter that, during the season, he occasionally started at first base and in the outfield and was used as a pinch-hitter. With a 1-1 count, the Brooklyn skipper flashed the hit-and-run sign, and with Kilduff and Miller on the move, Mitchell hit a line drive up the middle. Second baseman Bill Wambsganss had headed toward second base in case the ball was not put in play and O'Neill threw down to second to try to nail Miller. Wambsganss leaped and caught Mitchell's liner with his outstretched glove. Kilduff had almost reached third base, and Wambsganss had to take only two strides to step on second and double him up. Miller was nearing second and came to a halt, knowing he was a dead duck. Wambsganss ran over and tagged him out.

The fans took a moment to grasp what had happened and then burst into loud applause when they realized that Wambsganss had pulled off an unassisted triple play. It was only the second in the twentieth century and the first in World Series action; since then, the feat has not been accomplished again in the Series—or in any postseason game. In fact, there have been fewer than 20 unassisted triple plays in history—it is less common than a perfect game or a player hitting four home runs in a game.

The triple play deflated Brooklyn's hopes of getting back into the game. If Mitchell's line drive had made it beyond the reach of Wambsganss, Kilduff would have scored, and the Dodgers might have tacked on some more runs in the inning. But the game remained 7–0, and it ended 8–1.

With the momentum on their team's side, Cleveland fans were gearing up for their first World Series title. The Indians took care of business in the sixth and seventh games, blanking Brooklyn behind Duster Mails and Stan Coveleski and winning the Series, 5–2. Robinson had considered starting Marquard in Game 7, but the manager was furious about the arrest and the distraction it caused for the team. He scratched Marquard and went with Grimes on one day's rest. Brooklyn scored just eight runs in the seven-game Series. Marquard's team went down in defeat in the World Series for the fifth consecutive time. The Indians, moved by Ray Chapman's death, agreed to pay his widow the same full World Series share as the rest of the players.

Marquard had his day in court on Tuesday, October 12, the same day as the final game of the Series. The hearing was pushed back from Monday to Tuesday. Before the hearing, baseball officials convened a special meeting and decided to hold up Marquard's World Series check until the matter was disposed of.

Judge Samuel Silbert, just thirty-seven years old and in the early stages of a long judicial career, presided over the hearing. Marquard was represented by the lawyer Joseph Heintzman. Judge Silbert did not buy Marquard's story that his offer to sell the tickets was made in jest and found the pitcher guilty of scalping. "You acted like a rube, and I am fully convinced of your guilt." In rendering his verdict, Judge Silbert stated that the scalping ordinance was designed to ensure that people could buy tickets to a World Series game at a reasonable price. And then, alluding to the indictments of the White Sox players, the judge stated the following:

> It is an unfortunate thing, because baseball is going through its test period. For fifty years baseball has been regarded as a clean sport, but now the effect of a sudden scandal has made many people dubious.

Judge Silbert imposed on Marquard a fine of $1.00 and payment of $3.80 in court costs. In explaining his rationale for the light penalty, the judge referenced the considerable publicity that the arrest had garnered over the previous few days, as well as the upcoming presidential election—just three weeks away—between two Ohio natives, Warren Harding, the eventual winner, and James Cox:

> I believe he has been punished enough by being written up more than any Presidential candidate and feel that has been a lesson for him.

The National League president John Heydler had no tolerance for the pitcher's indiscretion:

> Marquard has hurt Brooklyn and he has hurt the National League by his action. Baseball doesn't want men of his caliber and I don't think he'll be back in the league next season, although I probably won't take any official action myself.

Charlie Ebbets, owner of the Dodgers, was even more scathingly critical of Marquard:

> I am through with him absolutely. He hasn't been released, however, and if anyone else wants him he can have him. But Marquard will never again put on a Brooklyn uniform.

Three days after Marquard was found guilty and his team lost the World Series, his wife, Blossom Seeley, appeared in court, requesting a divorce from her husband and custody of their son. Seeley claimed that Marquard had abandoned her two years earlier.

Neither Ebbets nor major-league officials blocked Marquard's World Series share, but John Bruce, the secretary of the National Commission, entrusted with distributing World Series checks to the players on both teams, was served with an order garnishing his check because of outstanding legal fees that he owed to the lawyers who represented him in his divorce. Marquard fought the charges and lost. The divorce decree dissolving Marquard and Seeley's marriage was entered in 1921.

The league did not suspend Marquard or take any other action against him for his scalping infraction, but in December, two months after the court hearing, Charlie Ebbets, true to his word, traded Rube to the Cincinnati Reds. The Dodgers received pitcher Dutch Ruether in return.

Despite all the drama in which Marquard had been embroiled over the previous year, he was one of the Reds' best starters in 1921, winning 17 games. But, at the start of spring training in 1922, the Reds shipped him to the Boston Braves, where he spent his final four major-league seasons. He had losing records in all four years; his 2–8, 5.75 ERA performance in 1925 marked the end of his major-league career. Still, at the time of his retirement, he ranked number three among left-handers in strikeouts, trailing only his namesake Rube Waddell and Eddie Plank, another outstanding Athletics pitcher.

In 1971, almost half a century after he threw his last pitch, Marquard was inducted into the Baseball Hall of Fame by the Veterans Committee. Many questioned the selection, noting that his 201–177 record and 3.08 ERA were good but did not qualify him for induction into the Hall. Statistician Bill James bluntly characterizes Marquard as "probably the worst starting pitcher in the Hall of Fame."

Shoeless Joe Jackson's involvement in the Black Sox scandal and Pete Rose's betting on baseball games in the 1980s kept them out of the Hall of Fame. Marquard's scalping debacle did not bar him from Cooperstown and may not have tarnished his reputation much in the long run, but it sure created plenty of controversy in the fall of 1920.

Rube Marquard was a three-time 20-game winner and won more than 200 games in the majors during a Hall of Fame career, but his actions before Game 4 of the 1920 World Series led to his arrest by the police. *National Baseball Hall of Fame and Museum*

12

Subway Ride to Greatness

In the long and storied history of the World Series, only one pitcher has thrown a complete game victory in which he struck out at least 10 batters, issued no walks, and allowed no earned runs. It was not Walter Johnson, Pete Alexander, or Lefty Grove. It was not Whitey Ford, Bob Gibson, or Sandy Koufax either. Curt Schilling, Greg Maddux, and Madison Bumgarner also didn't do it. The only pitcher to accomplish this impressive feat was the quick-working lefty with the fluid motion, Cliff Lee, in the 2009 World Series. Considering the sad state of Lee's career just two years earlier, it's remarkable that he was even pitching in the majors, let alone starting the opening game of a World Series.

Lee was drafted by the Washington Nationals' predecessor, the Montreal Expos, in 2000. He pitched in their minor-league system until June 2002, when he was traded to the Cleveland Indians in a six-player deal that included pitcher Bartolo Colon. Lee pitched for Akron and Buffalo in the Indians' minor-league system before getting called up to the majors in September and making two starts. Lee spent much of 2003 in the minors but made nine starts for Cleveland, all but one in the second half of the season. He showed promise in his major-league outings those two seasons, posting a 3.30 ERA.

In 2004, he earned a spot in the Indians' starting rotation and sprinted out to a 10–1 start. But then he was lit up in three straight games and showed his frustration when he was pulled in the fifth inning of the third one. While walking off the mound after allowing eight hits and six runs against the Toronto Blue Jays, Lee heaved his glove twenty rows deep into the stands. Fans often take foul balls home as souvenirs; some lucky Blue Jays fan corralled Cliff Lee's glove that day. Lee continued floundering for the rest of the season, finishing with a 14–8 record and a 5.43 ERA.

Lee bounced back big in 2005, winning 18 games against only five losses. He was aided by strong run support as his ERA was a modest 3.79. But he was inconsistent the following year, going 14–11 with a 4.40 ERA.

His 2007 season got off to a bad start. In spring training he suffered an abdominal strain that landed him on the disabled list for the first month of the regular season. By early July, he was 5–4, but then things got worse. After getting hit hard by the Chicago White Sox, allowing seven runs in 5⅓ innings, he was roughed up by the Texas Rangers for five runs in the first inning. In the bottom of the third, he hit Sammy Sosa in the head with a pitch. Sosa, who was playing his final season in the majors, lay on the ground for several minutes before stumbling to the dugout with the assistance of a trainer. Catcher Victor Martinez went to the mound and gave Lee an earful for not coming to the plate to check how Sosa was doing. Lee got pulled in the seventh inning, having surrendered seven runs.

In his next start against the Boston Red Sox in Cleveland, Lee allowed four runs through the first four innings. When the first five Boston batters reached base in the top of the fifth, Indians manager Eric Wedge went to the mound to make a pitching change. Lee heard a chorus of boos when he walked from the mound to the dugout and responded by sarcastically tipping his hat. Following the game, Lee was sent down to the minors. After a start each in Single A and Double A and eight starts in Triple A, Lee was called back up to the Indians, and he made four relief appearances in September. His final numbers for the Indians in the 2007 season were brutal—a 5–8 record and a 6.29 ERA. He allowed a home run every 5½ innings.

Meanwhile, the Indians as a team had a banner season—they won 96 games to capture the American League Central Division. CC Sabathia led the way, going 19–7 and winning the Cy Young Award. Lee had such a dismal season that Wedge did not include him on the postseason roster. With Lee on the sidelines, the Indians came within a hair of making it to the World Series, beating the New York Yankees in the Division Series and blowing a 3–1 lead to the Red Sox in the League Championship Series, losing in seven games.

Lee had a lot to ponder in the offseason. He was twenty-nine years old, he had been in the majors for six years, and his career was going backward, not forward. The Indians considered trading him that winter, but general manager Mark Shapiro held off, still not ready to give up on him. In January, Carl Willis, who had been Lee's pitching coach for the Indians since 2003, invited the lefty to his home in rural North Carolina. Lee was a country boy himself, having grown up in Benton, Arkansas, outside of Little Rock. The two had a good rapport, and, on a warm afternoon, they went to the local high-school field to throw the ball around and talk baseball. Willis made no drastic suggestions—he just stressed to Lee that he still had what it took to become a top major-league pitcher.

At spring training of 2008 in Winter Haven, Florida, Lee battled for the fifth spot in the Indians' rotation, competing against two young lefties, Jeremy Sowers and Aaron Laffey. While Lee was not dazzling in his spring training outings, he was good enough to beat out Sowers and Laffey. Lee followed Sabathia, Roberto Hernandez, Jake Westbrook, and Paul Byrd in the rotation. In his first start of the season against the A's, Lee was sharp, allowing four hits and no earned runs in 6⅔ innings and picking up the win. He kept throwing blanks—through his first seven starts, he was 6–0 with an 0.67 ERA, which included a streak of 28 innings without allowing a run. His control, sometimes shaky in prior seasons, was impeccable. He walked a batter every other start and painted the corners with a variety of pitches—a fastball, a curve, a change-up, and a new pitch that he had added to his repertoire, a cutter. Kelly Shoppach had spent most of his career as a backup catcher, but, that season, he started to catch Lee's games and the pair developed excellent chemistry. Lee's 12–2 record and 2.31 ERA through the first half earned him his first berth on the American League All-Star team and the honor of starting the game. He threw two scoreless innings, striking out three National League hitters.

Lee was equally dominant in the second half and finished the season 22–3 with a 2.54 ERA. He won the Cy Young Award going away, earning 24 out of 28 first-place votes. Despite Lee's outstanding season, the Indians staggered home with an 81–81 record. They effectively threw in the towel when they traded Sabathia, who was in the last year of his contract and eligible to become a free agent after the season, to the Milwaukee Brewers on July 7 for four players.

With Sabathia gone, Lee, coming off his brilliant 2008 season, was the undisputed ace of the staff heading into the 2009 season. But he wasn't as dominant—hurt by a lack of run support, he had a 7–9 record and a 3.14 ERA early in the second half of the season. But then, on July 29, right before the trade deadline, Lee received the surprising news that the Indians had traded him and outfielder Ben Francisco to the Philadelphia Phillies for four players, including Carlos Carrasco. The trade gave Lee the opportunity to pitch in the postseason for the first time. At the time, the Indians were going nowhere, mired in fourth place, 17 games under .500 and 11 games out of first place. The Phillies, however, who boasted one of the best infields in the majors, with first baseman Ryan Howard, second baseman Chase Utley, and shortstop Jimmy Rollins, were the defending world champions, having triumphed over the Tampa Bay Rays in the 2008 World Series. At the time of the trade, they were in first place in the National League Eastern Division, up by seven games. Charlie Manuel, white-haired and chubby with a West Virginia drawl, managed the Phillies. Years earlier, he had spent two-and-a-half seasons as manager of the Indians but was fired halfway through the 2002 season, two months before Lee made his major-league debut for Cleveland. Manuel's easygoing and folksy manner endeared him to the Phillies' players and fans.

For the Phillies in 2008, two left-handed pitchers, separated in age by more than twenty years, spearheaded the rotation. Jamie Moyer, forty-five years old and in his twenty-second major-league season, led the staff with 16 wins. Twenty-four-year-old Cole Hamels, a toddler when Moyer broke into the majors, won 14 games during the regular season and then was the star of the postseason, winning the MVP of the National League Championship Series and World Series. Intense, hard-throwing right-hander Brad Lidge was "lights out" as the Phillies' closer, 41-for-41 in save opportunities during the season and 7-for-7 in October.

But Moyer, Hamels, and Lidge struggled in the first half of the 2009 season, and the Phillies brass looked to bolster their pitching staff. Two weeks before the Phils acquired Lee in the trade, the team signed three-time Cy Young Award winner Pedro Martinez as a free agent on July 15. Pedro had not pitched at any level since he'd completed a four-year stint with the New York Mets the previous season. He was coming off his worst year, 5–6 and a 5.61 ERA, but the Phillies were willing to gamble that the thirty-seven-year-old still had some gas left in the tank. Pedro needed a few tune-up starts in the minors before he was ready to pitch in the majors and started his first game for the Phillies in mid-August.

Lee, however, was raring to go, and he took the mound for the Phillies in a game in San Francisco against the Giants on July 31, two days after the trade. He threw a complete game win, allowing only one run. Over his first five starts with his new team, Lee regained his 2008 form, winning all five and permitting just three earned runs in 40 innings. He did not fare as well the rest of the season, losing four of his last seven starts, but the Phillies won the division, and Manuel named him as his Game 1 starter against the Colorado Rockies in the best-of-five Division Series. The Rockies, led by first baseman Todd Helton and shortstop Troy Tulowitski, ranked second in the National League behind the Phillies in runs scored.

At Citizens Bank Park, with the raucous Phillies crowd cheering loudly—the fans had quickly embraced Lee—the Phillies won, 5–1. Lee tossed a complete game, losing a shutout with two outs in the ninth inning when the Rockies scored a run. Lee pitched well in his next start, in Game 4, allowing one earned run in 7⅓ innings. The Phils won the game—and the Series—coming from behind by scoring three runs in the top of the ninth inning to prevail, 5–4.

Lee was brilliant in Game 3 of the League Championship Series against the Los Angeles Dodgers, another strong-hitting team who finished fourth in the National League in runs scored. Lee threw eight shutout innings, striking out 10 batters, as Philadelphia routed the Dodgers, 11–0. Lee and catcher Carlos Ruiz, a very good defensive backstop, were completely in sync. The Phillies, on a roll, took out Joe Torre's Dodgers in five games to advance to the World Series to square off against the team that Torre managed for twelve years, the New York Yankees.

The Yankees, led by Torre's replacement, Joe Girardi, were a formidable opponent. They led the majors with 103 wins, 10 more than the Phillies. Their offense was particularly potent—they led the majors in runs scored and home runs, and they finished second in batting average. Seven Yankees hit 20 or more home runs. Mark Teixeira tied for the American League lead with 39 long balls, while Alex Rodriguez hit 30. The Yankees' keystone combination, Derek Jeter and Robinson Cano, hit .334 and .320 to finish third and sixth, respectively, in the American League. The Yankees swept the Minnesota Twins in the Division Series and beat the Los Angeles Angels of Anaheim in a six-game League Championship Series.

Game 1 of the World Series featured two former Cy Young Award winners. Manuel started the red-hot Cliff Lee, while Girardi named Lee's friend and former teammate CC Sabathia, who had signed a seven-year, free-agent contract with the Yankees before the season. Sabathia won 19 games during the season and three more in the playoffs against the Twins and Angels. At 6'6", 300 pounds, Sabathia towered over the 6'3", 205-pound Lee.

Because the American League won the All-Star Game in July, the Yankees had home-field advantage, and the Series started in New York, at the "new" Yankee Stadium, which opened its doors that season. It was a chilly, overcast late October day in New York. The Phillies team and staff stayed at the Parker Meridien Hotel in midtown Manhattan, on 56th Street near 6th Avenue. The game was slated to begin at 8 p.m., and, at about 3:30 in the afternoon, a police-escorted bus transported the players, coaches, trainers, and manager from the hotel to Yankee Stadium in the Bronx, ten miles away. With lights and traffic, the trip took about a half hour, and the bus arrived at about 4 p.m.

It was not mandatory for players to take the team bus; they were allowed to go to the ballpark on their own. Lee chose to forego the bus and, after lingering at the hotel for a while, hailed one of New York's many yellow taxi cabs. Lee got in the cab outside the hotel a little before 5 p.m., right in the heart of rush-hour traffic in New York City. The cab made its way north to the Bronx, and, after traveling about a third of the way, became stuck in a massive traffic jam. For twenty minutes, the cab did not move. The cabbie, along with drivers of other gridlocked vehicles, honked his horn in frustration. The cabbie, who was in communication with his dispatcher, told Lee it might take two hours to reach the stadium.

In the backseat, Lee grew worried. It was 5:45 p.m. If the cabdriver's forecast were right, Lee would arrive at Yankee Stadium just a few minutes before the first pitch. By the time he made it to the Phillies locker room, dressed, and went to the field, the game would be getting under way. There would be no time to warm up. Worse yet, if the cab ride took longer than two hours, he would be late for the game. Lee thought to himself: *I'm scheduled to pitch in my first World Series game, Game 1 at Yankee Stadium, and I am going to be scratched because I got stuck in traffic. It will be humiliating.*

Lee pulled out his cell phone and called his agent, Darek Braunecker, in Little Rock, Arkansas, and explained his dilemma. Braunecker suggested that Lee try to find a police officer, tell him who he is, and ask that the officer drive him to Yankee Stadium. Lee considered that suggestion but instead called Frank Coppenbarger, the Phillies' longtime, highly respected director of travel and clubhouse services. Coppenbarger had proved his trustworthiness when the Phillies beat the Rays to become world champions the previous October by going to extraordinary lengths to protect the World Series trophy. After the presentation of the trophy, team president David Montgomery locked it up in the trainer's closet. The next night, the team had a party in a tent right outside Citizens Bank Park. Jamie Moyer, the esteemed elder statesman on the team, carried the trophy from the trainer's closet to the party. A parade celebrating the team's World Series victory was scheduled to be held in Philadelphia the next day; about a million rabid fans would attend. The trophy would be proudly displayed by players riding in cars on Broad Street in Center City, Philadelphia. Montgomery entrusted Coppenbarger with the important responsibility of holding onto the trophy overnight and bringing it to the parade. Coppenbarger, flattered but nervous, wrapped a belt around the trophy to keep it secure in the front seat of his car and drove it over the Walt Whitman Bridge to his house in New Jersey. The next morning, Coppenbarger, his wife, and his two teenage kids ate breakfast at the kitchen table, gazing admiringly at the beautiful trophy.

Coppenbarger had taken a bus from the hotel to Yankee Stadium with the team brass—owners, executives, and their families. He was on the field, which was swamped with reporters, when his cell phone rang. When he heard Lee's voice on the other end of the call, Coppenbarger assumed the pitcher was in the trainer's room getting pregame treatment. He expected that Lee wanted him to leave tickets at the will-call window for family members. Instead he heard the following:

"I'm in a taxi and haven't moved for twenty minutes."

Coppenbarger was dumbfounded. "You're kidding."

"No," Lee replied. "I'm serious."

They discussed the predicament, and Lee, worried that an emergency pitcher might have to replace him as starter, told Coppenbarger, "You might want to let Charlie know."

Coppenbarger gave Lee the same advice Braunecker had: find a cop and ask if he will bring you to the stadium. Then he hung up. Lee looked around but saw no police cars and no police officers patrolling on foot.

At the same time, Coppenbarger was deciding what to do on his end and whether he should alert Charlie Manuel about the phone call. Coppenbarger glanced at his watch—it was almost 6 p.m., two hours until game time. Manuel was surrounded by reporters, and it was not going to be easy to get his attention. But he found the pitching coach, Rich Dubee, and told him about Lee's call. "This is what you get paid for," Coppenbarger added jokingly. Dubee recalled in a recent conversation that he ran through the possibilities in his mind if Lee didn't make it to the ballpark on time. Dubee also confirmed that he did not alert Manuel about Lee's absence. Maybe Pedro Martinez, scheduled to start Game 2, or Brett Myers, who pitched as both a starter and a reliever, could fill in.

After his futile search for a police officer, Lee was struck by an idea. During his years in the American League, when the Indians were in town to play the Yankees, Lee would occasionally take the New York subway from the team hotel to Yankee Stadium, and he knew how to navigate the subway system. He wondered whether the subway might be his best option. The cab had begun to creep forward, and Lee asked the driver to take him to the closest subway station. The driver took some turns and, within five minutes, reached an intersection with a subway sign. Lee paid the fare, jumped out, bounded down the steps leading to the subway, paid his fare, and boarded a train. He got off at 138th Street and hopped on the 4 train to Yankee Stadium. Lee, dressed in jeans, a flannel shirt, and a leather jacket, rode the subway with hordes of Yankees fans wearing the team's hats, jerseys, and jackets, yet he went unrecognized. If anybody spotted the pitcher, they didn't let on.

Lee alighted at the 161st Street-Yankee Stadium stop. When he had taken the subway to the old Yankee Stadium before, he knew the location of the visiting team's entrance. The new stadium was next door, but Lee didn't know where the visiting team's entrance was and couldn't locate it after circling the stadium on foot. It was now about 6:45 p.m., and Lee couldn't waste any more time. He called Coppenbarger again. "I'm here," said Lee, "but I don't know how to get in." Coppenbarger told Lee to find the McDonald's a block from the stadium and wait outside—somebody would come and get him. Coppenbarger quickly called the Yankees clubhouse and explained the situation. One of the clubhouse attendants walked over to the McDonald's, found Lee, and escorted him to the visiting team's entrance.

Lee hurried to the Phillies clubhouse. "Where have you been?" a couple of his teammates asked.

"It's a long story," Lee said. He put on his uniform, cleats, and hat and headed to the Phillies bullpen to warm up.

If Lee's escapade in making it to the ballpark caused him any anxiety, he didn't show it when he took the mound. He got in a groove quickly with Carlos Ruiz, striking out Jeter and Teixeira in the bottom of the first, followed by Rodriguez and Hideki Matsui in the second. Chase Utley hit a solo homer off Sabathia in the top of the third to give the Phillies a 1–0 lead. Lee kept dealing, whiffing Teixeira, Rodriguez, and Jorge Posada in succession in the fourth.

Lee benefited from some nice defense in the fifth. After Matsui led off the frame with a single to center, Robinson Cano hit a line drive that Jimmy Rollins snared at shortstop and then fired to first to double up Matsui.

Utley hit his second bases-empty home run of the game off Sabathia in the sixth to make it 2–0. In the bottom of the sixth, Johnny Damon hit a pop-up toward the mound. Pitchers usually step aside and let their infielders catch pops, but Lee nonchalantly stretched out his glove and made the grab.

Sabathia gave way to Phil Hughes in the eighth, and Raul Ibanez extended Philadelphia's lead to 4–0 with a two-run single off David Robertson, the Yankees' third pitcher of the inning. Cano led off the bottom of the eighth by hitting a ground ball that looked off the bat like it might be headed up the middle. But Lee snagged the ball with a slick behind-the-back move with his glove and threw Cano out at first.

The way Lee was pitching—and fielding—the Phillies didn't seem to need any more runs, but they added two in the top of the ninth on RBI hits by Shane Victorino and Ryan Howard.

With Lee's pitch count at 106, Manuel sent him back out for the ninth, hoping his ace could nail down the shutout. For the first time in the game, Lee allowed two Yankee batters to reach base in the same inning. Jeter and Damon led off with back-to-back singles, Teixeira then hit a ground ball to Utley, who threw to second to force Damon, but Rollins threw the ball away trying to double up Teixeira. Jeter crossed the plate for an unearned run. Lee, unfazed, struck out Rodriguez for the third time and Posada for the second time to end the game.

It was a masterpiece by Cliff Lee of historical significance. In the first World Series game ever played, in 1903, Deacon Phillippe of the Pittsburgh Pirates threw a complete game, beating the Boston Americans. He walked no batters and struck out 10. In the 106 years since, no pitcher in the World Series had ever thrown a complete game win in which he issued no walks and struck out 10 batters—until Lee. Lee set himself apart by not giving up any earned runs, while Phillippe had allowed two. The National Baseball Hall of Fame Museum deemed Lee's accomplishment so noteworthy that they asked for the cap he wore that night. Lee complied with the request, and his cap was sent to Cooperstown.

Years later, Mark Teixeira, who hit more than 400 home runs in his stellar fourteen-year major-league career, was surprised to learn for the first time about Lee's misadventures on his way to Yankee Stadium that night. This story only heightened Teixeira's praise for Lee's achievement in Game 1. "It was one of the best pitching performances I ever saw," he gushed. "Cliff had pinpoint control, and he was hard to hit because he hid the ball so well; you couldn't pick up his pitches until they were halfway to the plate."

Lee joined some other select company with his performance in Game 1. In all four of his postseason starts—two against the Rockies, one against the Dodgers, and one against the Yankees—he had pitched at least seven innings and given up no more than one earned run. Before Lee, only the early twentieth-century great Christy Mathewson pitched seven or more innings and surrendered one or fewer earned runs in each of his first four postseason starts.

Lee's effort in Game 1 was one of the few highlights for the Phillies in the World Series. The Yankees won four of the next five games to win the Series. Lee won Game 5 in Philadelphia, though he allowed five runs in seven innings. Matsui won Series MVP honors by hitting .615 with three home runs, including one off Pedro Martinez in the decisive Game 6, and eight RBIs. It was Martinez's last major-league game. Jeter also hit .407 in the Series, and A-Rod drove in six runs. Mariano Rivera saved two of the Yankees' four wins and closed out the finale with 1⅔ innings of shutout ball.

Despite Lee's postseason heroics, the Phillies traded him in the offseason to the Seattle Mariners for three minor leaguers. Lee was dispensable because the Phillies acquired perennial All-Star Roy Halladay in a trade from the Blue Jays the same day.

The Mariners ended up trading Lee to the Rangers halfway through the 2010 season. The Rangers won the American League Western Division, and, for the second straight year, Lee shone in the playoffs. He was 3–0 with a 0.75 ERA against the Rays and Yankees to help the Rangers advance to their first World Series in thirty-nine years and face the San Francisco Giants. But all did not end well for Lee in the 2010 postseason—the Giants torched him in both of his World Series starts.

Lee was a free agent after the season, and Phillies fans were delighted when the team signed him to a five-year contract in December. The Phils didn't make it back to the World Series during Lee's second stint with the club, but he teamed up with Halladay, Cole Hamels, and Roy Oswalt to form a superb starting rotation in 2011. The Phils won a team record 102 games that season, but they lost to the St. Louis Cardinals in the Division Series. Lee was an All-Star in 2011 as well as in 2013, but an elbow injury ended his career in 2014. He was offered surgery but chose rest and rehab instead. Unfortunately, that didn't work, and he announced his retirement in 2016.

Cliff Lee hit rock bottom in 2007. But, with determination and resilience, he bounced back to become one of the elite pitchers in baseball for a few years. His gem in the opening game of the 2009 World Series—after a circuitous trip to the ballpark—may have been the pinnacle.

Carlos Ruiz congratulates Cliff Lee on his complete-game masterpiece in Game 1 of the 2009 World Series. Earlier that day, Lee's taxi to Yankee Stadium got stuck in a traffic jam, causing concern that he might be late for his start. *AP Photo/Elise Amendola*

13

The War, the Flu, and the Babe

BY THE TIME THE 1918 WORLD SERIES WAS PLAYED, THE MODERN game was not yet even twenty years old. The era of the "live ball" was still a ways off, and baseball had already lost one World Series to a boycott, endured a threat from the upstart Federal League, and now saw play threatened by the advent of World War I and the Spanish flu pandemic. Maybe it was fitting, then, that the two most cursed franchises of the first hundred years of the modern game, the Boston Red Sox and the Chicago Cubs, would square off against each other after a shortened regular season in the only World Series ever to be played in its entirety during September.

Though the war began in September 1914, the United States didn't enter the fighting until April 1917, and the baseball season was largely unaffected. The full season of 154 games was played with rosters largely intact and with the majors showing support for the soldiers by staging marching drills for the fans, using bats instead of guns, in a show of unity for the war effort. By 1918, however, attitudes were changing and the public would no longer see these demonstrations as sufficient.

Backed by shifting public sentiment, the government issued a "work or fight" decree a month into the 1918 season. Announced by Provost Marshal General Enoch Crowder, the new mandate went into effect on July 1 and required that all draft-eligible men engaged in "nonessential" occupations apply for work directly related to the war or risk being drafted.

Secretary of War Newton Baker originally declared baseball players (along with entertainers) to be exempt. But in July he reversed himself, declaring baseball to be a nonessential business. The baseball owners petitioned Baker to at least let the season be completed, and, in a compromise, Baker agreed, providing that the season ended by Labor Day. After some additional back and forth with Baker, it was further agreed that the World Series could also be played, though with some minor travel restrictions. It would be the only World Series to be played during summer.

Despite the concessions by the government, major-league rosters had already been depleted, and the pennant races were greatly affected. In the National League, the defending league champion New York Giants lost three starting pitchers to the draft, and, though they started the season with an 18–1 record, they quickly sank to second place.

In the American League, the defending World Series champs and 1918 favorites, the Chicago White Sox, lost Joe Jackson, Eddie Collins, Lefty Williams, Red Faber, and Happy Felsch to the military, and they never challenged, falling rapidly to the second division. Jackson, Williams, and Felsch would later figure prominently in the Black Sox Scandal of 1919.

Though recordkeeping at the time was not great, it is estimated that as many as 38 percent of active players entered the service—mostly in 1918—and, depending on the account, anywhere from zero to eight players were killed in the war. In the background, the terrifying Spanish flu continued its advance.

The pandemic would ultimately claim an estimated 50 million victims globally, with an estimated 675,000 succumbing in the United States. The flu spread rapidly in the United States and was a threat to the 1918 season. Across the nation, people were asked to wear masks in public, avoid crowds, and go right home if they felt ill. The death rate was especially high even among healthy fifteen- to thirty-four-year-olds. There was no radio, television, or social media to help spread messages about health precautions. Messages that did get out were inconsistent and sometimes limited to the suggestion that handkerchiefs be carried in the event of sneezing or coughing.

Spring-training games continued to be played despite the virus. Some players wore masks, as did umpires and coaches. There was no players union to lobby for safer working conditions or protocols to protect the players or the public, and the owners, fearing a loss of revenue, plowed ahead with the season. Even in the aftermath of the pandemic, the major leagues faced little criticism for playing the season, perhaps because no active players died from the flu and because the virus had largely disappeared, at least in the Northeast, before the 1919 season started.

Attendance had already been slipping in 1917, largely in response to America's entrance into the war. In 1917, attendance was 5.2 million, down by 20 percent from 6.5 million in 1916. In 1918, attendance would reach just over 3 million, a significant drop, even when accounting for 20 percent fewer games being played in 1918. With no end to the pandemic in sight after the 1918 Series, baseball also faced the possibility of an indefinite work stoppage because of the war.

Some teams, such as the Red Sox and the Cubs, had begun to stockpile pitchers as a hedge against the draft and were rewarded for their forward thinking. The Red Sox had been the dominant American League team since the beginning of the new century, winning the World Series in 1903, 1912, 1915, and 1916, ceding dominance only to Ty Cobb's Detroit Tigers and then Connie Mack's Philadelphia Athletics before Mack dismantled one of his memorable American League championship teams, scattering several great players to the winds.

The Sox also found themselves in the peculiar situation of needing a new manager for the 1918 season when their player-manager Jack Barry (a member of Connie Mack's famed $100,000 infield) and star outfielder Duffy Lewis were drafted. Their owner, Harry Frazee, desperate to replace Barry, reached out to Ed Barrow to take over managerial duties. Barrow, though, hadn't managed in the majors for fifteen years. After a brief stint managing the Detroit Tigers early in the 1900s, he had returned to the minor leagues, where he'd held a number of positions, including president of the International League, until 1918.

When Barrow accepted Frazee's offer, he became the third manager in three seasons for the Sox. He managed two seasons before moving to the front office, eventually leaving Boston to go to the New York Yankees.

As Yankees manager, he oversaw the wholesale plundering of the Red Sox roster. His actions paved the way for the New York dynasty of the 1920s and launched his second act; he became a baseball executive and remained one for twenty-five years, culminating in his induction into the Hall of Fame.

In 1918, Barrow faced an immediate challenge. With the loss of the Sox' best hitter, Duffy Lewis, to the draft, Barrow had a big hole to fill in left field. Right fielder Harry Hooper suggested to Barrow that they play the twenty-three-year-old left-handed pitcher Babe Ruth in left field on the days when Ruth wasn't pitching. This was not some grand strategy or clever plan that had been thought about at great length but one apparently born of necessity.

Barrow did not follow Hooper's advice immediately and brought in journeyman George Whiteman to play left field. But he did come to rely on Hooper extensively during the season, and Hooper often advised on player positioning, pitching changes, and overall in-game strategy. Early in the season, Ruth played some at first base, but when Barrow eventually moved Stuffy McInnis back from third to his natural position at first, Ruth's days in the infield were limited. Ruth was not ascendant yet as a hitter, but Barrow slotted him into the starting lineup in 72 games when he wasn't the starting pitcher, mostly as an outfielder, and was rewarded when Ruth tied for the league lead in homers with 11 (collecting them all before the 4th of July) and far outpacing any other hitter, with a .555 slugging percentage. He also was sixth in the league in RBIs, with 61.

It's unclear whether Ruth actually contracted the Spanish flu, but he was definitely ill on May 19 when he went on a picnic with his wife. By that night he was in bed with a 104-degree fever. The situation was made worse by an early misdiagnosis of tonsillitis, which landed him in the hospital for a week or so. In early June, he was back, and Barrow began easing him into the lineup. But, when his turn in the rotation came up, Ruth balked, claiming that the stress of pitching and playing the field was too much for him to handle. He explained that he viewed himself as an everyday player now and that his pitching days were over.

Barrow relented and called on Sam Jones to fill in for Ruth. Jones did so admirably, but Barrow's peace of mind was short-lived. In mid-June, Dutch Leonard abruptly left the team to take a wartime job. Leonard had been pitching well, tossing three shutouts in a span of four starts, including a no-hitter. With Leonard now gone and his back against the wall, Barrow turned to Ruth and asked him to help for the good of the team. Ruth agreed, and in early July, after a month-long pitching hiatus, he was back on the mound. There was no doubt that one day Ruth's domination as a hitter would force a decision by the Red Sox, but Boston fans didn't realize that, for them, the decision wouldn't be between using him as a pitcher and using him as a hitter but between keeping him and selling him.

Ruth still shouldered his share of the pitching load, making 19 starts, completing 18 of them, and winning 13, with an ERA of 2.22. But it was "Bullet" Joe Bush and Carl Mays, along with Sam Jones, who led the rotation. Mays completed 30 games in 33 starts, going 21–13, with an ERA of 2.21 and a league-leading eight shutouts. Bush and catcher Wally Schang had been acquired from the A's in the offseason as part of Connie Mack's salary dump, and, while he went just 15–15, he led the team with a 2.11 ERA, throwing 26 complete games in 31 starts. He would be sidelined in 1919 with a sore arm but would resurrect his career with several more stellar seasons before fading during his final years.

Jones came to Boston from Cleveland in April 1916 in the deal that sent superstar outfielder Tris Speaker to the Indians. He had languished in the bullpen during his first two years with the Sox, making just one start, but was critical to their success in 1918, going 16–5 with a 2.25 ERA once Barrow added him to the regular rotation in June. Their pitching depth would also more than make up for the loss of right-hander Ernie Shore to the military before the season. Shore had been a reliable starter for the Sox since 1914, going a combined 3–1 in the 1915 and the 1916 World Series, but he would never be the same when he returned from service. By the start of the 1922 season, Mays, Bush, Jones, and Ruth would all be playing for the Yankees.

The Red Sox also had some offense. In addition to having Ruth in some of the games between pitching starts, they had Harry Hooper.

Hooper was a good hitter, collecting almost 2,500 lifetime hits, and a good defensive outfielder. He batted .289, second on the team to Ruth's .300 and first among the full-time starters.

The Red Sox also had Stuffy McInnis at first. The slick-fielding McInnis was a borderline Hall of Famer and an excellent hitter with a .307 lifetime average and more than 2,400 hits. Though his average had dipped to .272 in 1918, he was second on the team to Ruth in RBIs and to Hooper among regulars in hitting. His original claim to fame in the early part of the decade was with the Athletics as part of their "$100,000 infield." This infield, which included Jack Barry, was once judged by the statistician Bill James to be the greatest infield ever. The A's had fallen on hard times, however, and Stuffy escaped Connie Mack's most recent salary dump in Philadelphia when he was traded before the 1918 season to Boston, where he would hit over .300 twice in the next four years with the Red Sox.

Like the Red Sox, the Cubs had stocked up on pitching. They already had left-hander Jim "Hippo" Vaughn, who won 23 games in 1917, to go along with Lefty Tyler, who was acquired from the Braves before the beginning of the season. With the Braves, Tyler had proved himself to be a reliable workhorse. Vaughn was a great pitcher who would go on to win the 1918 pitching Triple Crown, leading the league in wins, ERA, and strikeouts. His nickname reflected his size—6'4" and 215 pounds—which was big for his day.

Chicago also had righty Claude Hendrix, who had led the Federal League with 29 wins and an ERA of 1.69 in 1914 before joining the Cubs in 1916. Though the Cubs were not a strong offensive team, with manager Fred Mitchell and with their superb pitching, they cruised to the pennant by 10½ games.

Mitchell was a baseball lifer who had pitched for the Boston Red Sox (then the Boston Americans) in their first game, an exhibition affair in April 1901. A one-time teammate of Cy Young, Mitchell had been signed by the current Sox manager, Ed Barrow, to a minor-league contract as a catcher before retiring to manage the Harvard University baseball team in 1916. He stayed for a year before taking over as the Cubs skipper.

The looming shadow of the left-handed–hitting Ruth as an offensive force would be a major factor in the Cubs pitching strategy. Mitchell decided to alternate his two lefties, Vaughn and Tyler, throughout the Series, basically benching Hendrix. Burt Whitman captured the tension in an article in the *Boston Herald and Journal*:

> The mighty shadow of Babe Ruth falls athwart Chicago tonight like a menace. But for the tremendous figure of the Boston Red Sox pitcher-outfielder and slugger, these parts of the United States would shout from the housetops the boast that Fred Mitchell's Cubs will smear the Boston hose in the world series which starts tomorrow afternoon at Comiskey's South Side Park.
>
> Never did one man count so heavily in the before-the-game pressure of a world series. A bigger, more important part he fills than did [Grover Cleveland] Alexander in 1915, [Rube] Marquard in '16, Eddie Collins in '17. Take him out of the way and the Cubs would be superior and would have enough confidence to do harsh things to the men from Massachusetts. But there he is, a huge, human, horrifying prospect for Mitchell and his men, absolutely unruffled and calm.

The Cubs, however, would play the Fall Classic without their greatest offseason acquisition and future Hall of Famer. Grover Cleveland "Pete" Alexander along with a number of other players had been traded to the Cubs after the 1917 season by the Phillies owner William Baker, who needed the money to meet expenses, and the Cubs were getting a star. In his first seven years in the National League, Alexander had already piled up 190 wins on his way to winning 373 games in his career. But, near the beginning of the 1918 season, Alexander was notified that he would be shipping out to Europe into combat in France in the next couple of months. After starting out with a 2–1 record and getting married, he departed for the war in early June. While serving as a sergeant in the 342nd field artillery, he was almost hit by an exploding shell on the front lines, and, when he returned, he was never the same person or pitcher. Already in a battle with alcohol, after the explosion, he was left struggling with hearing loss, seizures, and what we today would call post-traumatic stress syndrome.

Though he would have his iconic World Series moment eight years later at the age of thirty-nine as a member of the 1926 Cardinals, Alexander had earlier enjoyed postseason glory after winning Game 1 of the 1915 Series for the Phillies against the Red Sox—the last World Series game the Phils would win for sixty-five years! He pitched until he was forty-three, and, despite his physical struggles, won another 181 games once he returned from the war. One day he would be portrayed by future president Ronald Reagan in the movie *The Winning Team*.

The favored Cubs had easily won the pennant but had decided to rely on just the two lefty starters for the Series. It is inconceivable that Alexander would not have been in the rotation had he been available to pitch. After all, he was just coming off an incredible stretch during which he had won the National League Triple Crown of pitching for three consecutive years. We'll never know how much difference it would have made to have had Alexander pitching, since offense was the Cubs' biggest problem during the Series, but it's hard to imagine that the Cubs would not have been better off had he been there.

Though not one player on the Cubs roster remained from the team's last championship team in 1908, there was one link to that season for which Cubs fans would be grateful. In 1918, Fred Merkle was a twenty-nine-year-old first baseman who had been purchased from Brooklyn in April 1917. He led the Cubbies in RBIs and was second on the team in batting, with a .297 average during the shortened season.

In 1908, Merkle was a fresh-faced youngster playing for John McGraw's Giants and, at nineteen, was the youngest player in the league. A part-time player, he had missed nearly two months of the season after enduring two surgeries made necessary by a blood infection that almost caused doctors to amputate his foot. On September 23, with the Giants and Cubs locked in a heated pennant race, Merkle would stamp his name in baseball infamy. He started for only the second time that year against the Cubs at the Polo Grounds in New York with both teams tied atop the National League standings.

With two outs in the bottom of the ninth, the score was tied, 1–1. Moose McCormick was on first as a result of a fielder's choice, and Fred was due up. Merkle lined a single to right, sending McCormick to third with the potential winning run. When shortstop Al Bridwell singled to center to bring in McCormick, pandemonium ensued at the Polo Grounds. The delirious fans stormed the field, and Merkle, fearing that he would get trampled by the mob, cut away toward the Giants clubhouse in center field before touching second base. Cubs second baseman Johnny Evers saw what Merkle had done and began calling frantically for the ball.

Accounts begin to vary at this point, but Evers eventually retrieved a ball and stepped on second base in front of the home-plate umpire Hank O'Day, who called Merkle out on a force play. Merkle later claimed that he had returned to second when he saw what Evers was up to and left the bag only when Christy Mathewson came to get him off the field. Some players reported seeing Giants pitcher Joe McGinnity grab the ball before Evers could get it from center fielder Solly Hofman and heave it into the crowd, leaving open to debate whether Evers ever retrieved the actual ball that Bridwell hit. The play became known as Merkle's "boner" play.

With the fans still mobbing the field and the late-afternoon light fading, O'Day determined that the game would be declared a tie. His decision was held up on appeal. If the two teams ended up tied at the end of the season, the game would be replayed, with the winner representing the National League in the Series, and that's just what happened. On October 8, the Cubs beat the Giants, 4–2, before forty thousand fans at the Polo Grounds, with thousands more trying to get in. The win advanced the Cubs to the World Series, where they beat the Detroit Tigers for their last championship of the twentieth century.

The Series would start right after Labor Day. But, because of travel restrictions, it was decided that there would be only one road trip during the Series and that, by virtue of a coin flip, the first three games would be played in Chicago and the remaining games, including Games 5, 6, and 7, if needed, would be played in Boston. The Cubs would host the first three games at Comiskey Park rather than their home field, Weeghman Park (later renamed Wrigley Field), because Comiskey had greater seating capacity. The Sox would play their home World Series games at Fenway Park for the first time since 1912. Though they had been in the Series in

1915 and 1916, they had played their home games during those Series at the more spacious Braves Field.

Game 1 on September 5 would be a classic pitching duel between the two great lefties Vaughn and Ruth. Ruth had been relegated to the bench (except for one pinch-hitting appearance) for the 1915 Series because of the Phillies' reputation for murdering lefties. But, in the '16 Series, he'd pitched a 14-inning complete game gem in Game 2, giving up one run in the first, then pitching 13 scoreless innings (the last six without giving up a hit) in defeating the Brooklyn Robins, 1–0. It would be his last World Series game until the Series with the Cubs. He shut out the Cubs, 1–0, extending his scoreless innings streak to 22 innings and setting the tone for the Series.

Hippo Vaughn was the tough-luck loser in Game 1, giving up just one run on an RBI single to McInnis in the top of the fourth. Vaughn was no stranger to hard luck pitching though. Just the year before, in an early-May game against the Reds, he locked horns with Fred Toney in an epic duel, with both pitchers throwing no-hitters through the ninth inning. The game was decided in the top of the 10th when the Reds' Jim Thorpe (yes, that Jim Thorpe) hit a dribbler for an infield hit, knocking in Larry Kopf, who had broken up Vaughn's no-hitter with one out, for the lone run of the game, with Toney getting the victory in the only "double no-hitter" (through nine innings) in major-league history.

During the seventh-inning stretch of Game 1, the US Navy Band began to play "The Star Spangled Banner." Fred Thomas, the Boston third baseman, on furlough from the navy so that he could play in the Series, stood up and saluted. Soon the other players stood with their hands over their hearts as the crowd also stood and began to sing along. Though the song didn't become America's national anthem until 1931, the tradition of playing "The Star Spangled Banner" at baseball parks all over the country began at that first game of the 1918 World Series.

Game 2 would be much like Game 1. Joe Bush pitched for the Red Sox with Lefty Tyler going for the Cubs. Tyler and Vaughn would alternate games and, between the two of them, start every game for Chicago and pitch 50 of the 52 innings in the Series. The Cubs' strategy was clear—keep Ruth on the bench when he wasn't pitching, and to do so they would feed Boston a steady dose of left-handed pitching. As far as it goes, they accomplished that; after his Game 4 start, Ruth made only a brief appearance as a defensive replacement in Game 6.

Offense would be at a premium throughout the Series, with neither team hitting a home run (one of only three times and the most recent) or scoring more than three runs. Game 2 ended in Chicago's favor, with Tyler winning, 3–1, as both pitchers threw complete games. Tyler was the hitting hero as well, singling in two runs in the bottom of the second for the winning margin.

Game 3 followed the same pattern as the first two games, and Vaughn lost another tough one. This time it was Carl Mays who bested him, 2–1, in the last game played in Chicago. Both pitchers threw complete games, with Vaughn giving up seven hits and just one walk in his second losing effort of the Series.

The most excitement came in the bottom of the ninth when, with the Red Sox clinging to a one-run lead, Charlie Pick (a late-season acquisition who would lead the Cubbies with a .389 average for the Series) singled with two outs and stole second. With the tying run on second, Boston catcher Wally Schang let a Mays pitch get away from him, but Pick, aggressively coming around third, got caught in a rundown between third and home, finally getting tagged out by Schang for the final out of the game. The two Bosox runs would be the last that Vaughn would surrender during the Series. But, after two complete games, he had two losses on his record, despite throwing two great games and giving up only three runs.

Game 4 was slated for Fenway Park on September 9, and though the final score was just 3–2, there was no lack of drama before, during, or after the game. On the train back to Boston from Chicago, Ruth, who was scheduled to start against Lefty Tyler, injured a finger on his throwing hand during what the *Boston Globe's* Edward F. Martin described as "some sugarhouse fun with [Red Sox batting-practice pitcher] W. W. Kinney." Martin added, "All the world should know, Babe said, that it was not the finger that was troubling him, but the stuff that was on it, and the stuff that was on it was putting too much stuff on the ball." Martin had reported that Ruth had missed Kinney with an errant punch that broke a window. In his seminal biography of Ruth, *Babe*, Robert Creamer says it was a steel wall that Ruth hit, and still another story was circulated that a sudden jolt on the train caused Ruth to somehow hurt his hand. Whatever the cause of his injury, with the Series at 2–1 and his consecutive innings streak now at 22 innings, Ruth would pitch Game 4 with a finger injury that was almost certainly self-inflicted.

He pitched well again despite the injury, though he was a little wild, issuing six walks. In the bottom of the fourth, he also reminded the Cubs why they so desperately wanted to keep him sidelined between starts when he whacked a triple to right center, driving in the first two runs of the game. Before the at-bat, Tyler tried to move right fielder Max Flack further back toward the fence, but Flack repeatedly ignored Tyler and then paid the price. Flack had a notably bad game. He was picked off at first base in the top of the first and then off second in the top of the third to become the only player in major-league history to get picked off twice in the same World Series game. Along with his bad judgment on Ruth's triple, his play fed into another ugly narrative that was in the offing: perhaps the fix was in.

Ruth would nurse the two-run lead through the seventh. But, in the eighth, he got into trouble and gave up a couple of runs when he walked Bill Killefer and then gave up a single to Claude Hendrix, a pitcher who was pinch-hitting for Tyler. Ruth then threw a wild pitch sandwiched between two singles, the second one plating Bill McCabe, who came on to run for Hendrix, with the tying run.

In the bottom of the inning, the Sox took a stranglehold on the Series. Pinch-hitter Wally Schang singled and then advanced to second on a passed ball with Harry Hooper at the plate. Hooper then bunted back to Phil Douglas, who had come on in relief of Tyler. Douglas fielded the ball but overthrew first, allowing Schang to score from second with the go-ahead run.

Ruth took the mound for the ninth with a one-run lead but gave up a leadoff single to Fred Merkle before issuing his last walk of the afternoon. With no outs and two on, Joe Bush replaced Ruth in a double switch, with Ruth moving to left field. Chuck Wortman tried to advance the runners with a sacrifice, but first baseman Stuffy McInnis fielded the bunt and threw to third, getting the first out and keeping the potential tying run at second. Bush then induced a double-play grounder by pinch-hitter Turner Barber to wrap up the game and give the Sox a commanding 3–1 lead in the only game in which neither starter threw a complete game.

Ruth's scoreless innings streak had ended at 29⅔ innings and would become the record he cherished above all others. It would last until Yankee Whitey Ford broke it in 1961 against the Reds—the same year that his single-season home-run record of 60 was eclipsed by Yankee Roger Maris. As Ford quipped, 1961 was a tough year for the Babe.

It's worth noting here that, though the Black Sox scandal was still a year away, gambling in baseball was far from unknown or even rare. Sometime after the 1918 Series, claims were made that the Cubs may have thrown the Series or at least may have considered it. But, unlike in 1919, during the lead up to the 1918 Series, there were no real rumors that anything nefarious was afoot. In the 1919 Series, observers who had heard rumors of a fix noticed several plays throughout the Series that supported the notion that the Sox weren't playing the games on the level. In the 1918 Series, however, with the possible exception of Game 4, there was little to suggest that the Cubs had done anything but their best to beat the Red Sox.

Despite the lack of evidence, players on both sides may have had some motivation to fix some games or the Series, because they were unhappy that the owners seemed to be continually evasive when asked what the players' shares would be. For several reasons, however, those numbers did change often. Attendance during the Series wasn't what it had been in previous years, and, as a result, ticket prices had been reduced. In addition, 1918 was to be the first year during which players from all first-division finishers would also get a piece of the winners' and losers' shares. Thus, players would receive decidedly less than they had in previous years, with early estimates of $900 for the winners and $300 for the losers.

Since the Cubs made no secret of the fact that they were going to use two pitchers almost exclusively in the Series, gamblers would have to have had at least one of the Cubs starters in their hip pockets. But there is nothing that would have led anyone to think this was true. Both Tyler and Vaughn pitched exceptionally well, each yielding only three earned runs over six games for a combined ERA of just over 1.00.

Nevertheless, in a 1920 deposition obtained by the Chicago History Museum in 2007, Chicago White Sox pitcher Eddie Cicotte (one of the first players to confess to throwing the 1919 Series) was quoted as saying, "The ball players were talking about somebody trying to fix the National League ball players or something like that in the World Series of 1918. There was talk that somebody offered this player $10,000 or anyway the bunch of players were offered $10,000 to throw this series."

Though Cicotte never named any names or cited specific incidents that would support his claims, the terrible plays by Flack in the field and on the bases in Games 4 and 6 as well as reliever Phil Douglas's overthrow of first base that allowed the winning run to score late in Game 4 certainly stood out. Flack led National League right fielders in fielding percentage in three of the next four years, and intensifying the conspiracy theory was the fact that years later Douglas was banned from baseball for life for offering to let another contending team pay him to "go fishing" for the remainder of the season.

Of more immediate concern to baseball in the wake of Game 4 was the player unrest that was about to surface around the winning and losing shares. With the Series now standing at 3–1, it was possible that Boston could clinch the title with a win in Game 5. The players saw that they had some leverage but that it could quickly disappear. In 1916, winning Red Sox players received almost $4,000 per man, and in 1917 winning players received $3,500, with losing players getting $2,400.

For 1918 it was originally agreed that winning players would get $2,000 and losers $1,500, with the remaining player shares being allocated to the remaining first-division teams. This agreement was based on a formula that would give the players 60 percent of the proceeds for the first four games (less a 10 percent kickback to the National Commission, earmarked for wartime charities), with the balance going to the owners. With Series attendance down from previous years and ticket prices flatlining, players saw their payday slipping away.

Harry Hooper and Dave Shean of the Red Sox and Leslie Mann and Bill Killefer of the Cubs formed a committee to represent the players in an effort to get the owners to reconsider the splits. Talks began between the players' committee and the three-man National Commission about concessions or renegotiations. But the commission would have none of it, claiming that it could face legal repercussions from team owners who had already signed on for the original payout formula. With game time approaching on September 10 and twenty-four thousand fans in the stands, the players were nowhere to be seen. Only the bat boys were on the field. In a 2015 article in the online magazine *VICE*, Jack Moore describes the scene:

> The game was scheduled to start at 2:30 PM. At 2:45, the commissioners and the four players' representatives, accompanied by some sportswriters, met in the umpires' room. Perhaps the players would have had a chance if the country hadn't been at war. The fans in Boston, including some wounded soldiers, had understandably little patience for the delay. The players weren't unsympathetic. Hooper even told the commission that the entire players' share could go to the war charities if they would just restore the previous revenue sharing deal, between two teams instead of eight. The commissioners, their confidence boosted by some pre-gaming at the hotel bar, refused to budge. An "absolutely smashed" Johnson (according to Stout) told the players that they owed it "to the soldiers in the stands."

There would be no real labor union for more than fifty years to negotiate for the players, and they correctly understood that, with a stadium filled with veterans and the public still living in fear of the Spanish flu, striking over money wasn't going to get them any sympathy and it would be a losing public-relations battle. Though that battle was over, with the winners getting only $1,102 per player and the losers getting $671, the owners would eventually restore the "old" formula for the next season, with the winners getting more than $5,200 per player.

When Game 5 was finally played, Hippo Vaughn received some measure of revenge. He gave up only five hits and one walk in spinning a shutout and beating Sam Jones, 3–0, to bring the Cubs to within one game of the Sox and forcing a Game 6 for the following day. The offensive "explosion" for the Cubs came by virtue of a one-run double by Les

Mann in the third and a two-run double by Dode Paskert in the top of the eighth. It was all Vaughn would need in what would be his final Series performance before turning things over to Lefty Tyler for Game 6.

Unfortunately for Tyler, he would get almost no offensive support in Game 6, losing, 2–1, when, in the bottom of the third, Flack committed an error in right on a line drive by George Whiteman, allowing two Red Sox to score with all the runs Carl Mays would need to lock down Boston's fifth World Series championship since 1903. When an outbreak of the flu at Fort Devens, which was about forty miles away, left soldiers confined to their quarters, to help keep up the spirits of the ailing troops, arrangements were made to send carrier pigeons every half inning from Fenway with updates about the game.

Boston wouldn't win another title in the twentieth century, enduring an eighty-six-year drought before finally winning the Series again in 2004. For the Cubs, the wait would be even longer. They had last won in 1908 and wouldn't win again until 2016, an astounding 108-year span. Books written about the Curse of the Bambino and the Curse of the Billy Goat must only have added to the torment of the fans for these two iconic franchises.

The numbers told the story of the 1918 Series. And, if you weren't a fan of great pitching, there were at least enough subplots to capture even the casual fan's interest. The statistics pointed oddly in Chicago's favor, with the Cubs outhitting the Red Sox with a team average of .210 to Boston's .186. The Cubs' team ERA of 1.04 was also better than Boston's 1.70, and the Cubs even outscored the Red Sox, 10–9 over the six games. The difference was that Boston was tougher in the clutch situations. There were four one-run games, and the Sox won every one of them. When Mays or Ruth took the mound, they were every bit the equal of Vaughn and Tyler, who, with Phil Douglas, were betrayed at times, by some shaky defense (including Douglas's own error) that led to three of Boston's nine runs being counted as unearned.

One also wonders why, at some point, Barrow didn't take a chance on playing Ruth in the field on days when he didn't start. Offensively they couldn't have done much worse, and he did have two of their six runs batted in, though he played in just two games with five at-bats. It could be that, with McInnis and his great glove at first and with Whiteman in left (Ruth's "other" field positions) hitting reasonably well at .250, Barrow saw no need to make a move that possibly could have tired Ruth between starts. The fact that the Sox never trailed in the Series may have also swayed Barrow from tinkering with something that was working.

With trench warfare still raging in France, the immediate fate of baseball was undecided, but the game was spared any prolonged indecision when the armistice was signed in November, effectively bringing World War I to an end. In the aftermath of the 1918 season, both franchises took a downturn. The Cubs, even with the return of Alexander, fell to third place before heading for the second division in '20 and '21. By 1922, none of the starting pitchers from the 1918 team remained, and Vaughn was out of the game completely at the young age of thirty-three. The lineup in the field was almost totally different as well. The Cubs wouldn't get back to the Series again until 1929, when they lost to the Philadelphia Athletics in five games.

The Red Sox immediately fell to sixth in the last year of the "dead-ball era," despite the emergence of Ruth as baseball's preeminent slugger, with an astounding 29 home runs (almost three times as many as the league runner-up). The years immediately after 1918 were especially painful to Boston fans as they watched owner Harry Frazee, desperate for cash, unload Ruth and seven of his teammates to the Yankees between 1919 and 1922. The Yankees dynasty that emerged at the beginning of the 1920s was built on the backs of former Red Sox Babe Ruth, Wally Schang, Joe Bush, Everett Scott, Sam Jones, Carl Mays, and future Hall of Fame pitchers Herb Pennock and Waite Hoyt.

Mays had an especially tragic moment of infamy with the Yankees in 1920. When pitching for New York in the Polo Grounds against the Indians in a mid-August game, he hit Cleveland's Ray Chapman in the head. Though he was helped off the field, Chapman died the next morning, becoming the only player killed in a game-related incident in history.

The pandemic never did have much of an effect on the 1918 season, mostly because of the premature ending to the season. No active major leaguers died from the flu, but several minor leaguers and former major leaguers did die that year. The American League lost umpire Silk

O'Loughlin in December when he succumbed to the Spanish flu at his home in Boston.

In Boston, things took a turn for the worse starting in late September. Over the next three months, the number of cases and deaths mounted. Hospitals were overwhelmed with patients as more and more nurses and doctors were infected every day. In Chicago, the big spike came just a week or two after the one in Boston, and by mid-October new cases exceeded 2,400 a day and all kinds of precautions were put into place, though schools remained in session. Fortunately for both cities, the worst would be over by late in the winter of 1919, and, despite the harsh impact of the flu, the 1919 season was never seriously threatened.

Though the Black Sox scandal of 1919 would be a dark endcap to the first two decades of the modern era of baseball, the advent of the "live ball" era and the emerging star power of Babe Ruth along with his arrival in New York helped baseball recover from its greatest scandal. The owners acted quickly to restore order to the national game at least from a public-relations standpoint by eliminating the National Commission and replacing it with an omnipotent commissioner, Kenesaw Mountain Landis, who would remain in office until his death in 1944.

The modern game, though still young in many ways, was changing rapidly, and, as hard as it would have been to believe, it would not be the last time that war and a global pandemic would leave indelible marks on America's pastime.

Hall of Fame outfielder Harry Hooper was instrumental in convincing the Red Sox to convert Babe Ruth from a pitcher to an outfielder in 1918. He also played a key role as a player representative during the 1918 Series when it was learned that the owners were attempting to shortchange the players on their winning and losing shares. *National Baseball Hall of Fame and Museum*

14

The Pitcher Who Went AWOL

MANAGERS GET FRUSTRATED WITH THEIR PITCHERS FOR A VARIETY OF reasons. They hang a curveball that is hit out of the park, they walk a batter with the bases loaded, or they forget to hold a baserunner and he steals an easy base. In a 1990 World Series game, manager Lou Piniella was frustrated with his pitcher for an especially unusual reason—he wanted his pitcher to warm up in the bullpen *but could not find him.*

When he was hired as manager of the Cincinnati Reds shortly after the 1989 season ended, Lou Piniella was faced with an imposing task. The team had been rocked by a scandal just a few months earlier when allegations surfaced that Pete Rose had bet heavily on sports games, particularly Major League Baseball games, while he was managing the Reds. Rose had managed the Reds since 1984 and had broken Ty Cobb's all-time hits record in 1985 while he was a player-manager.

Bart Giamatti, the former president of Yale University, became the commissioner of baseball in April 1989. Soon after he took office, Giamatti appointed John Dowd as special counsel to investigate the matter involving Rose. In a lengthy report submitted on June 27, 1989, Dowd concluded unequivocally that Rose had bet on baseball. There was already no love lost between Giamatti and Rose. In 1988, Giamatti, while serving as president of the National League, suspended Rose for thirty days—quite a harsh suspension—for shoving an umpire during a game.

In August 1989, the two men reached an agreement in which Rose did not admit that he had bet on baseball but accepted a lifetime ban from the sport. He was allowed, however, to apply for reinstatement a year later. Just eight days after the agreement with Rose was finalized, Giamatti, only fifty-one years old, died of a heart attack.

Coach Tommy Helms replaced Rose and served as the Reds' interim manager for the last 37 games of the 1989 season. The Reds finished in fifth place in the six-team National League Western Division, 17 games behind the San Francisco Giants.

Piniella had an eighteen-year career as an outfielder and designated hitter, the last eleven of which were with the New York Yankees. He was a .291 lifetime hitter and played on World Series winners for the Yankees in 1977 and 1978. He retired in 1984, and two years later, owner George Steinbrenner hired "Sweet Lou"—Piniella's nickname facetiously referenced his temperament—as manager of the Yankees. After second- and fourth-place finishes in 1986 and 1987, Steinbrenner relieved Piniella of his managerial duties and moved him to the general manager position. He then rehired Billy Martin as manager of the Yankees, for the *fifth* time; however, just 68 games into the 1988 season, with the team at 40–28, Steinbrenner humiliated Billy by firing him again. He brought back Piniella as manager. Under Piniella, the Yankees played below .500 ball for the remainder of the season, finishing in fifth place, and again Steinbrenner axed Piniella.

Piniella was still under a personal-services contract with the Yankees, and he spent the 1989 season working as a broadcaster for the MSG Network and tutoring some of the Yankees hitters. Other teams expressed interest in bringing on Piniella as manager in 1989. Among them were the Toronto Blue Jays, who wanted to pull the plug on Jimy Williams in May. Piniella would have taken the job, but, because he was still under contract with the Yankees, Steinbrenner demanded compensation from the Blue Jays, and the deal broke down.

Following the 1989 season, however, Steinbrenner released Piniella from his contract, paving the way for the Reds to hire him as their skipper. Marge Schott, the owner of the Reds who sometimes stirred up controversy with her rude and off-color comments, gave Piniella free rein to choose his own coaching staff. He retained Tony Perez, one of the big guns on "the Big Red Machine" in the 1970s, as hitting coach but replaced the other coaches. His most important pick was Stan Williams as pitching coach—Williams was Piniella's pitching coach for the last two seasons that he managed the Yankees.

In the offseason, the Reds acquired Randy Myers, a hard-throwing, left-handed reliever from the New York Mets, and Hal Morris, a promising young first baseman from the Yankees. In 1990, Piniella had to wait a month to get his squad on the field in Florida, because a lockout by the owners delayed the start of spring training by thirty-two days, until March 19. As a result, the start of the regular season was pushed back a week, and three days were tacked on at the end of the season to ensure that teams played 162 games. In the final week of the abbreviated spring training, the Reds made another trade, picking up speedy outfielder Billy Hatcher from the Pittsburgh Pirates.

Though the Reds were optimistic that their additions of Myers, Morris, and Hatcher would improve the team, they were still pegged to finish in the middle of the pack in the National League West. Sometimes, however, the baseball pundits miss the mark with their predictions, and this was one of those times—the Reds held down first place, wire-to-wire, from Opening Day until the last day of the regular season. The Reds jumped out of the gate with six wins on the road, followed by three victories, for a 9–0 start. By June, they had built up a 10–game lead; it reached 11 games in July. Despite some bumpy stretches during the second half of the season, the Reds still finished atop the National League West, five games ahead of the Los Angeles Dodgers.

Cincinnati's bullpen was its strong suit. Randy Myers joined two third-year pitchers in the bullpen, righty Ron Dibble and lefty Norm Charlton. Myers was the team's primary closer; he saved 31 games, and Dibble chipped in with 11. Charlton saved only two games, but he was effective out of the bullpen, too, and started a few games. All three pitchers threw hard, but Dibble threw especially hard, averaging 12.5 strikeouts per nine innings in 1990. Myers also averaged more than one strikeout per inning. The trio were christened the "Nasty Boys" for their disposition on the mound.

Southpaw Tom Browning, the longest-tenured pitcher on the Reds, paced the team with 15 wins. Though he had not yet made an All-Star Game appearance, Browning was a reliable starting pitcher and a workhorse. From the time he broke in with a 20-win season in 1985, finishing second in the Rookie of the Year vote, until 1990, Browning started more games than any other pitcher in baseball, beating out rubber-armed hurlers Jack Morris, Bert Blyleven, and Orel Hershiser. Browning led the National League in games started four times during that six-year stretch.

Browning did not match his 20-win performance again, but he went 18–5 in 1988 and became the first left-hander since Sandy Koufax in 1965 to throw a perfect game, which he tossed against Sandy's old team, the Dodgers. Browning showed it was no fluke by almost duplicating the feat in a 1989 game when he retired the first 24 Philadelphia Phillies batters before Dickie Thon led off the bottom of the ninth with a double.

Right-hander Jose Rijo ably complemented Browning in the Reds' starting rotation. In 1990, he won 14 games and posted a 2.70 ERA. Rijo had such phenomenal talent growing up in the Dominican Republic that the Yankees signed him when he was *fifteen years old*. He pitched in the minors at sixteen and made his major-league debut at eighteen for the Yankees in 1984. Despite his tremendous potential, the Yankees used Rijo as a bargaining chip to acquire Rickey Henderson from the Oakland A's in a trade after the '84 season. Rijo struggled for three years in Oakland, and, after the 1987 season, the A's traded him to the Reds in a deal for Dave Parker. In Cincinnati he found his groove—1990 was his third straight season with a sub-3.00 ERA.

Cincinnati native Barry Larkin was in his fifth season of a nineteen-year Hall of Fame career, all with the Reds. He hit .301, stole 30 bases, and played a stellar shortstop. Third baseman Chris Sabo led the team with 25 home runs. Eric Davis, who split time between left and center fields, had an impressive blend of power (24 home runs) and speed (21 stolen bases). Right fielder Paul O'Neill, who later played for four world champion Yankees teams, was a solid contributor. Hal Morris quickly paid dividends for the Reds by hitting .340 as a part-time first baseman.

The Reds went head-to-head with the Pittsburgh Pirates in the League Championship Series; it was both teams' first postseason appearance since 1979. Jim Leyland managed the Bucs; Barry Bonds won his first of seven MVPs. The Reds lost the opener but won four of the next five games to take the Series. Randy Myers and Rob Dibble, with their shutdown relief pitching, were named co-MVPs of the LCS.

The Reds faced a stiff challenge in the World Series—Tony La Russa's juggernaut A's were appearing in their third straight Fall Classic. The A's had lost to the Dodgers in the '88 World Series but swept the San Francisco Giants in the following year's Series. The 1990 A's won 103 games during the regular season and bowled over the Boston Red Sox in the American League LCS, allowing just four runs in the four-game sweep. While the Reds boasted the "Nasty Boys," the A's featured the "Bash Brothers," Mark McGwire and Jose Canseco. Both young sluggers came close to hitting 40 homers, finishing with 39 and 37, respectively. Rickey Henderson, who was traded back to the A's from the Yankees the year before, won the MVP, hitting .325 and leading the American League in runs scored and stolen bases.

Bob Welch had a breakthrough year, winning 27 games—he's the only pitcher to reach that total since 1972—and Dave Stewart rattled off his fourth consecutive 20-win season. Dennis Eckersley came out of the bullpen to save 48 games. As if the A's were not good enough already, for insurance, at the end of August, they traded for two more star players, Willie McGee and Harold Baines. The A's, who won 12 more games than the Reds during the season, were overwhelming favorites to win the World Series.

Lou Piniella, forty-seven years old, and Tony La Russa, forty-six, when the 1990 World Series kicked off, grew up not far from each other in West Tampa, Florida. They played baseball against each other as boys, and, in 1961, when they were in high school, they were teammates on a PONY League team and traveled together to California that summer to compete in the Colt League World Series. La Russa had a brief and undistinguished career as a major-league player, but, as a manager, he had become one of the best in the business. Though Piniella and La Russa had remained friendly, they were both fiercely competitive and determined to beat each other in the World Series.

The Series opened up at Cincinnati's Riverfront Stadium, on the banks of the Ohio River. La Russa opted to start Dave Stewart, who was on a roll with six straight postseason wins, over Bob Welch. Piniella started Jose Rijo. The game was never a contest. Eric Davis launched a long two-run homer in the bottom of the first to give the Reds a quick 2–0 lead. They added two more in the third, and Stewart was gone after four innings. Rijo threw seven shutout innings, and Dibble and Myers each threw a scoreless inning to secure a 7–0 win for the Reds. Billy Hatcher also played a vital part in the Reds' opening game victory—the center fielder went 3-for-3 with two doubles, three runs, and an RBI.

It was an auspicious start to the World Series for the Reds. The A's were in a good position to even the Series in Game 2 when Bob Welch took the mound against Danny Jackson for the Reds. Jackson won 23 games for the Reds in 1988, but injuries and inconsistency had limited him to six wins in each of the past two seasons. He pitched well in the LCS against the Pirates, and the Reds won both his starts, so Piniella gave him the starting assignment against Oakland's 27-game winner.

Jackson did not make it out of the third inning. The A's peppered him for six hits and four runs before Piniella pulled him with two outs in the third and the Reds down, 4–2. The Reds got one back in the bottom of the fourth, and the game remained 4–3 into the bottom of the eighth inning. Piniella was already on his fourth pitcher, having used Scott Scudder, Jack Armstrong, and Norm Charlton following his early hook of Jackson.

Billy Hatcher led off the eighth against Welch, still toiling for the A's. He had banged out two more doubles and dropped down a bunt single and was now 6-for-6 for the Series. He hit a fly ball, which was catchable, to right-center field, but right fielder Jose Canseco got a bad jump and the ball fell in. Hatcher used his speed to motor into third base with a triple, his seventh straight hit. Canseco's failure to make the catch infuriated La Russa. Welch walked Paul O'Neill and induced Eric Davis into hitting a short fly ball to Canseco. Jose caught this one, and Hatcher had to stay at third. With left-handed-hitting Hal Morris coming up, La Russa took out Welch and brought in a lefty, Rick Honeycutt.

The wheels were turning in Piniella's head. If the Reds scored the tying run, the game could go into extra innings. The A's had three right-handed hitters due up in the ninth, so Piniella planned to replace

Charlton with Dibble, his fifth pitcher. Piniella knew that if the game went deep into extra innings, he might need to use several more pitchers. Jose Rijo was unavailable because he had pitched seven innings the night before. That left Piniella with only three more available pitchers. Piniella planned to start Tom Browning in Game 3 in Oakland but was considering bringing in Browning to help the Reds win Game 2. He asked his pitching coach, Stan Williams, to tell Browning to head out to the bullpen and to be ready to come in if necessary. Williams did not see Browning in the dugout, so he sent someone to the clubhouse to find him.

When Honeycutt had finished his warm-up pitches, Piniella countered La Russa's move by sending in a right-handed hitter, Glenn Braggs, to bat for Morris. Braggs grounded into a force out, and Hatcher scored to tie the game at 4–4. Honeycutt recorded the third out, and the game went to the ninth inning.

Piniella was happy the Reds had evened the score but did not like the perplexing news Stan Williams gave him: Tom Browning was nowhere to be found. He was not in the Reds clubhouse or the bullpen. "What the hell is going on?!" Piniella barked to Williams.

Answering Piniella's question requires a rewind to the afternoon before the start of Game 2. Tom Browning's wife, Debbie, was pregnant with their third child. At about 4 p.m., she began to experience labor pains. Because the baby was not due for another week, she thought it was false labor. Debbie's obstetrician had recommended against her attending that night's game, but she wanted to support her husband's team. She drove to the stadium and was in her seat behind home plate, in a section with some of the other wives of Reds players, for the first pitch at 8:30 p.m.

As the game progressed, Debbie's contractions grew stronger, and by the seventh inning she came to the inevitable realization that she was going to have her baby that night. She hurried out of the stadium to the parking lot reserved for Reds players, staff, and their family members. Her plan was to drive herself to St. Elizabeth South Hospital in Crestview Hills, Kentucky, about a fifteen-minute drive from Riverfront Stadium. When Debbie reached the parking lot, she saw a team van blocking her car, preventing her from leaving. She went in the team entrance and down a runway to the Reds clubhouse. When the clubhouse attendant answered her knock on the door, she told him that she wanted to see her husband, Tom Browning. The pitcher was in the clubhouse, watching the game on TV. The attendant told Browning that his wife was in the waiting room outside the clubhouse and wanted to see him right away. Browning knew immediately why she was there, jumped up in a panic, and bolted to the waiting room. Debbie told him that she had gone into labor and needed to go to the hospital. "All she wanted was to get somebody to move the van so she could move her car," Browning recalled later. "She didn't want me to leave the game."

Browning was not going to let his wife go to the hospital alone. Even though it was a World Series game, Browning, without telling anybody, walked out of the stadium in uniform with his wife. They got in his car, and he drove them to the hospital in Kentucky. At that point, the Reds had not yet tied the game, and Browning assumed there was no chance he would pitch in this game. "I was supposed to pitch the next game," Browning said. "They're not going to miss me."

Word got back to Piniella about Debbie's knock on the clubhouse door, and Tom's disappearance soon after. He knew that Browning had left to take his pregnant wife to the hospital. A young staffer for the Reds was asked to call all of the hospitals in the area to determine where the pitcher had taken his wife. For privacy reasons, the hospitals could not confirm or deny whether Debbie Browning had been admitted.

While he understood the importance of Tom Browning's wife's delivering a healthy baby, Piniella was livid that his pitcher had left the stadium without his permission, in a World Series game no less, when his services as a pitcher might be required.

By this time, the game had entered the 10th inning since neither team had scored in the ninth. Rob Dibble was in his second inning of work for the Reds. Piniella, through a person in the Reds' public relations department, conveyed a message to the team's radio booth to issue a statement—an all-points bulletin of sorts—demanding that Browning return to the stadium immediately. Marty Brennaman, radio broadcaster for the Reds, delivered this message over the air:

We have a rather unusual message. We understand Tom Browning's wife, Debbie, has gone into labor and he has left the ballpark, and a call has apparently come up from the Reds' airwaves to have Tom Browning come back to the ballpark in the event they have to use him to pitch tonight.

Soon after, Tim McCarver, who was broadcasting the game on national TV for CBS, made a similar announcement. Browning, watching the game on a TV in the labor room at the hospital while his wife was being prepared to deliver their baby by C-section, was flabbergasted. It occurred to him that, in his rush to take his wife to the hospital, he had told no one where he was going. With his manager insisting that he return to the stadium and his wife on the brink of giving birth, Browning knew he had to make a quick decision. He decided to stay with his wife and make sure that she and the baby were fine.

In the bottom of the 10th inning, Dennis Eckersley, who was nearly unhittable during the season with an ERA of less than 1.00, came in out of the bullpen for the A's. After Eric Davis grounded out, Piniella sent up Billy Bates to bat for Dibble. A reserve infielder who was used primarily as a pinch-runner because of his wheels, Bates would collect just six regular-season hits in his major-league career. Bates hit a chopper toward third base, and Carney Lansford couldn't make a play on it. Bates was credited with a hit. Chris Sabo followed with a ground ball single through the hole between third and short into left field, advancing Bates to second. Catcher Joe Oliver, just a .231 hitter during the season, grounded a single down the left-field line to score Bates. Delighted Cincinnati fans celebrated the win by launching rolls of toilet paper from the stands onto the field.

At St. Elizabeth South Hospital, Browning clapped his hands when Oliver delivered his game-winning hit to give the Reds a surprising 2–0 lead in the Series. He also felt a sense of relief about his decision to leave Riverfront and drive to the hospital—and stay there after he heard the announcement on TV that he was expected to return to the ballpark. The game ended a minute after midnight; Browning was then fitted for a gown to wear over his uniform and taken into the delivery room.

Twenty-five minutes later, Debbie Browning, with her husband by her side, delivered a healthy baby boy, Tucker.

The next day, the Reds boarded a plane to Oakland. Browning received congratulations on the birth of his baby and ribbing for his surreptitious midgame departure from the stadium. If the Reds had lost the game in 16 innings, and Piniella had had to bring an infielder in to pitch, he probably would not have been forgiving. But the Reds won in 10 innings, so all was well, and Browning, as planned, started Game 3 at Oakland-Alameda County Coliseum. Chris Sabo hit a solo homer off Mike Moore in the top of the second, but Harold Baines answered with a two-run homer off Browning in the bottom of the second to put the A's ahead.

In the top of the third, the Reds as a team batted for the cycle—hitting a single, double, triple, and home run—and added three more singles. Mark McGwire helped the Reds' cause by making a costly error at first base, and Scott Sanderson, called upon to relieve Moore, threw a wild pitch. When it was over, the Reds had scored seven runs and Browning had himself a comfortable 8–2 lead. The Reds cruised to an 8–3 win. Browning pitched six innings, and Dibble and Myers combined for three shutout innings to seal the win.

Despite the A's loss, at least their pitchers finally figured out a way to get Billy Hatcher out. His streak of seven consecutive hits ended in the top of the first when he grounded into a double play. Hatcher singled in the third, though, to start the Reds' seven-run rally, and added a single in the eighth to complete his 2-for-5 night.

The Reds had the momentum and were poised for a sweep. Piniella sent Jose Rijo to the mound in Game 4, even though he was nursing a blister on his pitching hand. Dave Stewart tried to keep the A's alive. La Russa benched Jose Canseco, who was 1-for-11 in the Series. In the top of the first, Stewart hit Billy Hatcher in the left hand with a pitch. Hatcher relied on adrenaline to fight off the pain and stay in the game. He tried to steal second but was thrown out.

In the bottom of the first, Willie McGee hit a sinking line drive to left field. Eric Davis sped in and tried to make a diving catch. He got his glove on the ball and appeared to make the catch, but the ball popped out, and McGee made it into second for a double. Davis remained face down on the ground in intense pain but was able to get on his feet and stay in the game. McGee scored on a single by third baseman Carney Lansford. When the inning ended, Davis had trouble jogging off the field and needed assistance from his teammates to make it to the dugout. He was due up first in the top of the second, but Piniella brought Glenn Braggs off the bench to pinch-hit. Davis was taken to a hospital in Oakland, along with Hatcher, whose hand pain had intensified. Herm Winningham replaced Hatcher in the lineup. It was only the second inning, and two Reds outfielders, who were two of their hottest hitters, had left the game with injuries.

In the bottom of the second, the A's put runners on second and third with two outs, but Rijo struck out McGee to thwart the threat. Stewart and Rijo then locked horns in a pitchers' duel, and the game stayed 1–0 in favor of the A's into the eighth inning.

The Reds used two bunts to load the bases off Stewart in the top of the eighth inning with no outs. Barry Larkin singled up the middle, and Herm Winningham bunted for a hit. Paul O'Neill laid down a sacrifice bunt, and when Stewart's throw pulled second baseman Willie Randolph, covering first, off the bag, everybody was safe. Glenn Braggs followed with a ground ball force out, scoring Larkin and sending Winningham to third. Hal Morris delivered a sacrifice fly to right, plating Winningham, and the Reds owned their first lead of the game, 2–1.

When Rijo struck out Dave Henderson to lead off the bottom of the ninth, it was the 20th straight batter that he had retired. With Rijo's pitch count high and the blister on his hand bothering him, Piniella summoned Randy Myers to pitch to left-handed-hitting Harold Baines. Jose Canseco pinch-hit for Baines and grounded out weakly to third base. Myers then retired Carney Lansford on a foul pop fly to first baseman Todd Benzinger, and the Reds had completed a convincing and improbable sweep of the A's.

The X-rays of Billy Hatcher's hand were negative, so he was able to return to the ballpark and celebrate with his teammates. Eric Davis was not so lucky. Tests showed that he had a lacerated kidney, which required surgery. Davis stayed five days at the Oakland hospital before he flew back to Cincinnati. A rift developed between Davis and Reds owner Marge Schott. From his hospital bed, Davis tried to make arrangements to fly home, but Schott would not return his calls. Davis ended up booking a private plane that cost him several thousand dollars out of pocket. Davis spent five more days in a Cincinnati hospital and then was discharged to complete his recovery at home.

Though Davis played ten more seasons in the majors, he was not the same player after he sustained his kidney injury. But he earned a World Series ring for the '90 Reds and made a major contribution when he drove in five runs in the Series and hit a first-inning home run in Game 1, setting the tone.

Billy Hatcher set two World Series records—most consecutive hits and highest batting average in a Series, .750, breaking Babe Ruth's record, which was set in 1928. For those accomplishments, one of the bats Hatcher used in the Series is displayed at the Hall of Fame in Cooperstown, New York. Hatcher's records were all the more remarkable, because, all in all, he was a modest hitter. He hit .276 during the regular season for the Reds in 1990, and he never hit .300 in a season during his twelve-year career.

Chris Sabo also greatly overperformed in the World Series. A career .268 hitter, Sabo hit .563 in the Series, with two homers and five RBIs.

The Nasty Boys—Myers, Dibble, and Charlton—made their mark in the World Series, collectively pitching 8⅔ innings and allowing not a single run.

Though all of these Reds players significantly contributed to one of the greatest upsets in World Series history, Jose Rijo was awarded MVP of the Series for his 2–0 record and 0.59 ERA.

Tom Browning's stats in the '90 Series paled in comparison to those of many of his teammates, but he pitched well enough in Game 3 to pick up the win. Injuries got the better of him in the following years, and after four more years with the Reds and part of a season with the Kansas City Royals, Browning retired during spring training in 1996. Browning reached the peak of his career when the Reds won the World Series; after 1990, he did not pitch in another postseason game, did not pitch another no-hitter, and did not lead the league in games started. But he did leave the ballpark in the middle of another game without his manager's permission.

In 1993, Davey Johnson had replaced Tony Perez, who lasted only 44 games as Piniella's successor. The Reds were playing the Chicago Cubs at Wrigley Field on a warm July afternoon. Browning, who had started and won three days earlier, was in the bullpen. A known jokester, Browning snuck out of the bullpen midgame, left Wrigley Field, and went across the street to join a group of Cubs fans, watching the game and drinking on the roof of a nearby apartment building. Browning made himself at home by dangling his legs over a railing. His teammates in the dugout spotted him, laughed, and waved to him. He tipped his hat and waved back. An inning later, Browning returned to the Reds bullpen.

It was an amusing stunt by Tom Browning, but, for sheer drama, nothing could compare to his disappearing act in Game 2 of the 1990 World Series.

Tom Browning, a mainstay in the Cincinnati Reds' starting rotation for almost a decade, won Game 3 of the 1990 World Series. In Game 2, he exasperated his manager and confounded the baseball world when he left the ballpark late in the game and did not return. Browning passed away in 2022 at the age of sixty-two. *The Cincinnati Reds*

PART IV
HEARTBREAK AND TRIUMPH

15

The Gold Glover's Gaffe

A PASSED BALL BY BROOKLYN DODGERS CATCHER MICKEY OWEN IN the 1941 World Series and first baseman Bill Buckner's error for the Boston Red Sox in the 1986 Series rank as two of the most renowned blunders in World Series history. Though less well known, a misplay by an outfielder with a slew of Gold Gloves in his trophy case turned the tide in the 1968 Fall Classic.

In 1967, Bob Gibson, the exceptionally talented and fiercely competitive right-hander for the St. Louis Cardinals, established himself as one of baseball's premier postseason pitchers by becoming the first hurler to win two World Series Game 7s; the feat has not been achieved since. In '64, Gibson won Game 5 against the New York Yankees with a complete game, 10-inning, 13-strikeout gem in which he allowed only two unearned runs. Back in St. Louis three days later, he went the distance in the seventh game to lead the Redbirds to their first world championship in eighteen years. He set a record for most strikeouts by a pitcher in a World Series with 31.

Gibson was even more unhittable in the '67 Series against the Red Sox, tossing complete game victories in Games 1, 4, and 7. He permitted just three runs and 14 hits in the three games and fanned 26 batters.

Center fielder Curt Flood was another star on the Cardinals' 1964 and 1967 championship teams and was one of Bob Gibson's closest friends. The two men had an inextricable bond, because they were both subjected to egregious racial prejudice in the minors and early in their major-league careers.

Flood was signed out of high school in 1956 by the Cincinnati Redlegs (the team was called the Redlegs for five years in the 1950s before they were renamed the Reds). At his first spring training, white players stayed at a team hotel while Flood and the other Black players lodged at a boarding house. Flood also endured the indignity of being blocked from eating at the same restaurants as his white teammates and being forced to play in a soaked uniform in the second game of a doubleheader because he was not allowed to shower between games. Once, while Flood was playing for High-Point Thomasville, Cincinnati's Class-B affiliate in the Carolina League, a white man and his sons jeered at him from the front row and pelted him with racial epithets. Flood received little support from his teammates and manager. But he tolerated the mistreatment and flourished on the field in 1956 and 1957, earning late-season call-ups to the Redlegs both seasons. Despite the promise Flood seemed to hold for the team, Cincinnati traded him to St. Louis after the 1957 season, and, in 1958, when he was only twenty years old, he started in center field for the Cardinals.

When Bob Gibson played in the minors, he also suffered the humiliation of having to live apart from his teammates who did not share his skin color. Like Flood, Gibson was determined to succeed, so he endured the prejudice, persevered, and made the majors, debuting with the Cardinals in 1959. Gibson's first major-league manager, Solly Hemus, piloted the Cards from the beginning of '59 until halfway through the '61 season, when he was fired. Gibson and Flood were both targets of Hemus's bigotry. He told them they would never make it in the majors. In his autobiography, *Stranger to the Game*, Gibson writes, "Hemus's treatment of [B]lack players was the result of one of the following, either he disliked us deeply or he genuinely believed that the way to motivate us was with insults." Flood described the environment as "racist poison." Gibson and Flood quickly developed a close friendship and always roomed together while on the road.

When Johnny Keane, a kind, unprejudiced man, replaced Hemus, he made an immediate difference in the team's performance. St. Louis posted a losing record the first half of the '61 season under Hemus, but they played almost .600 ball once Keane took the reins.

Gibson and Flood both blossomed under Keane's guidance. In 1962, Gibson, in his first full season pitching for his new manager, won 15 games, threw five shutouts, and struck out more than 200 batters. Flood, who played semiregularly when Hemus managed the club, played every day for Keane. In '62, he hit .296 with 70 RBIs and developed into a top defensive center fielder.

With Gibson and Flood front and center, the Cardinals improved each season, culminating in the 1964 World Series win. Johnny Keane had such confidence in Gibson that when, in the top of the ninth inning of Game 7, with the Cardinals leading the Yankees, 7–3, Gibson allowed two solo homers to reduce the lead to 7–5, Keane stuck with his ace. Most managers would have pulled him. Gibson rewarded his manager's confidence by nailing down the last out and the world championship.

Keane got along swimmingly with Gibson, Flood, and the rest of the Cardinals players, but he did not see eye-to-eye with the owner, Gussie Busch. That incompatibility led to his resignation less than twenty-four hours after the Cardinals won the World Series. Ironically, four days later he was hired as manager by the team he had just beaten in the Series, the Yankees. Cardinals coach Red Schoendienst, who had played most of his stellar nineteen-year career for St. Louis before retiring in 1963, was promoted from coach to manager. Like Keane, Schoendienst was easygoing and unbigoted and had excellent rapport with his players.

The Cardinals hovered around .500 in their first two years under Schoendienst but broke through in 1967 by winning 101 games and defeating the Red Sox in the World Series. They repeated as National League champions in 1968, and though Curt Flood hit .301 and left fielder Lou Brock stole 62 bases, it was all about Bob Gibson. In what was dubbed the "Year of the Pitcher," when seven starting pitchers compiled an ERA lower than 2.00, Gibson was otherworldly. He won 22 games with a microscopic 1.12 ERA, the lowest ERA for a starting pitcher since 1914. His 13 shutouts were the most for a hurler since 1916. In one stretch of 95 innings, Gibson allowed *two* runs. He won the Cy Young Award unanimously and also captured the MVP.

The Cardinals' opponent in the World Series, the Detroit Tigers, were playing their first October baseball since 1945, when they beat the

Chicago Cubs in seven games. In the summer of '67, a race riot broke out in Detroit after police raided an after-hours establishment frequented largely by Black patrons. The mayhem, which lasted nearly a week, compelled the Michigan governor to declare a state of emergency and President Lyndon Johnson to send in five thousand federal troops. When order was finally restored, forty-three people were dead and more than four hundred buildings were destroyed. Racial tensions were heightened in Detroit and around the country.

When the Tigers clinched the American League pennant before a full house in Detroit on September 17, 1968, fourteen months after the riots, fans, Black and white, stormed the field and engaged in a joyous celebration. The revelry marked a step toward the uniting of the city.

That the Tigers would win the pennant in '68 was never in much doubt. Manager Mayo Smith's club led the league pretty much from wire-to-wire. In contrast to Red Schoendienst, who amassed more than 2,400 hits, Smith collected just 43 hits in the majors. Smith played pro baseball for nineteen years, but his time was spent entirely in the minors, save a half season in 1945, in which he hit .212 for the Philadelphia Athletics. He managed the Philadelphia Phillies and Cincinnati Reds for five years in the 1950s with little success and then worked as a scout for the Yankees for eight years before the Tigers offered him the manager's job after the 1966 season. The Tigers came up short in '67, when they were eliminated during the last weekend of the season but then dominated in '68, winning 103 games.

The Tigers lineup featured a strong nucleus of veterans, who had played together for several years. Outfielder Al Kaline was the elder statesman, having broken in with Detroit in 1953. He was the face of the franchise and a hero to Tigers fans. He was a perennial All-Star; he failed to be named to the team in only three of his first sixteen seasons. First baseman Norm Cash joined the Tigers in 1960 and was followed soon after by catcher Bill Freehan and infielder Dick McAuliffe. Outfielders Willie Horton, Mickey Stanley, and Jim Northrup were all wearing Tigers uniforms by 1964. Freehan, Horton, Stanley, and Northrup all had Michigan roots.

Mayo Smith did some juggling and platooning in the outfield and at first base during the 1968 season. Al Kaline, the Tigers' regular right fielder, broke his arm in late May when he was hit by a pitch. Kaline spent more than a month on the disabled list, and when he returned in July, he had still not recovered completely from his arm injury. Smith used him in a reduced role for the remainder of the season, giving him periodic playing time in right field and some starts at first base in place of the left-handed-hitting Norm Cash when a southpaw started for the opposing team. Both before and after Kaline's injury, Mickey Stanley, a right-handed swinger, sometimes spelled Cash when a southpaw was on the mound. But he played the bulk of his time in center field. Catcher Bill Freehan also moved down and played first periodically. Jim Northrup played a lot of right field after Kaline's injury and also played some center when Stanley was not in the lineup. Willie Horton held down left field for most of the season, but Northrup got a few starts in left as well. Smith shuffled his players masterfully to get the most out of them.

While Al Kaline was the year-in-and-year-out star of the team, Denny McLain, a brash and cocky twenty-four-year-old right-handed pitcher, was the indisputable star of the 1968 Tigers. McLain became the first pitcher since Dizzy Dean in 1934 to reach the coveted 30-win mark. No hurler has attained that win total since. McLain's 31–6 record and 1.96 ERA earned him the Cy Young and MVP Awards, both by a unanimous vote.

The Tigers' only weakness in 1968 was at shortstop. Ray Oyler got most of the starts at short during the first half of the season. Though he was solid with the glove, he could not keep his batting average higher than .200, and, by June, it had sunk to .150. After the All-Star break, Mayo Smith switched things up and tried two other players at shortstop: Dick Tracewski, who had picked up World Series rings for Sandy Koufax's Los Angeles Dodgers in 1963 and 1965, and rookie Tommy Matchick. Tracewski and Matchick did not fare much better at the plate than Oyler, hitting .156 and .203, respectively. Tracewski topped the trio with four home runs and 15 RBIs. Oyler was hitless in his last 37 at-bats, finishing the season with a paltry .135 average.

With virtually no production at the shortstop position, Mayo Smith hatched a plan to beef up the team's offense for the World Series. With a week and a half left in the regular season and the pennant already sewed up, he began to play Mickey Stanley at shortstop. Stanley started seven of the last 10 games at short, and, while he committed two errors in one of the games, he played capably overall even though he had not played the position before in the majors or the minors, except for eight innings in August.

In Baltimore, between games in the next-to-last series of the season, Smith gave Stanley the news: "You are going to be my shortstop in the World Series." It was quite a gamble by Smith because Stanley was flawless in center in 1968, committing no errors in more than 300 chances and winning the Gold Glove. Jim Northrup took over in center. While Northrup was an above-average defensive outfielder, Stanley was better, and some writers and fans thought that, by making the move, Smith was weakening the Tigers defensively at two key positions. This move, however, allowed Smith to get Stanley, Horton, Northrup, Kaline, and Cash in the starting lineup at the same time.

Smith weighed the risks and benefits, and, when the World Series got under way at Busch Memorial Stadium in St. Louis before nearly fifty-five thousand fans, he went ahead with his plan, starting Stanley at shortstop and Northrup in center between Horton and Kaline, with Cash at first base. Ray Oyler, Dick Tracewski, and Tommy Matchick were on the bench. It was a marquee pitching match-up, Denny McLain versus Bob Gibson. The Cardinals wasted no time testing Stanley at shortstop. The leadoff batter, Lou Brock, hit a sharp ground ball to short, and Stanley threw out the speedster.

The day belonged to Gibson. He threw a five-hit shutout and allowed a runner past first base only once, in the sixth inning when Dick McAuliffe singled and Al Kaline doubled before Norm Cash struck out to end the inning. By then, the Cardinals led, 3–0, and Smith had pulled McLain for a pinch-hitter after five innings. Gibson's strikeout of Cash was his 11th of the game. In the eighth inning, he struck out pinch-hitter Eddie Mathews, a member of the 500-home-run club. Mathews was released by the Tigers after the Series, which marked the end of his career. Gibson kept dealing and, entering the ninth inning, his K total was 14, one short of Sandy Koufax's record, which he set in the 1963 World Series against the Yankees. Mickey Stanley hit a leadoff single, but then Gibson struck out Kaline to tie Koufax's record and struck out Cash to break the record. He made it three in a row by whiffing Willie Horton to finish with 17 strikeouts. Eleven Tigers struck out swinging, five looking, and one on a foul bunt. Many years later, Denny McLain praised Gibson's accomplishment, "It was the single greatest pitching performance I have ever seen."

Mickey Lolich, a twenty-eight-year-old left-hander, helped the Tigers even things up in Game 2 with his arm and bat. During the season, he had finished a distant second to McLain in wins on the staff with 17. Lolich was not as dazzling as Gibson had been the day before, but he held St. Louis to one run and struck out nine batters. A career .113 hitter going into the World Series, Lolich hit a solo home run—it would be the only homer in his sixteen-year career—and added a single and another RBI in the Tigers' 8–1 win.

The Series shifted to the Motor City, and the Cardinals used the long ball to prevail in the third game, 7–3, as catcher Tim McCarver and first baseman Orlando Cepeda each hit a three-run homer. Curt Flood delivered two hits and scored on both home runs.

The MVPs squared off again in Game 4, and, once again, Gibson was dominant and McLain labored. The Cardinals knocked out McLain in the third inning, leading 4–0. Of McLain's 41 starts during the regular season, he failed to make it to the sixth inning only twice. In his first two World Series starts against the Redbirds, he exited before the sixth. Meanwhile, Gibson mowed down the Tigers hitters with precision. Aside from a bases-empty home run by Jim Northrup in the fourth, Gibby was not touched for any runs. Number 45 also piled up 10 more strikeouts. After McLain's departure, the Cardinals tacked on more runs against Tigers relievers, one on a home run by Gibson, who hit well for a pitcher, and won the game, 10–1. Leading in games, 3–1, St. Louis was on the brink of winning its second straight World Series.

Denny McLain was not getting the job done, but Mayo Smith counted on Mickey Lolich to pick up the slack and duplicate his Game

2 effort so that the Tigers could stay alive. Lolich was overshadowed by McLain during the season, but the free-spirited southpaw nevertheless made a strong contribution. Relegated to the bullpen in August after a stretch of rocky starts, he pitched his way back into the rotation and closed the season on a strong note, tossing three shutouts in his last seven starts.

After Jose Feliciano's soulful rendition of the national anthem, which drew some boos from the crowd and provoked a bit of controversy after the game, the Cardinals pounced on Lolich in the top of the first, as Curt Flood singled in Lou Brock and Orlando Cepeda followed with a two-run dinger to stake the Cardinals to a fast 3–0 lead.

The Tigers got two back in the fourth off the Cardinals' number-two starter, Nelson Briles—triples by Mickey Stanley and Willie Horton were the big hits. A baserunning mistake by Lou Brock likely cost the Cardinals a run in the top of the fifth. After Brock doubled against Lolich with one out, Julian Javier laced a hit to left field. Brock rounded third and headed for home but, instead of sliding, he went in standing up. Catcher Bill Freehan blocked the plate, took Willie Horton's throw, and tagged Brock out. The consensus was that if Brock had slid, he would have gotten underneath the tag and touched the plate before Freehan could put the ball on him, which would have increased the Cardinals' lead to 4–2.

When it was stretch time at Tiger Stadium, the Cardinals clung to a 3–2 lead. The first batter for the Tigers in the bottom of the seventh, Don Wert, took a called third strike, and the Cardinals were eight outs away from closing out the Series. Mickey Lolich had pitched six scoreless innings since getting roughed up in the first, and Mayo Smith let him bat. The normally weak hitter came through again by singling to right field.

Red Schoendienst replaced Nelson Briles with Joe Hoerner, a side-winding lefty. It proved to be an unpropitious move by Red. Dick McAuliffe singled, and Mickey Stanley drew a walk to load the bases. Al Kaline, who had waited sixteen years to play in a World Series, came through with the hit of his life, a single to right-center field, to score the tying and go-ahead runs. Schoendienst kept Hoerner in, and Norm

Cash hit an RBI single to up the Tigers' lead to 5–3. The Cardinals put two runners on base with one out in the ninth, and Schoendienst sent up Roger Maris as a pinch-hitter. Maris had broken Babe Ruth's single-season home-run record for the Yankees in 1961, but 1968 was the end of the line for him. Lolich struck out Maris and retired Lou Brock on a ground out to bring the Tigers to within a game.

It was a gut-wrenching, come-from-behind win for the Tigers, but they still needed to win two games in St. Louis to take out the Cardinals. Mayo Smith banked on Denny McLain not to falter for a third time in the Series and decided to start the righty on two days' rest in Game 6. Smith's hunch was right—McLain redeemed himself with a complete game win, allowing only one run. The Tigers put up a 10-spot in the top of the third to ice the game early. Jim Northrup had the big blow, a grand slam, his fifth of the year; three of the four came in the *same week* in the regular season. In a June game against the Cleveland Indians, Northrup hit grand slams in consecutive at-bats and, five days later, socked another slam against the Chicago White Sox.

The Tigers' 13–1 shellacking of the Cardinals set up a seventh game. For the second straight Series, Bob Gibson would make the Game 7 start for St. Louis. Mayo Smith would go with his hot hand, Mickey Lolich. Because Lolich had pitched nine innings in Game 5 and would have only two days of rest, Smith was hoping to get five good innings out of his lefty and then turn things over to the bullpen.

The weather in St. Louis was nice on that Thursday afternoon, but the field conditions at Busch Memorial were not ideal. It had rained between the sixth and seventh games, and the grass in the outfield was still wet. The field had also taken a beating from the NFL game played between the St. Louis football team, also named the Cardinals, and the Dallas Cowboys four days earlier.

Gibson had carried the Cardinals on his back throughout the season and in the World Series, and Red Schoendienst needed him to rise to the occasion one more time. Gibson was a sight to behold on the mound. He wore his hat low on his forehead and gripped the ball tightly behind his right hip. When he released the ball, his body hurtled violently toward the first-base line. He glared at each hitter with ferocity. He considered opposing players to be the enemy; he never fraternized with them, even when they were his teammates on the National League All-Star team. Gibson would have cringed at the friendly banter exchanged between opposing players in today's game. A player will reach first base and then exchange small talk and maybe a laugh with the first baseman.

Gibson set down the Tigers in order in each of the first three innings. When he struck out Mickey Lolich in the third for his fifth K of the game and his 32nd for the Series, he broke his own record for most strikeouts in a World Series, which he had established in 1964.

Mickey Stanley got the first hit off Gibson in the top of the fourth, an infield single, but he did not advance. Through six innings, Stanley was the only Tiger to reach base. The Cardinals were not doing much better against Lolich; they managed two singles and two walks through the first five innings but did not score. Because Lolich was sailing along with five shutout innings, Smith deviated from his original plan and kept his starting pitcher in the game. The Cardinals had a chance to break the scoreless tie in the bottom of the sixth when Lou Brock singled to left, tying the record for most hits in a World Series with 13. He was looking to etch his name in the record books in another category by stealing his eighth base of the Series. Brock took his usual sizable lead off first base while Norm Cash held him on. Lolich threw to first as Brock broke for second. Cash threw down to Stanley to erase Brock.

After Julian Javier lined out, Curt Flood beat out an infield single. Flood did not have Brock's speed, but he had stolen 11 bases during the season and swiped three more in the World Series. Lolich caught Flood leaning toward second and fired to Cash. A rundown followed, and Stanley tagged out Flood to end the inning. Lolich had picked off two very good baserunners in the same inning.

The Series was tied, 3–3, and the game knotted at 0–0 through six innings. It all boiled down to the last three innings. Bob Gibson disposed of Mickey Stanley and Al Kaline to start the seventh, but then Norm Cash and Willie Horton hit back-to-back singles. It was Gibson's 25th inning in the World Series, and it was the first time he had permitted consecutive hits.

Jim Northrup approached the plate, and Tim McCarver trotted out to the mound to talk to Gibson. Northrup was hitting only .192 in the Series, .111 off Gibson. The left-handed swinger dug in. Gibson threw a first-pitch fastball, and Northrup hit a line drive slightly left of center field and fairly deep. Center fielder Curt Flood, who had won his sixth straight Gold Glove in 1968 for his defensive prowess, misread the ball off the bat and broke in a step. Realizing that the ball was over his head, Flood tried to reverse direction but slipped on the wet grass. He recovered quickly and retreated back, but it was too late—the ball sailed over his head. Cash and Horton scored easily, and by the time Flood chased down the ball and threw it in, Northrup was at third base. Though Flood could have—maybe should have—caught the ball, it was scored a triple, the first three-bagger that Gibson had allowed all year. Bill Freehan kept the inning going with a double to the gap in left-center field, expanding the Tigers' lead to 3–0.

It was up to Mickey Lolich to protect the lead. Lolich worked around a two-base error by Northrup in the seventh and kept the Cardinals off the scoreboard. With one out in the bottom of the eighth and the score still 3–0, Red Schoendienst let Gibson bat for himself and he struck out. The Tigers added a run in the ninth, and Lolich came within an out of a shutout, allowing a solo homer by third baseman Mike Shannon with two outs. Tim McCarver then fouled out to his opposite number, Bill Freehan, and the Series was over.

The expectation going into the World Series was that Bob Gibson or Denny McLain would win the Series MVP, but it was the unsung Mickey Lolich who took home the award on the strength of his three complete-game victories. "Finally, somebody knows who I am," he remarked. Twenty thousand jubilant Tigers fans greeted the team at the Detroit airport. Many displayed signs, including "Lolich for president." John Fetzer, owner of the Tigers, acutely aware that racial tensions still pervaded Detroit, praised Mayo Smith. "You've not only won the pennant and Series; you might have saved the city." At another airport a week or so after the Series, an old lady asked Gibson, "Do you still speak to Flood?" Gibson, aghast, responded, "How can you ask that?"

Smith's gutsy decision to move Mickey Stanley to shortstop paid off. Stanley's two insignificant errors did not hurt the Tigers defensively, and his offense helped, as he delivered a key triple in the fifth game and scored four runs in the Series.

Smith also took advantage of Ray Oyler's glove at shortstop. Late in all four of the Tigers' wins, to shore up his defense, Smith inserted Oyler at shortstop, moved Stanley to center field, shifted Jim Northrup from center to left, and took left fielder Willie Horton out of the game.

Cardinals fans were bitterly disappointed—their team had squandered a 3–1 lead in the Series. In the subdued Cardinals clubhouse after the game, Curt Flood told reporters the following:

> I couldn't see it against the shirts [worn by fans sitting behind home plate]. The reason I started in, I just didn't know where the ball was. A ball hit right at me gives me trouble in day games. If I hadn't slipped, I might have got it. I loused it up. I don't want to make any alibis about it.

Following the 1968 season, because of the dominance demonstrated by pitchers—only six qualifying batters hit .300—Major League Baseball lowered the mound from fifteen inches to ten inches and reduced the size of the strike zone from the armpits to the letters.

Curt Flood and the Cardinals front office butted heads in the off-season. Flood's salary for the '68 season was $72,500, and he was offered a $5,000 raise for '69. Flood insisted that he would not play for less than $90,000, and Busch grudgingly met his player's salary demand.

During spring training in 1969, Flood was subjected to some negative publicity when his brother Carl, recently released from prison on parole and living in Curt's St. Louis apartment, tried to rob a jewelry store in an escapade that involved taking hostages. The police chase that ensued was televised in St. Louis, and Carl Flood was identified as the baseball player's brother.

Toward the end of spring training, Gussie Busch held a meeting with his players. Members of the media were invited. Busch chided his players for their greed and urged them to concentrate on their performances on the field.

Busch's diatribe demoralized the players, especially Flood. Relations between Flood and the front office worsened progressively during the season, but the center fielder turned in another good season, hitting .285 and winning another Gold Glove. The team fell to fourth place.

Six days after the conclusion of the regular season, Flood received a phone call from the Cardinals assistant to the general manager—a "mid-level front office coffee drinker" according to Flood—informing him that he had been traded to the Phillies in a seven-player deal. Disgruntled Phillies slugger Richie (he later went by Dick) Allen was the key player the Cardinals acquired from the Phillies. The trade would change the course of baseball history.

John Quinn, the general manager of the Phillies, offered Flood a $100,000 contract for the 1970 season, but he refused to report to Philadelphia. Flood considered Philly to be the country's "northern-most southern city." Flood knew well that Allen had been victimized by racial prejudice while playing in Philadelphia, and Flood did not want to endure the same treatment. He also disputed the fairness of Major League Baseball's reserve clause, which prevented a player from selling his services to another team. Flood characterized the players as "indentured servants."

Flood faced a conundrum—he did not want to play in Philadelphia, but he was also not ready to retire because he was only thirty-one years old. On December 24, 1969, he wrote a letter to Commissioner Bowie Kuhn, pleading his case. He stated that he is not a piece of property to be bought and sold regardless of his wishes, adding, "I believe I have the right to consider offers from other clubs before making any decisions. I therefore request that you make known to all major league clubs my feelings in this matter and advise them of my availability for the 1970 season." Kuhn declined Flood's request.

Flood stuck to his guns and did not report to spring training for the Phillies in February 1970. The Cardinals sent two minor leaguers to the Phillies as compensation for Flood's refusal to report. One of those players, Willie Montanez, went on to have a solid, fourteen-year major-league career.

Flood discussed the matter with Marvin Miller, the head of the players' union, and hired a lawyer to file a lawsuit, challenging the validity of the reserve clause. The antitrust suit was filed against Major League Baseball and Bowie Kuhn in federal court in New York, and a three-week trial proceeded before Judge Irving Ben Cooper in the spring of 1970. Instead of showing his skills on the baseball diamond, Flood sat with his lawyer in court and testified on his own behalf. Bob Gibson told Flood he was crazy for suing Major League Baseball, through which he had earned his livelihood. Judge Cooper ruled against Flood, upholding the integrity of the reserve clause. Flood's lawyer filed an appeal.

After the 1970 season, the Phillies, who retained the rights to Flood, traded him and a player to be named later to the Washington Senators for three minor leaguers. Flood and the Senators agreed to a contract for the 1971 season, according to which he would be paid $110,000, one of the highest salaries for a player in baseball.

Things did not go well for Flood in '71. He had not stayed in shape during his year out of baseball, and though he was in the Senators Opening Day lineup, manager Ted Williams benched him after five games because he was hitting only .150. Flood played sparingly over the next two weeks, and then, on April 26, he abruptly left the team, effectively ending his baseball career. He went to Spain, where he stayed for several years and encountered financial, drinking, and legal problems.

In 1972, while Flood was abroad, the United States Supreme Court, in a split decision (5–3), ruled against Flood. Flood's efforts, however, did not go for naught. In the coming years, the union continued to attack the reserve clause, employing a grievance and arbitration process to which the owners had agreed. In 1974, an arbitrator ruled that Oakland A's owner Charlie Finley had violated the contract of pitcher Jim "Catfish" Hunter, and he was granted free agency. Hunter signed with the Yankees.

A more significant ruling was issued in 1975. Pitchers Andy Messersmith of the Dodgers and Dave McNally of the Montreal Expos played the season without a contract. The union successfully convinced an arbitrator, Peter Seitz, that an owner's right to renew a player's contract is good for only a year; Seitz declared Messersmith and McNally to be free agents, effectively abolishing the reserve clause. Countless players have signed lucrative free-agent contracts since Seitz's ruling.

Years after the Supreme Court's decision and the birth of free agency, the question of whether Curt Flood should have caught Jim Northrup's line drive in the seventh game of the 1968 World Series was still being debated. Northrup agreed that it was slick in center field but always insisted that even if Flood had read the ball right and had not stumbled, he would not have made the catch: "You call that a misplay if you want. I call it a triple that won the World Series," he snapped.

Red Schoendienst and Bob Gibson never came out and said that Flood botched the play, but they agreed he should have caught Northrup's liner. Schoendienst said, "I'm sure he could have caught it if he had not charged in on it." And, in his book, *Stranger to the Game*, Gibson wrote, "As soon as the ball left the bat, I was confident Flood would track it down as he had done on so many similar occasions over the years. This time, though, Curt's first step was toward the infield, and when he realized he had underestimated the hit, he turned sharply, and for a split second lost his footing on the wet grass."

***

Mickey Owen was a four-time All-Star and a fine defensive catcher, but his career was marred by one pitch that he failed to catch in the 1941 World Series. Owen's Dodgers led the Yankees, 4–3, with two outs and nobody on in the top of the ninth inning of the fourth game of the Series. Hugh Casey threw a full-count curveball to Tommy Henrich, which he swung at and missed, seemingly ending the game and giving the Dodgers a Series-tying victory. But the ball hit the heel of Owen's glove and skittered toward the backstop, allowing Henrich to reach first. The Yankees rallied for four runs to win the game and stun the Ebbets Field crowd. They wrapped up the Series the next day.

Bill Buckner totaled more than 2,700 hits and won a batting title, but his reputation was forever sullied when he let a ground ball roll through his legs in the 1986 World Series. The Red Sox led the Mets, 5–3, heading into the bottom of the 10th inning of Game 6 at Shea Stadium. They were three outs away from winning their first World Series in sixty-eight years. The first two batters flied out, but the Mets then tied the game on three singles and a wild pitch. Mookie Wilson followed with a routine grounder to first base, and Buckner failed to get his glove all the way down. The ball went between his legs, and the winning run scored. The Mets beat the shell-shocked Red Sox two nights later to capture the Series.

Curt Flood's misplay, however, contributed more to the team's loss of the World Series than did Mickey Owen's and Bill Buckner's. Even after Owen let Tommy Henrich reach first base, the Dodgers would still have won the game if Hugh Casey had retired one of the next two batters, but he did not; he gave up a single to Joe DiMaggio, a two-run double to Charlie Keller, and another two-run double later in the inning. Owen shouldered the blame for the loss, but Casey played a big part, too.

Likewise, Red Sox pitcher Calvin Schiraldi deserved more flak for not putting the game away earlier in the inning when he needed only one more out.

Though these were crushing defeats, the '41 Dodgers remained in the Series after losing the fourth game, as did the '86 Red Sox after coughing up the sixth game. But there was no tomorrow for the '68 Cardinals if they did not win the seventh game. If Flood had made the play on Northrup's ball, the Tigers would not have scored in the seventh, and the Redbirds well may have won the game and the Series. If they had, Bob Gibson almost certainly would have been awarded his third World Series MVP. Because Flood did not make the grab, the Cardinals were put in a two-run hole that became three when Bill Freehan added an RBI double. To have a chance, the Cardinals had the difficult task of scoring three runs off a red-hot Mickey Lolich in the final three innings. They scored only one and lost the game.

Curt Flood has deservedly been hailed as the "Father of Free Agency" because his bold efforts in challenging the reserve clause laid the foundation for Peter Seitz's landmark ruling. Whether he should have been branded a "goat" for his misstep and stumble in the 1968 World Series is much less clear.

Curt Flood's great glove in center field for the Cardinals earned him seven Gold Gloves, but his misplay late in Game 7 of the 1968 World Series cost St. Louis dearly as the Tigers rallied to take the title after being down three games to one. *National Baseball Hall of Fame and Museum*

16

Ralph's Redemption

It was baseball at its very best: Game 7 of the World Series. The visiting team led by a run heading into the bottom of the ninth inning. The home team put two runners on base—the tying run on third, the winning run on second. There were two outs. The visiting team's manager went to the mound, considering whether to take out his starting pitcher and whether to walk the next batter intentionally. The crowd was on its feet screaming.

This was the setting in the 1962 World Series. The ending was dramatic, and it vindicated a pitcher who had allowed a World Series–winning home run two years earlier.

The New York Yankees represented the American League in the Series, fending off the Minnesota Twins for their twelfth pennant in fourteen seasons. Mickey Mantle won his third MVP to lead the way. Ralph Houk, in his second year as the Yankees' skipper, took over for Casey Stengel in 1961 and won the World Series in his first year at the helm. Houk had served for four years in World War II, ascending from lieutenant to captain to major; his highest rank became his postwar nickname—"the Major." Houk brought to the dugout some of the sternness that he had learned from his military experience, but, overall, he was considered to be an easygoing manager by his players.

The San Francisco Giants had to pull off quite a comeback to make it to the World Series. The Giants, in their fifth year in the Bay Area after moving from New York, trailed another East Coast transplant, the Los Angeles Dodgers, by four games with seven games left in the regular season. The Dodgers sputtered, losing six of their last seven games; they were shut out in their last two games at home. Meanwhile, the Giants won five of their last seven to force a tie. The Dodgers and Giants squared off in a three-game playoff series as they had eleven years earlier when the teams were in New York. That series ended with the Giants' Bobby Thomson's historic three-run homer.

In the 1962 playoff series, the teams split the first two games, and the Giants trailed, 4–2, heading into the ninth inning of the third game at Dodger Stadium. The Giants rallied, piecing together two hits, four walks, a sacrifice fly, a wild pitch, and an error to score four runs and win the pennant.

Alvin Dark was in his second season as manager of the Giants; his club finished in third place in 1961. At forty years of age, he was one of the youngest managers in the majors. Five of the players on Dark's team were later enshrined in Cooperstown. Legendary Willie Mays, thirty-one years old and in his eleventh season, was the veteran. He hit 49 home runs in 1962 and finished second in the MVP vote. Juan Marichal, Willie McCovey, and Orlando Cepeda were young and already accomplished. Marichal, in his third season, won 18 games in 1962. Cepeda was named Rookie of the Year in 1958; McCovey won the award in 1959. Gaylord Perry, who would go on to win more than 300 games, was a little-used rookie in 1962.

McCovey and Cepeda were natural first basemen, and it took some juggling to get them both in the lineup. To give their manager more options, both learned to play the outfield. Cepeda had really come into his own during the past two years; he hit 46 home runs in 1961 and 35 more in 1962. But a knee injury had slowed him down the stretch of the '62 season—after September 1, he hit only .223 with three home runs. McCovey had been mostly a part-timer in the majors, largely because he had difficulty in hitting lefties and usually sat when a southpaw was on the mound. In 1962, McCovey played a little first base and some outfield—he had only 229 at-bats, but he hit 20 home runs.

The Series opened at Candlestick Park. The Giants played their first two years in San Francisco at Seals Stadium, where a minor-league team had played for nearly thirty years. The stadium seated only about twenty-three thousand fans, and so the city built a larger park, Candlestick Park, which the team moved into in 1960. The park was on San Francisco Bay, and the breeze from the bay often created windy conditions at Candlestick. The year before, in one of the 1961 All-Star games (there were two games from 1959 to 1962), Stu Miller, a reliever for the Giants, came into the ninth inning of the game with runners on first and second and tried to save the game for the National League. But, when the scrawny Miller went into the stretch facing Rocky Colavito, a huge gust of wind hit him in the face, knocking him off balance. After Miller delivered the pitch, the umpire called a balk, and this helped the American League tie the game and force extra innings. Willie Mays, who ended up playing his home games at Candlestick for twelve years, lamented that the windy conditions cost him a hundred home runs.

The wind was mild for Game 1. Yankees starter Whitey Ford entered the game with a record 32 consecutive scoreless innings in the World Series, dating back to the 1960 Series. Ford's streak was snapped at 33⅔ when the Giants scored a run in the bottom of the second. Ford, though, breezed to a 6–2 complete-game win.

Game 2 featured the teams' winningest pitchers, right-handers Jack Sanford and Ralph Terry. Sanford, whose 24 wins ranked second in the National League to Don Drysdale's 25, started for the Giants. His exceptional season included a 16-game winning streak from mid-June to mid-September. He was unavailable to start Game 1 because he had pitched five innings in the second game of the playoff series two days earlier. Dark, not wanting to get down two games to the Yankees, decided to bring Sanford back on two days' rest in Game 2.

Terry, a tall right-hander who had led the American League with 23 wins, took the hill for the Yankees. A native of Oklahoma, Terry broke in with the Yankees as a twenty-year-old in 1956. Halfway through the 1957 season, he was traded to the Kansas City Athletics in a seven-player deal that included Billy Martin. In the 1957–58 offseason, Terry was involved in a near-fatal car accident; his injuries were so severe that he was in traction for seven weeks. But he recovered and was back on the mound in '58, winning 11 games for the Athletics. He was dealt back to the Yankees early in the 1959 season. He struggled, posting a 5–11 record for the Athletics and Yankees in '59. He turned things around in 1960, recording a 10–8 record for the Yankees, splitting time as a starter and a reliever. That fall, he surrendered one of the World Series' most famous home runs, Bill Mazeroski's drive over the left-field fence in the bottom of the ninth inning of Game 7 to win the Series for the Pittsburgh Pirates. Terry had come in out of the bullpen to record the final out in the bottom of the eighth inning after the Pirates scored five runs to take a 9–7 lead. The Yankees then scored two runs in the top of the ninth to tie the game, but Terry allowed Maz's leadoff home run in the bottom of the inning.

While Ralph Branca's career went downhill after he gave up Thomson's pennant-winning home run in 1951, Terry, only twenty-four when he was torched by Mazeroski, bounced back with a vengeance. He went 16–3 in 1961 and 23–12 in 1962. Houk could have started Terry in Game 1 but opted for Ford because of his Hall of Fame credentials, notably his extensive World Series experience (he had started five Game 1s) and recent October dominance.

Terry pitched well in Game 2, allowing two runs in seven innings, but Sanford was better, twirling a three-hit shutout to beat the Yankees, 2–0. McCovey hit a solo home run off Terry in the seventh inning. On the heels of his Game 7 loss in the 1960 Series and Game 2 defeat in the 1961 Series, Terry had now lost a game in three straight World Series.

The action moved to New York for Game 3, and Bill Stafford, a 14-game winner during the season, got the ball for the Yankees. He pitched the Yankees to a 3–2 victory but was injured in the process. With one out in the top of the eighth inning and the Yankees up, 3–0, the Giants' Felipe Alou hit a shot up the middle, which drilled Stafford in the shin. He recovered to throw Alou out at first. Houk and the trainer came out to the mound to make sure Stafford was okay. The pitcher was in pain but wanted to stay in the game, and Houk relented. Stafford got the third out in the eighth, and though he was touched for a two-run homer by catcher Ed Bailey in the ninth, he completed the game and held on for the win. When Stafford woke up the following morning, his shin and knee were bruised and swollen. It was questionable whether he would be able to pitch again in the Series.

Juan Marichal took the mound for the Giants in Game 4 to try to even the Series. He was on the cusp of becoming one of the game's most dominant pitchers; he would win 20 and post an ERA of less than 2.50 in six of the following seven seasons. Marichal, with his signature high leg kick, outdueled Ford, 2–0, through four innings. As he attempted to lay down a sacrifice bunt in the top of the fifth inning, Marichal smashed the thumb on his pitching hand. He struck out on the foul bunt attempt, was taken out of the game because of his injury, and missed the rest of the Series.

The Yankees tied the game with two runs in the bottom of the sixth, but Houk pinch-hit for Ford in the inning, so Houk had to go to the bullpen. In the top of the seventh, with two outs and the bases loaded, Chuck Hiller, second baseman for the Giants, became the first National League player in World Series history to hit a grand slam. He was not a likely player to accomplish the feat, since he had homered just three times in 602 at-bats during the regular season and would hit only 20 home runs in more than 2,000 career at-bats. Hiller's slam was the big blow in the Giants' 7–3 win.

With the Series knotted at 2–2 and the very real possibility that the Series would go seven games, the managers had to map out their pitching strategies for the remainder of the Series. They had to improvise because of the injuries to Stafford and Marichal. Houk had Terry pegged for Game 5. But for his injury, Stafford would have started Game 6, and Ford would go if there were a seventh game. With Stafford unable to start, Houk was leaning toward using Ford on short rest in Game 6 and Jim Bouton in Game 7, if the Series went to a seventh game. Bouton, the future best-selling author of *Ball Four*, was a rookie for the Yankees in 1962. As a spot starter, he compiled a 7–7 record with a 3.99 ERA.

Dark had Sanford lined up for Game 5 and veteran left-hander Billy Pierce, who had thrown six shutout innings before allowing three runs in the seventh inning in Game 3, for Game 6. Had Marichal not injured himself, he might have gotten the start if the Series went to the brink. But, with Marichal unavailable, Dark penciled in his Game 1 starter, lefty Billy O'Dell, for the seventh game.

Then Mother Nature intervened, on both ends of the country. Rain in New York caused the postponement of Game 5 by a day, which gave Terry and Sanford four days' rest instead of their usual three. Terry broke his three-game World Series losing streak by winning, 5–3. McCovey went 1-for-4 off Terry, with a leadoff single in the ninth, then came around to score on Tom Haller's one-out double. Terry retired the next two batters to nail down the win for the Yankees.

The teams flew back west, but it would be a while before they played again. Torrential rains in California delayed Game 6 for three days. When play resumed at Candlestick, Ford, the Yankees' money pitcher, now fully rested, got the start. Dark stuck with his plan and went with Pierce. He had been a steady starter for the Chicago White Sox for more than ten years before coming over to the Giants in a trade in the 1961–62 offseason. It was all Giants in Game 6—they knocked out Ford early with three runs in the fourth and two in the fifth, while the crafty Pierce held the Yankees to three hits and two runs.

The stage was set for Game 7. It had been an evenly matched Series, with the Yankees and the Giants alternating wins for the first six games. The Giants had scored 21 runs to the Yankees' 19.

Because of the lengthy rain delay in San Francisco, Bouton was denied the opportunity to start the seventh game. Terry, as well as Sanford, had had plenty of rest, so for the third time in the Series, they faced off against each other. While Terry was riding the team bus from the Jack Tar Hotel in San Francisco to Candlestick, he heard the broadcaster and former player Joe Garagiola predict, "The Giants will win because Terry will choke." The thick-skinned Terry ignored the dig, determined to prove Garagiola wrong.

Dark used a slightly different lineup against Terry in Game 7. In Games 2 and 5, McCovey played first, Cepeda sat, and the Alou brothers, Felipe and Matty, played alongside center fielder Mays in the outfield. In Game 7, Dark put Cepeda at first. Still suffering the effects of his knee injury, Cepeda started the Series 0-for-12 before breaking through with three hits and two RBIs in Game 6. McCovey played left field, Felipe Alou played right field, and Matty Alou was not in the lineup.

Houk had not varied his lineup much in the Series, though he didn't start the same catcher every game. Yogi Berra, in his seventeenth and next-to-last season for the Yankees, was a part-time player in 1962. He had started only one game at catcher in the Series; Elston Howard, a rising star, had caught the rest, and he was behind the plate in Game 7.

The wind, insignificant in the first three games of the Series at Candlestick, was a factor in the deciding game. A stiff thirty-five–mile-an-hour wind blew in from center field on this Tuesday afternoon. The fans bundled up—they felt as though they were watching a 49ers game in the winter.

Sanford and Terry traded zeroes through the first four innings. In the top of the fifth, the Yankees manufactured a run when Tony Kubek grounded into a double play with the bases loaded, scoring Bill Skowron.

Terry wasn't just keeping the Giants off the scoreboard—he had not allowed a batter to reach base. He maintained his perfect game into the sixth inning, vying to repeat Don Larsen's magic from the 1956 World Series. Larsen was now a Giant—he was the winning pitcher in relief in Game 4—and he applauded when Sanford became the Giants' first baserunner when he singled to center field with two outs in the sixth. Felipe Alou grounded out to end the inning.

It looked like the Giants might have their first extra-base hit with one out in the seventh when Mays hit a line drive toward the left-field corner. Tom Tresh, the Yankees' Rookie of the Year left fielder, raced to his right and snared the bullet to rob Mays of extra bases. McCovey, however, was not denied extra bases when he socked a Terry fastball over Mantle's head in center and legged out a triple. Take away the strong wind, and McCovey's drive may have cleared Candlestick's 420-foot center-field fence. Cepeda stranded McCovey at third by striking out.

The Yankees, looking to break the game open, loaded the bases against Sanford with no outs in the top of the eighth. Dark brought in lefty O'Dell to face left-handed-hitting Roger Maris. With the Giants' infield in, Hiller gloved Maris's ground ball at second and threw home to force out Bobby Richardson. Howard followed by grounding into a double play, and O'Dell had escaped the jam, with the score still 1–0. Terry retired the side in order in the bottom of the eighth, and O'Dell did the same in the top of the ninth.

It came down to the bottom of the ninth. Terry had allowed just two baserunners—Sanford's single in the sixth and McCovey's triple in the seventh. Dark sent up Matty Alou, a left-handed hitter, to pinch-hit for O'Dell. Alou dropped down a beautiful drag bunt toward second base and beat it out for a hit.

Leadoff hitter Felipe Alou was surprised when third-base coach Whitey Lockman flashed the bunt sign. Alou had sacrificed only twice all year, but he had hit 25 home runs and knocked in 98 runs. He was chomping at the bit to blast one through the wind out of the park and win the Series for the Giants. But he followed orders and laid down a bunt, which rolled foul. He looked down at Lockman and now saw the hit-and-run sign. Alou fouled off the pitch. He then went down on strikes for the first out. Terry fanned Chuck Hiller, and the Giants were down to their last out.

Mays gave the Giants life by stroking a line drive hit down the right-field line. Maris got to the ball quickly and threw a strike to the cutoff man, second baseman Bobby Richardson, and Lockman held Alou at third. Mays coasted into second with a double. Felipe Alou seethed in frustration on the Giants bench, knowing that, if he had laid down the sacrifice bunt, his brother would have scored on Mays's double.

McCovey was due up next, and Houk went to the mound to talk to Terry and Howard. Houk had action in the bullpen: Righty Bill Stafford (though unable to start because of his injury, he was available for a short relief stint) and lefty Bud Daley were furiously warming up. With right-handed-hitting Cepeda next in the lineup after McCovey, Houk had four viable options:

1. Leave Terry in and have him pitch to McCovey. McCovey had handled Terry well in the Series—he was 3-for-11 with a long triple two innings earlier and had homered off him in Game 2.

2. Leave Terry in, intentionally walk McCovey, and have Terry pitch to Cepeda. If this were later in McCovey's career, when he was in

his prime, he probably would have drawn an intentional walk. He led the National League in that category four times, and he is the only player besides Barry Bonds to receive 40 or more intentional walks in a season twice. At that point in McCovey's career, though, while he had power, he was not a feared slugger—he received just one free pass during the 1962 season. This was the first game of the Series in which Cepeda played against Terry—he was 0-for-3 with two strikeouts and a pop-up.

3. Bring Daley in to face McCovey for a lefty-versus-lefty matchup. McCovey was only a .220 career hitter against left-handed pitchers, but a .297 hitter against right-handers. Lefty Marshall Bridges led the Yankees in saves, with 18 in 1962—no other Yankee reached double digits. But he allowed Hiller's grand slam with the game tied in Game 4, so Houk was hesitant to bring him out of the bullpen in a pressure situation. Daley saved only four games in 1962, but he had thrown a scoreless inning in Game 2. He had also bailed out Terry in the decisive Game 5 of the 1961 World Series against the Cincinnati Reds. Terry was knocked out in the third inning, and Daley pitched the final 6⅔ innings, allowing two unearned runs and getting credited with the win.

4. Bring Stafford in, intentionally walk McCovey, and have Stafford face Cepeda for a righty-versus-righty matchup. Cepeda's track record in his career was about the same against lefties and righties. He had a career .309 average against lefties and a career .308 average against righties. Stafford had shut down Cepeda in Game 3, as he was 0-for-4 and hit the ball out of the infield only once. Jim Coates was Houk's primary right-handed reliever during the season, but he had allowed a double and issued a walk in the seventh inning in Game 4 before Bridges allowed Hiller's grand slam. Coates had also pitched 2⅓ innings in Game 6 the day before. So Houk chose to warm up Stafford rather than Coates.

Some managers would have walked McCovey, some would have pulled Terry, some would have done both. Houk weighed the factors and did neither. He talked to Terry and Howard and decided to leave his starter in and let him go after McCovey. It was a gutsy move, and Houk would have been second-guessed for the rest of his life if his strategy had backfired.

The 6'4" McCovey settled into the batter's box. McCovey later described the intense pressure that he felt. "Not only did I have a whole team on my shoulders in this at-bat, I had a whole city." On the first pitch, McCovey drove the ball, but he pulled it foul into the stands. The second pitch was a fastball inside. McCovey extended his arms and hit a screaming line drive. Off the bat, it looked like a hit, but the ball went right to Richardson, positioned perfectly at his second-base position. He caught it chest high before McCovey was two steps out of the batter's box. The Yankees had won a nail-biter, and Terry had redeemed himself.

Giants fans would have to wait until another day to celebrate a world championship. Little did they know it, but it would be twenty-seven years before the Giants returned to the World Series, and forty-eight years before their team won the World Series, in 2010, when manager Bruce Bochy notched his first of three titles for the Giants; he came out of retirement to win a fourth title for the Texas Rangers in 2023.

The creator of the *Peanuts* comic strip, Charles Schulz, lived in Sebastopol, California, fifty-five miles north of San Francisco. Schulz was twelve years into his fifty-year run writing *Peanuts*. He became a Giants fan when the team moved to California, and his alter ego, Charlie Brown, also was a diehard fan of the team. After the World Series, Schulz drew a strip in which a dejected Charlie Brown sits on a curb with Linus in the first three frames. In the fourth frame, Charlie Brown leaps to his feet and wails in despair, "Why couldn't McCovey have hit the ball just three feet higher?" If McCovey had, he would forever be a World Series hero in San Francisco, and Terry would have lived in infamy, as the pitcher who allowed two walk-off hits in Game 7 of the World Series within three years. Instead, Terry was the hero, earning World Series MVP honors for his clutch performance in Game 7. "Seldom does a man get a second chance; I'll be eternally grateful," an emotional Terry told reporters after the game. "This is a personal triumph for me. It wipes away two years of worry, two years of doubt."

Ralph Terry is carried on the shoulders of his teammates after Bobby Richardson snared Willie McCovey's ninth-inning line drive with two men on and two outs to end Game 7 of the 1962 World Series. Terry went all the way in the Series clincher just two years after giving up Bill Mazeroski's iconic Series-ending, walk-off homer for the Pirates. *AP Photo*

17

Jason Saves the Series

Between October 14, 1908, and November 2, 2016, a span of slightly more than 108 years, the New York Yankees won 27 World Series. The St. Louis Cardinals won 11 Fall Classics, and the Athletics, playing in Philadelphia and Oakland, took nine Series. All told, twenty-one different franchises won at least one World Series during that stretch. The Chicago Cubs were not one of those teams. Throughout the 108 years, they won *zero* World Series. *Zilch. Nada.* And, had it not been for an impromptu motivational speech by a Cubs player during a rain delay, the drought might not have ended.

The Cubs were a powerhouse during the first decade of the twentieth century. In 1906, the Cubs, led by player-manager Frank Chance, first baseman for the famous Tinker-to-Evers-to-Chance double-play combination, won 116 games but were upset in the World Series by their crosstown rivals, the Chicago White Sox. The Cubbies rebounded to win the Series in 1907 and 1908, handily defeating Ty Cobb and the Detroit Tigers both years. When the Cubs triumphed over the Tigers in five games in 1908, Teddy Roosevelt was finishing his second term as the country's twenty-sixth president, no one had heard of the *Titanic*, and the start of World War I was a few years away.

Over the next thirty-seven years, the Cubs made it to seven World Series—in 1910, 1918, 1929, 1932, 1935, 1938, and 1945—and lost every one of them. Their record in the seven October showdowns was a dismal 9–28, and they rarely held a lead in games in any of the Series. They were swept by the Yankees in the '32 and '38 Series. They never led in the '10 Series, falling to the Athletics in five games, or in the '18 Series, losing to the Boston Red Sox in six games, or in the '29 event, going down to the Athletics in five again.

The Cubs won Game 1 of the '35 World Series against the Tigers but then lost four of the next five games. They had a rematch against the Tigers ten years later and jumped out to a good start by winning the first and third games in Detroit to take a 2–1 lead. The action moved to Chicago for the remaining games. On the day of Game 4, the curse began—the "Curse of the Billy Goat." While there are various versions of the story, everyone generally agrees on the following facts: A Greek immigrant named Billy Sianis owned a restaurant in the Near West Side section of Chicago called the Billy Goat Tavern. Sianis was a Cubs fan, and he bought two tickets for Game 4 at Wrigley Field, one for himself and the other, not for his wife, not for his brother, but for his *goat*. He wanted Murphy to accompany him to the game to bring the Cubs good luck. Sianis had taken in the goat after it fell off a passing truck and wandered in the front door of his restaurant.

Sianis, with Murphy by his side, presented his two tickets at the entrance to Wrigley. An usher informed Sianis, "There are no animals allowed in the park."

Sianis was furious and demanded to speak to P. K. Wrigley, the owner of the Cubs. Wrigley agreed to talk to Sianis. The owner told the tavern owner that he could attend the game but the goat could not.

"Why not the goat?" Sianis snapped.

"Because he stinks," Wrigley replied.

Sianis threw up his arms in disgust and blustered, "The Cubs ain't gonna win no more. The Cubs will never win a World Series so long as the goat is not allowed in Wrigley Field." Sianis stormed away with Murphy and returned to his tavern.

The Cubs lost Game 4 and two of the next three games, bowing to the Tigers in seven games. Sianis shot off a nastygram to Wrigley: "Who stinks now?"

Sianis must have been gloating when the Cubs ran off *20 straight* second-division finishes from 1947 to 1966. They finally turned the corner after they hired feisty Leo Durocher as manager. Leo the Lip, who had managed the New York Giants to the world championship in 1954, led the Cubs to third-place finishes in 1967 and 1968, and, in 1969, the first year of divisional play, his team held a nine-game lead on August 16. But this was the year of the Miracle Mets, and they bulldozed the Cubs, winning the division going away. The Cubs went from nine up to nine down in just 42 games.

The stars seemed aligned for the Cubs to break the curse in 1984. Jim Frey, who managed the Kansas City Royals to the World Series in 1980, was in his first season as the club's skipper. He led Chicago to a National League best 96 wins. Rick Sutcliffe came over in a June trade and went 16–1 for the Cubs, including 14 straight victories, to win the Cy Young Award on a unanimous vote. The Cubs took the first two games of the best-of-five League Championship Series against the Western Division champion San Diego Padres. With a win in any of the next three games, the Cubs would advance to the World Series for the first time in thirty-nine years. The Padres were hungry as well; they had not won a National League pennant since they started as an expansion team in 1969. The Padres pulled the rug out from under the Cubs and won the last three games in San Diego. The Game 5 loss was a crusher as the Cubs held a 3–0 lead with Sutcliffe on the mound, but the Pads shelled the ace for six runs in the sixth and seventh innings to win the game and series.

The Cubs again made the postseason in 1989 as division champs and in 1998 as the wild-card winner but were walloped in both series, 4–1 and 3–0, respectively.

In October 2003, Cubs fans were jubilant, poised to celebrate. Their team was five outs away from winning the franchise's first pennant in almost six decades. Dusty Baker had taken the reins as manager at the beginning of the season. He had capped off a ten-year stint as manager of the San Francisco Giants by leading them to the World Series in 2002 but they had lost to the Anaheim Angels. When the Giants did not renew Baker's contract, the Cubs wisely snapped him up. With slugger Sammy Sosa leading the way, the Cubs won their division, beat the Atlanta Braves in the Division Series, and then took a 3–1 lead in the LCS against the Florida Marlins. They lost Game 5 in Miami and returned to Chicago, hoping to close out the series before the home crowd. In Game 6, their best pitcher, Mark Prior, carried a 3–0 lead and three-hit shutout into the eighth inning. Prior retired the first batter and allowed a double, and then Luis Castillo lifted a foul fly ball down the left-field line. Moises Alou might have caught the ball, but as he reached for it, Steve Bartman, a twenty-six-year-old lifelong Cubs fan sitting in the front row, reached for the ball at the same moment, and the Cubs outfielder was unable to make the catch. Alou slammed his glove down in frustration. The Cubs vigorously argued that Castillo should have been called out because of fan interference, but umpire Mike Everitt ruled that the ball broke the plane of the wall separating the field of play from the stands so it was fair game for Bartman to go for it.

The roof then caved in on the Cubs. Castillo ended up drawing a walk, and Ivan Rodriguez followed with an RBI single on an 0–2 count. Prior had a chance to get out of the inning when Miguel Cabrera, a twenty-year-old rookie, hit a routine ground ball to shortstop. It was a potential double-play ball, but Alex Gonzalez bobbled the ball, and everybody was safe. Baker pulled Prior after he allowed the next batter, Derrick Lee, to hit a game-tying double, and the Marlins went on to score five more runs in the inning and win the game, 8–3. Florida won Game 7 the next night. It was a demoralizing, gut-punching loss for the Cubs and the city of Chicago.

By 2007, Lou Piniella was managing the Cubs. Sweet Lou had managed the 1990 Reds to the world championship and the Seattle Mariners to three trips to the League Championship Series. In his first season in Chicago, the Cubs won the division title but were whitewashed in the first round of the playoffs by the Arizona Diamondbacks.

In 2008, Piniella's Cubs compiled the best record in the National League, winning 97 games. Determined to win their first World Series in a hundred years, at the start of the playoffs the team called on a Greek Orthodox priest to spread the Cubs dugout with holy water in an attempt to exorcise the curse. It did not work. For the second straight year, the Cubs were swept in the Division Series, this time by the Los Angeles Dodgers. In the two Division Series with Piniella at the helm, the Cubs recorded a 0–6 record and were outscored, 36–12.

By 2015, the Cubs had hired another manager with World Series experience, Joe Maddon. Among the few managers who had not made it to the majors as a player, Maddon had guided the Tampa Bay Rays to their first World Series berth in 2008, but they had lost to the Philadelphia Phillies. Morale among the Cubs faithful was quite low before Maddon took the job. The years leading up to his hiring had been tumultuous and unproductive. Piniella could not get the Cubs back to the playoffs, and so, with his club floundering, in August 2010, he resigned to take care of his elderly mother.

After another dismal finish in 2011, the Cubs hired Theo Epstein as their president of baseball operations. Epstein was the general manager who had engineered the Red Sox' successful World Series run in 2004, breaking the "Curse of the Bambino." The Bosox won the Series again in 2007 with Epstein as general manager.

One of Epstein's first orders of business in Chicago was to fire Mike Quade, who had replaced Piniella as skipper. Dale Sveum suffered the same fate two years later, as did Rick Renteria the following October. Two days after the axe fell on Renteria in 2014, Epstein hired Joe Maddon, who had just opted out of his contract with the Rays.

It took Maddon three years to transform Tampa Bay from a last-place team to a postseason participant; he did it for the Cubs in one year. Under Maddon, the Cubs improved by 24 wins in 2015. They beat the Pittsburgh Pirates in the Wild Card Game and the St. Louis Cardinals in the Division Series but were swept by the New York Mets in the LCS. Third baseman Kris Bryant, the second pick in the 2013 draft, won the Rookie of the Year Award. Jake Arrieta captured the Cy Young, and first baseman Anthony Rizzo finished fourth in the MVP vote.

Theo Epstein beefed up the Cubs' already strong roster in the offseason with three notable free-agent signings: pitcher John Lackey, infielder/outfielder Ben Zobrist, and outfielder Jason Heyward. The 2016 Cubs breezed to the National League Central Division title—they were in first place every day except for one day during the first week of the season. They finished 17½ games ahead of the Cardinals and won 103 games, the club's first 100-win season since 1935.

On July 25, even though the Cubs were atop the division by seven games and Hector Rondon was capably handling the closer role, they made a trade a week before the deadline, acquiring from the Yankees one of the game's premier closers, Aroldis Chapman. The undisputed hardest thrower in baseball, Chapman's fastballs were consistently timed at 100 miles per hour or faster. The left-handed Chapman, a native of Cuba, broke in with the Cincinnati Reds in 2010 and quickly became a dominant closer. In 2012, he began a string of four straight 30-save seasons, making the All-Star team each year. He also racked up staggering numbers of strikeouts, averaging about 15 per nine innings in his six-plus years before he came to Chicago.

As high as Chapman set the bar, he was even better than usual in the last two months of the '16 season for the Cubs, saving 16 games with an ERA just north of 1.00. Kris Bryant followed up his Rookie of the Year season with an MVP performance in 2016. Anthony Rizzo enjoyed his second consecutive 100-RBI, fourth-place finish in the MVP vote. The Cubs also got a lot of production out of their keystone combination as shortstop Addison Russell drove in 95 runs and second baseman Ben Zobrist added 76 RBIs.

Jason Heyward was one of the few Cubs who had a disappointing season at the plate. Expectations were high after he inked an eight-year, $184-million contract the previous winter. Heyward came up to the majors as a highly touted rookie for the Atlanta Braves in 2010. *Baseball America* named him Minor League Player of the Year in 2009, and he followed it up for the Braves in '10 by hitting 18 home runs, making the All-Star team, and finishing as runner-up for Rookie of the Year. Except for a stellar season in 2012, Heyward was spotty offensively for the Braves over the next few years. He did win two Gold Gloves for his excellent play in right field. After five years in Atlanta, Heyward was traded to St. Louis, where he had a strong season in 2015, both at the plate and in the field. He tested the free-agent market, and the Cubs rewarded him with a mammoth contract. Heyward may have been feeling the weight of the big contract during his first year with the Cubs. While he was splendid in the field, notching another Gold Glove, he did not get untracked at the plate and finished the season with a .230 average, seven homers, and 49 RBIs.

The Cubs had a tough foe in their opening playoff series—Bruce Bochy's Giants, which had won the World Series in 2010, 2012, and 2014 and were shooting to make it four in a row in even-numbered years. But it was not to be for the Giants. The Cubs knocked them off in four games, pulling out the clincher with four runs in the top of the ninth inning to beat the Giants, 6–5. Aroldis Chapman saved all three wins for Chicago.

The Cubs fell behind the Dodgers, 2–1, in the LCS, getting shut out in Games 2 and 3. Joe Maddon rallied his troops to win the next two in Los Angeles. Then, before a standing-room-only home crowd at Wrigley, the Cubs, at long last, broke the curse and advanced to the World Series by beating the Dodgers, 5–0. Kyle Hendricks, the 2016 National League ERA champion, and Aroldis Chapman teamed up to face the minimum of twenty-seven batters.

The Cubs had one more hurdle to overcome before the curse was fully broken—they had to defeat the American League champion Cleveland Indians in the World Series. The Indians had a prolonged drought of their own; they had not been victorious in a World Series in sixty-eight years, since 1948. They actually outdid the Cubs' string of 20 consecutive second-division finishes by recording 21 in a row from 1969 to 1989. The Cleveland sportswriter and journalist Terry Pluto wrote a half-serious book in 1994 entitled *The Curse of Rocky Colavito*, suggesting that the Indians' long run of futility was caused by the team's decision to trade Colavito, the popular slugger, to the Tigers in 1960. Ironically, after Pluto's book was published, the Indians turned things around, and they made it to the World Series in 1995 and 1997. But they lost both times.

The Indians were up and down for the next fifteen years, and, after a nearly last-place finish in 2012, the Indians hired the two-time World Series' winning manager Terry Francona, who had parted ways with the Red Sox in 2011 after the Sox squandered a nine-game wild-card lead in the last month of the season. Under Francona in 2013, the Indians improved from 68 wins to 92 in one year; they won a wild card but lost the one-game playoff. They missed the playoffs in the next two years, but, in 2016, they put it all together and won the Central Division title. First baseman Mike Napoli and designated hitter Carlos Santana each hit 34 home runs. Corey Kluber anchored the starting rotation by winning 18. Cody Allen was not in Chapman's class but still was a strong closer, picking up 32 saves.

The Cubs won nine more games than the Indians during the regular season, but, because the American League won the All-Star Game in July, home-field advantage went to Cleveland in the World Series, so the opener was played at Progressive Field. Something had to give—either the Cubs were going to break their seemingly interminable dry spell of 108 years, or the Indians were going to snap their lengthy sixty-eight-year skid. The Cleveland fans were fired up—their National Basketball Association (NBA) team, the Cavaliers, behind LeBron James, had won the NBA title in June, and they were rooting hard for a second championship in the city in one year.

When the Cubs last played in a World Series, in 1945, Jackie Robinson had not yet broken the color barrier, and so Jason Heyward, Dexter Fowler, Addison Russell, Aroldis Chapman, and Carl Edwards were among the first Black players to appear in a World Series for the Cubs.

The club made a roster change for the World Series—they replaced reliever Rob Zastryzny with catcher/outfielder Kyle Schwarber. The barrel-chested Schwarber was brought up from the minors in June 2015 and showed considerable promise by socking 16 home runs in 69 games and adding five more in the postseason. While playing left field in the third game of the 2016 regular season, however, Schwarber collided with center fielder Dexter Fowler when trying to make a catch and blew out his left knee. He tore two ligaments and required surgery. He was not expected to be back on the field until 2017, but he made significant progress in rehabbing his knee, and, after playing two games in the Arizona Fall League while the Cubs were playing the Dodgers in the LCS, Schwarber was deemed fit to return to the major-league diamond. Maddon and Epstein decided to replace Zastryzny with Schwarber.

Schwarber was in Joe Maddon's Game 1 starting lineup as the designated hitter, and he showed no rust from his long layoff when he banged a double off the right-field wall in his second time up. It was one of the few highlights for the Cubs, who were blanked on seven hits by Corey Kluber and two relievers; they struck out 15 times, seven of them looking. Jason Heyward had followed up his subpar regular season with a poor performance in the first two rounds of the National League playoffs—he hit .071 (2-for-28) with one RBI. Heyward was scuffling so much that Maddon did not start him in the opening game.

The Cubs did not want to return to Chicago in a 2–0 hole, and, thanks to a big-time start by Jake Arrieta and some timely hitting, they avoided that fate by beating the Indians, 5–1, in Game 2. Arrieta was stingy, allowing only a run and two hits, while Kyle Schwarber delivered two RBI singles and Ben Zobrist smacked an RBI triple.

Two nights later, something happened that generations of Cubs fans had long awaited—a World Series game was played at Wrigley Field. The fans were ready; the Cubs hitters were not. The Indians broke a scoreless tie in the top of the seventh by cobbling together a single, a sacrifice bunt, a wild pitch, a walk, and an RBI single by pinch-hitter Coco Crisp to score a run. The actor and comedian Bill Murray, a native of Chicago, rallied the crowd by singing "Take Me Out to the Ball Game" during the seventh-inning stretch, concluding with "Let's get some runs, suckers!"

Despite Murray's exhortations, the Cubs did not get on the scoreboard. In the bottom of the ninth, Jason Heyward, who pinch-ran in the seventh and stayed in the game, came up with Chris Coghlan on second and two outs. First baseman Mike Napoli could not handle Heyward's ground ball, and he was safe while Coghlan moved up to third. Heyward stole second base on the second pitch without a throw. A hit to the outfield well might have won the game, but Javier Baez whiffed on high heat by Cody Allen.

Corey Kluber made it two wins in a row in Game 4 by beating the Cubs easily, 7–2. Carlos Santana and Jason Kipnis each homered for the Indians. Normally sure-handed Kris Bryant made two errors in an inning, which contributed to a run. Jason Heyward made his first start of the World Series and, though he singled twice, he produced no runs. The Cubs were one loss away from elimination.

The Cubs played better than .700 ball at Wrigley during the regular season and were 4–1 in the National League playoffs, but, in the

World Series, they had lost two straight games at the Friendly Confines to the Indians in the World Series. No team had rebounded from a 3–1 deficit in the World Series since the Royals overcame the Cardinals in 1985; no team had accomplished that feat by winning the last two games on the road since the Pittsburgh Pirates battled back against the Baltimore Orioles and won the 1979 World Series. For the Cubs to prevail in the Series, they had to win the final two games in Cleveland.

Their first mission, though, was winning Game 5 in Chicago. Maddon entrusted veteran pitcher Jon Lester to start the win-or-go-home game. He was not sharp in the opening game, but he was rock solid during the season, posting a 19–5 record and a 2.44 ERA. The crafty lefty held the Indians to two runs in six innings. Carl Edwards got one out, and then Aroldis Chapman preserved the 3–2 lead with an impressive eight-out save in which he allowed just an infield single and struck out four. The 41,711 spectators in attendance at Wrigley were thrilled to witness a Cubs win in the World Series.

Travel day fell on Halloween, and the Series resumed at Progressive Field on November 1. President Barack Obama's successor would be determined the following week in the election that pitted Hillary Clinton against Donald Trump. Game 6 was the Addison Russell show—the Cubs' shortstop hit a two-run double in the first and a grand slam in the third. The Cubs never looked back and won, 9–3. Jake Arrieta picked up the W by striking out nine in 5⅔ innings.

It was an unseasonably warm November night in Cleveland for Game 7—the temperature was about 70 degrees for the first pitch at 8:02 p.m. There was a chance of rain later in the night. With the Series on the line, Terry Francona went with his best pitcher, Corey Kluber, on three days' rest; it would be the third time he pitched on three days' rest in the postseason after he had not pitched on less than four days' rest during the regular season. Kluber was trying to become the first pitcher since the Tigers' Mickey Lolich in 1968 to win three games in one World Series as a starter. Kyle Hendricks got the ball for the Cubs. He had started in Game 3 and had had his normal four days' rest.

Dexter Fowler started the game with a bang by hitting a leadoff home run over the center-field fence. The Indians tied the game in the bottom of the third, and then the Cubs notched a two-spot in the fourth. Javier Baez chased Kluber with a home run to start the fifth, and Anthony Rizzo's RBI single off Andrew Miller later in the inning increased the Cubs' lead to 5–1.

In the bottom of the fifth, Joe Maddon made a managerial move that later subjected him to significant criticism. Hendricks got the first two outs and then walked Carlos Santana. At this point, Hendricks had given up only four hits and one run in 4⅔ innings and had thrown just 63 pitches. Yet Maddon yanked his starting pitcher and replaced him with Jon Lester, who had thrown six innings in Game 5 three days earlier. David Ross, nearly forty years old and playing in his last big-league game, was Lester's preferred catcher and came in at the same time to take over for Willson Contreras behind the plate.

Jason Kipnis greeted Lester with a roller down the third-base line. Ross corralled the ball but overthrew first base, permitting Santana to reach third and Kipnis to move up to second. With Francisco Lindor at the plate, Lester uncorked a wild pitch—it bounced up and struck Ross in the mask. The ball careened away, and both runners scored. Ross made amends by hitting a solo home run in the top of the sixth to make it 6–3.

The Cubs maintained their three-run lead as the game headed into the bottom of the eighth inning. Cubs fans, elbow-to-elbow in bars throughout Chicago, were counting the outs to paydirt—it was down to six. Lester retired the first two Indians batters and then allowed a single to Jose Ramirez. Lester had thrown three innings and 55 pitches on short rest so Maddon brought in his workhorse Chapman to try to nail down the last four outs and send Chicago into hysteria.

Chapman's track record over his career made it a safe bet that he would hold the lead. Between regular season and postseason games, Chapman had pitched in exactly 400 games, all in relief, and the opposing team had scored at least three runs on his watch in only 15 games. In six of those games, Chapman was charged with three or more runs; in the nine other games, he allowed three or more runs counting both inherited runs and charged runs. The chance that the Indians would not score three runs against the Cubs' flame-throwing lefty was 96 percent.

Chapman, however, was feeling arm weary. Over the course of his career, he had pitched in roughly 40 percent of his team's games. This was the Cubs' 17th game in the 2016 postseason, and Chapman was making his 13th appearance—four were in the Division Series, four were in the League Championship Series, and this was his fifth game in the World Series. Thus, Maddon had given the ball to Chapman in 76 percent of the Cubs' postseason games. When Chapman got the last eight outs in Game 5, he threw 42 pitches. He was used in Game 6, though the Cubs had a big lead, and he tossed 20 more pitches. It remained to be seen whether Chapman had enough gas left in the tank to save Game 7.

Brandon Guyer was the first batter to face Chapman. Guyer had pinch-hit for Lonnie Chisenhall in the sixth inning, singled off Lester, and stayed in the game to play right field. The Indians had just picked him up in a trade with Tampa Bay on August 1. In limited play during the last two months of the season, Guyer made it count by hitting .333. He had maintained his stroke by hitting .294 in the postseason. The count ran full; Chapman's fastball appeared to be a tick behind. Guyer then laced a double to the alley in right-center to score Ramirez.

Center fielder Rajai Davis represented the tying run at the plate. Cleveland was the well-traveled Davis's sixth major-league stop. Davis's speed was his strong suit—he led the American League in stolen bases in 2016 with 43 and had swiped 365 bags in his 11 years in the majors, fourth among active players. But he had hit only 55 career home runs; his 12 for the Indians in 2016 marked his season high.

Davis dug in against Chapman. He had not hit well in the 2016 postseason, just 3-for-32. The count went to 2-2. Davis fouled off two pitches and then connected. It was not a colossal blast, but it was hit long enough to clear the left-field fence and tie the game. Davis tore around the bases with his tongue out, pumping his right fist.

While Indians fans went wild, the many Cubs fans in attendance sat in stunned silence. Moments earlier, the Cubs had held a three-run lead, and, with two swings of the bat, the Indians had knotted the game. Coco Crisp followed with a single off a shaken Chapman. Maddon stuck with his pitcher, and he recovered to strike out Yan Gomes.

In the top of the ninth, while Chapman sat disconsolately in the Cubs dugout, Cody Allen walked David Ross. Chris Coghlan pinch-ran but he was erased when Jason Heyward grounded into a force out. Francona brought in Bryan Shaw for Allen, who had thrown two innings. Heyward stole second and scurried to third on catcher Yan Gomes's throwing error. The Cubs were ninety feet away from retaking the lead, but Javier Baez struck out attempting to bunt and Dexter Fowler grounded out.

Chapman went out for the bottom of the ninth. With one out, Jason Kipnis hit a long fly down the right-field line that, off the bat, looked like it might be a homer. Cubs fans exhaled as the ball sailed foul. Chapman eventually struck out Kipnis and retired Lindor to send this riveting game into extra innings. Then it began to rain. Soon the rain was coming down hard enough that the crew chief, Joe West, ordered play halted and the field covered. The grounds crew quickly went to work.

The Cubs, looking glum, filed out of the dugout and down a hallway to a set of stairs that led up to the visitors clubhouse. Aroldis Chapman and Willson Contreras were the last two players to leave the dugout. Chapman was tearful, and Contreras's arm was draped around his broad-shouldered teammate.

Then, suddenly, someone shouted, "Guys, weight room! Won't take that long!" It was Jason Heyward. The players obliged, turning into the weight room, located off the hallway. Joe Maddon kept walking toward the visiting manager's office. The last player in closed the door of the weight room. Theo Epstein lingered outside and tried to listen.

At 6'5", 240 pounds, Heyward was a commanding presence. The players paid rapt attention as he spoke. "I know some things may have happened tonight you don't like. We're the best team in baseball, and we're the best team in baseball for a reason. Now we're going to show it. We play like the score is nothing-nothing. We have to stay positive and fight for your brothers. Stick together and we're going to win this game."

Jon Lester, John Lackey, and David Ross earned World Series rings for the Red Sox in 2013. Lester was also a member of the Red Sox 2007 championship team. Lackey had also picked up a ring for the Angels in 2002. Ben Zobrist was part of the world champion Kansas City Royals team the year before. Yet it was Jason Heyward, playing in his first World Series, the high-priced free agent who was a flop during the season and whose 0-for-4 effort so far that night lowered his batting average in the postseason to .106, who spoke up.

He spoke for less than a minute. He said nothing grandiose. He did not quote Vince Lombardi. But his words were just what the Cubs needed. Heyward quickly transformed the team's mood from somber to upbeat. Other players fed off Heyward's talk and chimed in with words of encouragement. When the team returned to the dugout, they were energized, ready to put the disastrous eighth inning behind them and finish off the Indians.

The rain delay lasted just seventeen minutes. No sooner had the grounds crew put the tarp on the infield then they were told to remove it. The Indians took the field, with Bryan Shaw still on the mound.

Kyle Schwarber was due up first for the Cubs. With a bat in his hand, he assured catching coach Mike Borzello, "I've got this, Borzie." And he did. With three Cleveland infielders on the right side of the diamond, the left-handed swinger hit a line drive through the shift into right field for a single. Rookie Albert Almora, who had not seen much playing time in the postseason, ran for Schwarber. Kris Bryant, battling cramps that he attributed to nerves all night, belted a long fly to center field that Rajai Davis hauled in on the warning track. Almora tagged and moved up to second.

Francona intentionally walked Rizzo so Shaw could go after Ben Zobrist and try to induce a double-play grounder. The switch-hitting Zobrist, batting left against the right-hander, sliced a 1-2 pitch down the left-field line for a double, which scored Almora. Francona again decided on the free pass; this one went to Addison Russell. Miguel Montero, the Cubs' third catcher of the night, singled to left to score Rizzo and increase the lead to 8–6. That is the way it stayed heading into the bottom of the 10th.

Maddon replaced Chapman, who was spent, with Carl Edwards Jr., a tall, slender rookie right-hander. He was the losing pitcher in Game 3, having allowed the only run in the Cubs' 1–0 loss. Edwards was not normally called on as a closer—he saved only two games during the season in 36 appearances out of the bullpen.

Edwards disposed of Mike Napoli on strikes and Jose Ramirez on a groundout. The Cubs were one out away from the moment the city had waited so long for. But the pesky Indians would not go down without a fight. Brandon Guyer walked and advanced to second on defensive indifference, and Rajai Davis again came through when it mattered by stroking a single to left-center to score Guyer.

The distinguished-looking sixty-two-year-old Maddon, wearing horn-rimmed glasses above a gray mustache and goatee, took a walk to the mound to lift Edwards. It was his third midinning pitching change of the game. He brought in another non-closer, southpaw Mike Montgomery, who was acquired by the Cubs from the Seattle Mariners in July. In his brief career, he had not recorded a save, yet he was tasked with trying to get the last out in the seventh game of the World Series for a team that had not won in more than a century. Just a little pressure on the young pitcher.

Michael Martinez, who had come into the game to play right field in the top of the ninth inning, stepped to the plate to face Montgomery. Martinez, a switch-hitter, batted right against the lefty. Francona had seldom used him in the 2016 postseason; he had just three at-bats, and he struck out all three times. His only contribution of note was scoring the lone run in Game 3 after he came in as a pinch-runner.

Martinez's career batting average as a six-year reserve was below the Mendoza Line—just .197, with six home runs. He began the 2016 season with the Indians, went to the Red Sox in July, and, a month later, Cleveland reacquired him on waivers. Francona was out of position players, so he had no choice—other than sending up a pitcher as a pinch-hitter—but to let Martinez bat.

Martinez took a strike and then hit a chopper to third base. Kris Bryant charged the ball and threw a strike to first base, which Anthony Rizzo squeezed for the last out. Rizzo raised his arms and dashed to the area between the pitcher's mound and second base where his teammates had congregated to celebrate. On the way, he had the wherewithal to put the ball in his back pants pocket so that it could be saved for posterity.

The ghosts of postseasons past were vanquished. The "Curse of the Billy Goat" was purged. *The Cubs had won the World Series.* Bedlam broke out in Chicago—fireworks were set off, and people poured into the streets, screaming joyously. Two days later, a parade that a reported five million people attended was held in Chicago. It was one of the largest gatherings in human history.

Jason Heyward downplayed his weight-room speech, insisting that the Cubs would have won regardless of whether he had spoken up. His teammates disagreed. Anthony Rizzo acknowledged that he had been a nervous wreck throughout the game until that point. "I thought about all the people in Chicago and how much this meant to them. But after we had that meeting, I knew we were going to win. It was only a matter of how and when." Kris Bryant also tipped his hat to his teammate: "Jason doesn't say much so when he does, it gets everybody's attention." Theo Epstein added, "That [Jason] stayed not only connected to the team, but in the middle of everything, despite his offensive struggles, he stepped up. It speaks to his character and professionalism."

In the offseason, Aroldis Chapman signed a five-year, $86-million contract with the Yankees—the biggest free-agent contract ever dished out to a relief pitcher. Dexter Fowler also took his ring and left the Cubs, signing a five-year deal with the Cardinals.

Despite losing Chapman and Fowler, the Cubs had the horses to return to the World Series. They made it to the LCS the following year but were defeated by the Dodgers. They lost the Wild Card Game to the Colorado Rockies in 2018. After the Cubs failed to make the playoffs in 2019—a nine-game losing streak down the stretch was the team's death knell—Maddon and the team parted ways. David Ross replaced Maddon as manager. Theo Epstein left the Cubs after the pandemic-shortened 2020 season.

The Cubs' World Series triumph in 2016 will be forever cherished by the organization and the city. Ben Zobrist, who grew up in central Illinois two hours from Wrigley Field, was named MVP of the World Series for his .357 average and game-winning RBI in Game 7. Jason Heyward deserved an honorable mention for his passionate pep talk in the Progressive Field weight room while the rain fell.

After delivering an inspiring speech during a rain delay, Jayson Heyward (right) celebrates with teammates Anthony Rizzo (left) and David Ross (on shoulders) after the Cubs beat the Indians in a hard-fought Game 7 of the 2016 World Series. *Icon Sportswire via AP Images*

18

Glory Denied

THE 1947 BASEBALL SEASON BEGAN WITH JACKIE ROBINSON BREAKING the color barrier and ended with a World Series that featured one of the greatest games ever pitched in the Fall Classic.

In October 1945, Branch Rickey, the progressive president and general manager of the Brooklyn Dodgers, determined to desegregate the major leagues, signed Robinson to a minor-league contract. Robinson, who starred for the Kansas City Monarchs of the Negro Leagues in 1945, would join the Dodgers' Triple-A affiliate, the Montreal Royals of the International League, the following spring. Robinson showed he was major-league material for the Royals in 1946 by leading the International League in hitting and runs scored and finishing second in stolen bases. He was on target to move up to the parent club in 1947.

Rickey, preparing for Robinson's major-league debut, chose Havana, Cuba, as the site of the team's spring-training camp. He had seen the racial hatred that Robinson had faced when he trained with the Royals in Daytona Beach, Florida, the previous spring. Rickey chose Cuba because some Negro League greats, including Josh Gibson and Satchel Paige, had played there and were greeted warmly by the Cuban fans; Rickey expected Robinson would receive the same reception. And though he did receive a welcome from the Cuban locals, a few of his Dodger teammates protested. A group of players, led by outfielder Dixie Walker, circulated a petition opposing the addition of Robinson to the roster. Rickey, along with Leo Durocher, the Dodgers' gruff, no-nonsense manager, confronted the petitioners and told them bluntly that Robinson was going to open the season with the team, and, if they didn't like it, they would be traded. The players behind the petition backed off.

During the first week of April, the team broke camp in Cuba and headed to Brooklyn. Robinson's usual position in the Negro Leagues and minors had been second base, but because Eddie Stanky was entrenched in that position for the Dodgers, Robinson was pegged to start at first base. On April 9, six days before Opening Day, Commissioner Happy Chandler made a bombshell announcement: Durocher was suspended for the season. He had committed a number of transgressions, Chandler explained, most notably consorting with gamblers. But he also had a history of engaging in heated arguments with umpires and very likely was guilty of striking a fan during an altercation in 1946.

Rickey was in a predicament because he had less than a week to find a manager for his team. He first asked Joe McCarthy, who had won seven World Series for the New York Yankees but stepped down early in the 1946 season. McCarthy, less than a year into his retirement, turned down the offer. (He came out of retirement in 1948, however, when he was offered the job as manager of the Boston Red Sox.) Rickey asked two of the Dodgers' coaches, Clyde Sukeforth and Ray Blades, whether they were interested, but they declined. Sukeforth, though, agreed to manage the team on an interim basis until Rickey found a permanent manager.

After playing some exhibition games against the Yankees at Yankee Stadium, the Dodgers opened the season at Ebbets Field on April 15 by beating the Boston Braves, 5–3. Robinson, batting second behind Stanky, went 0-for-3 with a sacrifice bunt and run scored. In the next game, Robinson picked up his first major-league hit, a bunt single, as the Dodgers trounced the Braves, 12–6.

Rickey's team was 2–0, but he was still without a permanent manager. He had another man in mind for the job: Burt Shotton. Rickey and Shotton had been friends since 1913, when Shotton played outfield for the St. Louis Browns and Rickey took over as manager of the club late in the season. Rickey managed Shotton for two more years with the Browns and, later, for five years with the St. Louis Cardinals. Rickey, who admired Shotton's even disposition, his knowledge of the nuances of baseball, and his good rapport with younger players, hired him as manager of one of the Cardinals' minor-league teams in 1926. This job was a springboard to Shotton's being named as manager of the Philadelphia Phillies in 1928. He held the position for six years, and, though he was not particularly successful, Rickey hired him again to manage in the minors and fulfill other jobs in the Cardinals organization from the mid-1930s to the early 1940s.

When Rickey left the Cardinals and became president and general manager of the Dodgers in 1942, he considered replacing Durocher, who had been the manager since 1939, with Shotton. But he stuck with Durocher and hired Shotton as a scout. In 1947, Shotton assumed the position of supervisor of the Dodgers' minor-league training camp in Pensacola, Florida. Shotton, sixty-two years old and content with his low-stress position in Florida, was surprised to receive a telegram from Rickey on April 17 with a direct message: "Be in Brooklyn tomorrow morning. See nobody. Say nothing." Shotton, who held Rickey in high regard, boarded a plane early the following morning and, by late morning, was seated across from the longtime executive in his Ebbets Field office.

Rickey, dapperly attired in his usual jacket and bow tie, peered at his old friend through wire-rimmed glasses, explained his dilemma, and implored him to take over as manager of the Dodgers. Shotton, enticed by the prospect of managing a strong Dodgers team that included Jackie Robinson in his first season, readily accepted. He was announced as the Dodgers' manager and boarded a bus with the team to the Polo Grounds so that he could be on the bench for that afternoon's game against the New York Giants. Shotton lost his first game, 10–4, as well as his second game at the helm. But then he guided the Dodgers to wins in eight of their next nine games. Like Connie Mack, Shotton wore street clothes rather than the team's uniform in the dugout, though sometimes he wore the Dodgers' team cap, along with its jacket or windbreaker.

Under Shotton's firm leadership, the Dodgers won the National League pennant in 1947 by five games. Robinson withstood cruel taunts, vile insults, and knockdown pitches to win the Rookie of the Year Award, hitting .297 and leading the league in stolen bases. Dan Bankhead, whom Rickey had purchased from the Memphis Red Sox of the Negro leagues, had become the first Black pitcher in the majors when he took the mound for the Dodgers in August.

Over in the American League, another first-year manager, Bucky Harris, led the Yankees to the flag. In June and July, the team went on a 27–2 roll, capped off by a 19-game winning streak, taking a commanding lead in the league, one that they never relinquished. Center fielder Joe DiMaggio won his third MVP, and lefty reliever Joe Page finished fourth in the MVP vote on the strength of his 14 victories and a league-leading 17 saves.

This was Shotton's first World Series—as a player or manager. Harris was player-manager of the Washington Senators, which won the World Series in 1924 and lost it in 1925. He had two separate stints as manager of the Senators (and would later have a third) and also piloted the Detroit Tigers, Boston Red Sox, and Phillies.

Harris's team jumped off to a strong start, as the Bronx Bombers won the first two games at home. In Game 3 at Ebbets Field, the Dodgers' cozy ballpark in the Flatbush section of Brooklyn, the Dodgers jumped out to a 6–0 lead in the second inning and then fought off a fierce comeback by the Yankees, hanging on to win the game, 9–8. Harris pulled starter Bobo Newsom in the six-run second and went deep into his bullpen, using five pitchers in the loss.

For Game 4, Harris decided to start Floyd "Bill" Bevens, a husky 6'3" right-hander. Bevens struggled during the regular season, posting a 7–13 record and a 3.82 ERA, a big drop from his 16–13, 2.23 season the year before. Bevens knew the ups and downs of life as a pitcher, having toiled in the minors for seven-plus years, throwing two no-hitters along the way, before cracking the majors for the Yankees in 1944.

Even though Bevens was the only pitcher on the staff with a losing record in 1947, Harris had faith that his reserved, hard-nosed pitcher could beat the Dodgers and give the Yankees a 3–1 lead in the Series. It was Bevens's first appearance in a World Series; the Yankees, uncharacteristically, had not won the pennant in any of his first three seasons in the majors. Yogi Berra, playing in his first of 14 World Series, caught Bevens that day. Rookie Harry Taylor started for the Dodgers. Taylor lasted just four batters. After two hits and an error, a flustered Taylor walked DiMaggio with the bases loaded, forcing in a run. Shotton, trying to stave off a big inning, yanked his ineffective hurler in favor of Hal Gregg, a five-year veteran who had bounced between the Dodgers' starting rotation and bullpen during the season. Gregg quickly escaped the jam, inducing a pop-up to short and then a ground-ball double play.

Bevens, three weeks shy of his thirty-first birthday, walked to the mound to begin his work against the Dodgers. He was much less effective in 1947 than he had been in 1946, largely because of his control. In 1946, he averaged 2.8 walks per nine innings; that number jumped to 4.2 in 1947. He started the game with spotty control, walking leadoff man Eddie Stanky and cleanup hitter Dixie Walker, but retired the other three batters.

In the top of the third, the Yankees tried to parlay another Dodger error into a run, but Walker threw DiMaggio out at the plate. They scored a run in the fourth off Gregg on a triple by Billy Johnson and a double by Johnny Lindell.

Bevens continued to struggle with his command. His free passes to Spider Jorgensen and Gregg to lead off the bottom of the fifth inning brought his walk total to six. Stanky bunted the two runners over, and Pee Wee Reese, shortstop and future captain of the Dodgers, brought Jorgensen in with a ground ball to short, and Gregg was thrown out at third. The Dodgers had a run on the scoreboard to close the gap to 2–1 but were still hitless. Reese stole second and advanced to third on Berra's throwing error, but Bevens struck out Robinson to thwart the rally.

Gregg, after a strong seven innings in relief of Taylor, was pinch-hit for in the bottom of the seventh by Arky Vaughan, a longtime Pirates star now in the twilight of his career. Vaughan worked a walk, the eighth of the game for Bevens, but the righty got out of the inning.

When right fielder Tommy Henrich made a nice catch on Gene Hermanski's long fly ball to end the eighth, Bevens, an ordinary pitcher with a career record of 40–36, became the first pitcher in the forty-four-year history of the World Series, covering 250 games, to take a no-hitter into the ninth inning. Yankee Red Ruffing had come the closest—he allowed his first hit with two outs in the eighth inning of Game 1 of the 1942 World Series.

The Yankees, trying to plate some insurance runs for Bevens in the top of the ninth, loaded the bases off Dodgers reliever Hank Behrman with one out. Shotton brought in Hugh Casey to face Henrich, who was nicknamed "Old Reliable" for his steady and dependable play, both offensively and defensively. Henrich hit a ground ball to Casey, who threw home for the force out, and catcher Bruce Edwards threw down to first to complete the double play and keep the score at 2–1.

The Dodgers had their 6-7-8 hitters coming up in the bottom of the ninth against Bevens. Edwards led off by hitting a long fly to left that Lindell leaped to catch in front of the wall. Bevens sighed in relief—his no-hitter and lead were still intact. Bevens walked Carl Furillo, tying a World Series record for most walks allowed by a pitcher in a game with nine; Jack Coombs of the Philadelphia Athletics had set the record in 1910.

Spider Jorgensen hit a pop that George McQuinn caught in foul territory, back of first base. It was Bevens's 26th out. With a mixture of fastballs, curves, and changeups, he had retired the Dodgers hitters in a variety of ways—eight by groundout, seven by pop out, five by strikeout, five by fly out, and one by line out. He had thrown 130 pitches. He was tired and felt some soreness in his right arm, but with a no-hitter in sight, adrenaline propelled him to keep battling.

After Jorgensen's foul out, Shotton made two moves—he sent in reserve outfielder Al Gionfriddo to run for Furillo at first, and he pinch-hit Pete Reiser for pitcher Hugh Casey. Reiser had twisted his ankle the day before when he was caught stealing in the first inning, and he had left the game. He was still favoring the ankle and hobbled up to the plate, much the way Kirk Gibson of the Los Angeles Dodgers would later do in the ninth inning of Game 1 of the 1988 World Series before hitting his famous game-winning home run. Reiser was regarded as one of the game's best pure hitters. A left-handed swinger, Reiser won the batting title for the Dodgers in 1941 with a .343 mark. In 1947, he, as a part-timer, hit .309 with five home runs.

Reiser dug in and worked the count to 2-1. On the next pitch, Gionfriddo got the steal sign and dove into second safely. The pitch was called a ball. With first base open, Harris, concerned that Reiser would smack a game-tying hit to the outfield, decided not to take any chances—he intentionally walked Reiser. He instructed Berra to move over so Bevens could lob in ball four. The 10th walk by Bevens broke Coombs's record. Shotton promptly pinch-ran twenty-one-year-old Eddie Miksis for the gimpy Reiser.

Some baseball purists questioned Harris's strategy of putting the potential winning run on first base. But Harris felt more comfortable having Bevens pitch to Eddie Stanky with two runners on. Stanky was nicknamed "the Brat" for his gritty, in-your-face style of play. He had a solid season in 1947, as he hit .252, scored 97 runs, and drew 103 walks. He was named to the All-Star team and finished 13th in the National League MVP vote. He had collected a hit in each of the first three World Series games and he banged a two-run double in the Dodgers' Game 3 win. Against Bevens that afternoon, he had walked twice, laid down a sacrifice bunt, and popped out.

Shotton, in a highly debatable move, called Stanky back for a pinch-hitter, a grizzled veteran, thirty-four-year-old Cookie Lavagetto. Like Stanky, Lavagetto swung from the right side. Earlier in his career, from 1938 to 1941, Lavagetto was an All-Star third baseman for the Dodgers. His best year was 1939, when he hit .300 with 10 home runs and 87 RBIs. His career was interrupted when he served for four years in World War II, and after he returned in 1946, he saw less playing time. In 1947, he played sparingly—he started only 13 games and totaled 69 at-bats, hitting .261. As a pinch-hitter, he was 6-for-22, with a home run, a double, and six RBIs. Shotton chose Lavagetto because he was a clutch hitter and had a slight power edge over Stanky.

Lavagetto was 0-for-2 in the Series—he pinch-hit for Jorgensen in Game 1 and popped out to second. He stayed in the game and later struck out. In his only other World Series, in 1941, he had gone 1-for-10. So, he brought to the plate an .083 batting average in the World Series.

As Pee Wee Reese waited on deck, Lavagetto dug in. Bevens checked the runners and delivered, and Lavagetto swung and missed for strike one. Here is how Red Barber, venerable Dodgers broadcaster, described what happened next:

Gionfriddo walks off second, Miksis off first. They're both ready to go on anything. Two men out, last of the ninth. The pitch . . . swung on, there's a drive hit toward the right field corner. Henrich is going back. He can't get it! It's off the wall for a base hit! Here comes the tying run, and here comes the winning run! Friends, they're killing Lavagetto, his own teammates, they're beating him to pieces, and it's taking a police escort to get Lavagetto away from the Dodgers.

And then, Barber summed up his emotions and, referencing his Mississippi roots, exclaimed, "Well, I'll be a suck-egg mule"—Southern for "That is just unbelievable."

With one pitch, one agonizing pitch, Bevens lost not only his no-hitter but the game, too. At the crack of the bat, Henrich headed toward Ebbets' nineteen-foot right-field wall, which was festooned with advertisements. He had to make a split-second decision—try to make a difficult catch or hold up and play the ball off the wall. Henrich later described it as "the toughest five seconds of my life." He lunged but the ball was out of reach—it soared over his head and hit the wall. After the ball caromed back to him, he juggled it momentarily. By the time he threw it in to the cutoff man, McQuinn, who then fired to Berra, Eddie Miksis had slid across the plate with the winning run.

As Dodgers players and fans mobbed Lavagetto, a downcast Bevens walked off the field and headed to the Yankees clubhouse. The team, stunned by the loss, closed the clubhouse doors for a half hour as they tried to fathom the dramatic turn of events. Bevens later lamented, "I felt like a guy who had dropped 10 stories in an elevator." He made another grim observation, "Those bases of balls will kill you." Three of the 10 batters that he walked came around to score, and that was the difference in the game. The game was such an anomaly for Bevens because, in the 46 complete games that he had thrown in his career, he had averaged allowing 6.6 hits and walking 2.3 batters. In Game 4 of the '47 World Series, however, he permitted only one hit and issued a double-digit number of walks.

The next game was strangely similar to Game 4. The Yankees, behind starter Spec Shea, again carried a 2–1 lead into the bottom of the ninth inning. The Dodgers put a man on second base, and, with two outs and the pitcher's spot up, Shotton called on Lavagetto to pinch-hit. DiMaggio, from center field, yelled over to Henrich in right, "For Christ's sake, say a prayer." This time, Lavagetto struck out, and the Yankees took a 3–2 lead in the Series.

Back at Yankee Stadium for Game 6, with the Dodgers leading, 8–5, in the bottom of the sixth with two on and two outs, DiMaggio hit a shot to deep left-center field. Gionfriddo, who had entered the game as the Dodgers left fielder at the start of that inning, sprinted toward the ball and made a terrific one-handed catch two steps from the fence. DiMaggio, sure that he had an extra-base hit, kicked the dirt in disgust between first and second when Gionfriddo made the grab. The Dodgers maintained their lead to force a Game 7 showdown.

The night before the game, Bevens's wife massaged his sore right arm so that he would be ready in case Harris called on him to pitch. Shea, pitching on just a day's rest, allowed three straight hits and a run in the second, and Harris motioned to the bullpen for Bevens. He allowed a run-scoring double to Jorgensen (the run was charged to Shea) but then pitched 2⅔ innings, allowing no runs. Joe Page took over and showed why he was an MVP candidate by pitching five scoreless innings with the season on the line. The Yankees, aided by a strong game by shortstop Phil Rizzuto (three hits and two runs scored), won the game, 5–2, to capture the Series. Bevens redeemed himself by pitching well in relief, contributing to the Yankees' victory. Lavagetto pinch-hit in the seventh inning and popped out to second. Robinson hit .259 in the Series, with three RBIs and two stolen bases.

Rickey had a dilemma after the 1947 season—keep Shotton as manager or reinstate Durocher. Even though Shotton led the Dodgers to within a game of winning the World Series, Rickey brought back Durocher. Shotton remained with the organization as a consultant in the farm system. About halfway through the 1948 season, the Dodgers were struggling at 35–37. Mel Ott, manager of the Giants, with his team also hovering around .500, resigned. Horace Stoneham, owner of the Giants, called Rickey and asked for permission to speak to Shotton about his team's managerial opening. Rickey, having second thoughts about not rehiring Shotton, gave Stoneham permission to speak to Durocher. In a shocker, Durocher abruptly switched teams and became manager of the Giants. Rickey then brought Shotton back as manager of the Dodgers. The Boston Braves ended up winning the National League pennant that year—the Dodgers finished third, and Durocher's Giants finished fifth.

Bevens, Lavagetto, and Gionfriddo each played a memorable role in the 1947 World Series. Ironically, none of the three ever played another major-league game. Gionfriddo was only twenty-five when he stole second and scored on Lavagetto's hit off Bevens and later made the spectacular catch on DiMaggio. But the Dodgers sent Gionfriddo to Triple-A Montreal in 1948, and he played nine years in the minors without ever getting the call back to the majors.

Lavagetto was released by the Dodgers in 1948, and he played three more seasons for the Oakland Oaks, an unaffiliated minor-league team, before he retired.

Like Gionfriddo and Lavagetto, Bevens never stepped on a major-league diamond again after the 1947 World Series. The sore arm that he felt during the 1947 Series persisted and prevented him from pitching at all in 1948 or 1949. He returned to the minor leagues, where he pitched from 1950 to 1953. Bevens's travels during his second tour in the minors spanned from Sacramento and San Diego, California, to Salem, Oregon, which was about twenty-five miles from Hubbard, Oregon, where he grew up. He was a 20-game winner for Salem in 1951 but still could not make it back to the majors. After a season with San Francisco, he returned to pitch for Salem but called it quits early in the 1953 season.

Bevens was asked years after his near no-hitter how he felt about coming so close to achieving immortality. The humble pitcher responded, "I was just lucky to be out there."

A dejected Bill Bevens, with Joe DiMaggio trailing behind, in the runway leading to the Yankees clubhouse after he came within an out of throwing the first no-hitter in World Series history in Game 4 of the '47 Series. He then lost the no-hitter and game on one pitch. Bevens, soon to be thirty-one years old at the time of his heartbreaking loss, never pitched in a major-league game after the '47 Series. *AP Photo/ John Lindsay*

ACKNOWLEDGMENTS

From Dave and Jeff—We want to thank numerous people for their significant contributions to the writing and publication of *Shadows of Glory*: our agent Tim Hays for his strong belief in this project and his tireless efforts to find a publisher; the entire team at Lyons Press, including our editor Ken Samelson for his zealous enthusiasm for this book as well as his impeccable editing and fact-checking, editorial director Gene Brissie for believing in our concept and putting the project in Ken's capable hands, production editor Jenna Dutton, and copy editor Alison Browdie for their great work helping to bring the manuscript to its final form, and Neil Cotterill for the outstanding job designing the cover. We also want to thank our copy editor in the early stages of the project, Debby Smith, for greatly improving the initial draft of the manuscript.

Thanks to the late Sal Bando and to Larry Bowa, Frank Coppenbarger, Rich Dubee, Tom Herr, Ron Mayer, and Rich Westcott for their recollections and insight. Thanks also to Mickey Rivers for two hours of entertainment and interviews. A huge thanks to Mark Teixeira for his recollections and for stepping in for Sal Bando to deliver an excellent foreword.

A special thanks to Sal Bando's gracious wife, Sandy, and their son, Sal Jr., for their kind assistance under difficult circumstances. Our sympathies to the entire Bando family for Sal's passing.

We appreciate the assistance of the following people from Major League Baseball media relations and alumni relations departments for facilitating interviews: Kevin Gregg, Bonnie Clark, Debbie Nocito, and Jim Hogan of the Philadelphia Phillies; and Larry State of the St. Louis Cardinals.

Thank you to these nice folks for assisting with the book's photo section: John Horne of the Baseball Hall of Fame, Tricia Gesner of the Associated Press, Sarah Christie of Getty Images, Taka Yanagimoto of the St. Louis Cardinals, and Michael Anderson of the Cincinnati Reds.

And finally, thanks to our friend and baseball aficionado Chris Kupst for helping to develop the theme for this book. This project would not have gotten off the ground without his contributions.

From Dave—First, I want to offer a big thanks to my longtime friend and college fraternity brother Jeff Rodimer for coming out of the bullpen early in the game to collaborate with me on this project. Your time and effort were invaluable to the completion of this book.

I appreciate the time and effort given by the following people for graciously reading chapters of the manuscript and offering sage suggestions and positive feedback: Evan Aidman, Bob Anderson, Garrett Brindle, my brother Doug Brown, Rob Elias, Lee Fiederer, Mitch Golding, Marc Harrison, John Mitchell, and Scott Olin. Sadly, Bob Anderson and John Mitchell, two longtime friends and baseball junkies, passed away during the writing of this book. I miss them both. My sympathies to their families.

A shout-out goes out to my mother Nancy Brown, sister Kristin Brown, and friend Mike Jones for their encouragement over the years. Last, but certainly not least, the biggest thanks goes to my family of All-Stars for their patience, support, and encouragement: my wife Kim and children Alex, Jack, and Caroline. Thank you for allowing me to pursue my lifelong passion.

From Jeff—I can't thank Dave Brown enough for bringing me into the world of writing. Having read every word he has ever published, I am honored to be his partner in this venture. I'd like to thank Monica Pisacano, Michael Margolis, and Kaitlyn Brennan of the New York Yankees for their help and kindness throughout my involvement in *Shadows of Glory*. I'd like to also thank Andrew Levy (an original Conehead) for his ongoing interest in our project.

Bob Cvornyek was helpful to us early on with his ideas, expertise, and thoughtfulness, which ultimately led to a chapter about the Negro World Series. Thanks to Kevin McVey for his enthusiasm and willingness to dig in and help connect us to some key people who could relate to our efforts in significant ways. Thanks also to John Messina, a great friend who took time out to spitball with us when the well of ideas was running dry, and to my late friend Tom Greene, for his thirty-five years of friendship and shared love of Yankee baseball.

I'd be remiss if I didn't thank Jon Latzer (a real CTHS Gladiator) as well for his promotional ideas and willingness to help an old friend.

Thanks, finally, to my family: my big brother, Steve, who set me on the road to baseball (and Yankees) fandom many years ago; my sister, Trish, who remains my biggest fan, adviser, and supporter; and my wife, Peggy, for indulging me in a "second act."

Bibliography

Authors' Interviews
Bando, Sal
Bowa, Larry
Coppenbarger, Frank
Dubee, Rich
Herr, Tom
Rivers, Mickey
Teixeira, Mark

Books
Anderson, Dave, and Bill Pennington, eds. *New York Times Story of the Yankees: 1903–Present: 390 Articles, Profiles & Essays*. Rev. ed. New York: Black Dog & Leventhal, 2021.

Bisher, Furman. *Strange but True Baseball Stories*. New York: Random House, 1966.

Clark, Tom. *Champagne and Baloney: The Rise and Fall of Finley's A's*. New York: Harper & Row, 1976.

Coffey, Wayne. *They Said It Couldn't Be Done: The '69 Mets, New York City, and the Most Astounding Season in Baseball History*. Illustrated ed. New York: Crown Archetype, 2019.

Deveney, Sean. *The Original Curse: Did the Cubs Throw the 1918 World Series to Babe Ruth's Red Sox and Incite the Black Sox Scandal?* New York: McGraw Hill, 2009.

Dickey, Glenn. *The Story of the First Two Oakland A's Dynasties—and the Building of the Third*. Chicago: Triumph Books, 2013.

Enders, Eric. *Ballparks Then and Now*. New York: Pavilion, 2019.

———. *100 Years of the World Series*. New York: Barnes & Noble Books, 2003.

Gibson, Bob. *Stranger to the Game: The Autobiography of Bob Gibson*. New York: Viking, 1994.

Golenbock, Peter. *The Spirit of St. Louis: A History of the St. Louis Cardinal and Browns*. New York: Harper Entertainment, 2000.

Hirsch, James. *Willie Mays: The Life, the Legend*. New York: Scribner, 2010.

La Russa, Tony, and Rick Hummel. *One Last Strike*. New York: William Morrow, 2013.

Leventhal, Josh. *Take Me Out to the Ballpark: An Illustrated Tour of Baseball Parks Past and Present*. New York: Black Dog & Leventhal, 2006.

Maddon, Joe, and Tom Verducci. *The Book of Joe: Trying Not to Suck at Baseball and Life*. New York: Twelve, 2022.

McGraw, Tug, and Joseph Durso. *Screwball*. New York: Houghton Mifflin, 1974.

Nemec, David. *Players of Cooperstown: Baseball's Hall of Fame*. 1st ed. Lincolnwood, IL: Publications International, Ltd., 1994.

Nemec, David, and Saul Wisnia. *100 Years of Major League Baseball: American and National Leagues, 1901–2000*. Morton Grove, IL: Publications International, Ltd., 2000.

Peterson, Robert. *Only the Ball Was White: A History of Legendary Black Players and All-Black Professional Teams*. New York: Oxford University Press, 1992.

Pluto, Terry. *The Curse of Rocky Colavito: A Loving Look at a Thirty-Year Slump*. New York: Simon & Schuster, 1994.

Rapoport, Ron. *Let's Play Two: The Legend of Mr. Cub, the Life of Ernie Banks*. New York: Hachette Books, 2019.

Ribowsky, Mark. *A Complete History of the Negro Leagues: 1884 to 1955*. 1st ed. New York: Birch Lane Press, 1995.

Veeck, Bill, with Ed Linn. *Veeck as in Wreck*. Chicago: University of Chicago Press, 1962.

Verducci, Tom. *The Cubs Way: The Zen of Building the Best Team in Baseball and Breaking the Curse*. New York: Crown, 2017.

Zachter, Mort. *Gil Hodges: A Hall of Fame Life*. Lincoln: University of Nebraska Press, 2015.

PUBLICATIONS

Boston Herald
Chicago Tribune
Deseret News (Salt Lake City, UT)
Detroit Free Press
Evening Standard (Uniontown, PA)
Los Angeles Times
New York Daily News
New York Times
Newsday (Long Island, NY)
Philadelphia Inquirer
Sports Illustrated
St. Louis Dispatch
Sun Sentinel (Ft. Lauderdale, FL)
USA Today
Wall Street Journal

WEBSITES

Away Back Gone. https://awaybackgone.com

Barstool Sports. https://www.barstoolsports.com/blog
Baseball Almanac. https://www.baseball-almanac.com
Baseball Egg. https://baseballegg.com
Baseball Fandom. https://baseball.fandom.com
Baseball Hall of Fame. https://baseballhall.org
Baseball History Comes Alive. https://www.baseballhistorycomesalive.com
Baseball Reference. https://www.baseball-reference.com
Bleacher Report. https://bleacherreport.com
Call to the Pen. https://calltothepen.com
CBS Sports. https://www.cbssports.com/mlb
CDC. https://www.cdc.gov/flu
Cincinnati Enquirer. https://www.cincinnati.com
Covering the Corner. https://www.coveringthecorner.com
Daily Cal. https://www.dailycal.org
Did the Tribe Win Last Night. https://didthetribewinlastnight.com
Encyclopedia.com. https://www.encyclopedia.com
ESPN. https://www.espn.com
Fox Sports. https://www.foxsports.com
Gaslamp Ball. https://www.gaslampball.com
History Locker. https://historylocker.com
History.com. https://www.history.com
I70 Baseball. http://www.i70baseball.com
KY3. https://www.ky3.com
Lonestar Ball. https://www.lonestarball.com
Medium. https://medium.com
Metsmerized Online. https://metsmerizedonline.com
Military. https://www.military.com
MLB. https://www.mlb.com
Mlive. https://www.mlive.com
NBC Philadelphia. https://www.nbcphiladelphia.com/news
News Yahoo. https://news.yahoo.com
Philadelphia Inquirer. https://www.inquirer.com
Philly Voice. https://www.phillyvoice.com
Pinstripe Alley. https://www.pinstripealley.com
Redbird Rants. https://redbirdrants.com
Retrosimba. https://retrosimba.com
SABR. https://sabr.org
SB Nation. https://www.sbnation.com
Sports Ha. https://sports.ha.com
Sports Illustrated. https://www.si.com
Sports Illustrated Vault. https://vault.si.com
Sports of Yore. https://www.sportsofyore.com
Sportscasting. https://www.sportscasting.com
St. Louis SBNation. https://stlouis.sbnation.com

Syracuse. https://www.syracuse.com
The Sports Arsenal. https://thesportsarsenal.com
This Great Game. https://thisgreatgame.com
THT Fangraphs. https://tht.fangraphs.com
Vice. https://www.vice.com
Wickersham's Conscience. https://wickershamsconscience.wordpress.com
Wikipedia. https://en.wikipedia.org/wiki
YouTube. https://www.youtube.com

Index

Note: page numbers in *italics* indicate photographs.